SPIN
GREATEST HITS

SPIN
GREATEST HITS

25 Years of Heretics, Heroes, and the New Rock'n'Roll

EDITED BY DOUG BROD

WILEY

John Wiley & Sons, Inc.

Published by John Wiley & Sons, Inc., Hoboken, New Jersey
Published simultaneously in Canada

Design by Forty-five Degree Design LLC

For general information about our other products and services, please contact our Customer Care Department within the United States at (800) 762–2974, outside the United States at (317) 572–3993 or fax (317) 572–4002.

Wiley also publishes its books in a variety of electronic formats. Some content that appears in print may not be available in electronic books. For more information about Wiley products, visit our web site at www.wiley.com.

Library of Congress Cataloging-in-Publication Data:
Spin greatest hits: 25 years of heretics, heroes, and the new rock'n'roll / edited by Doug Brod.
    p. cm.
  Includes index.
  ISBN 978-0-470-63996-2 (pbk.:alk. paper); ISBN 978-0-470-89094-3 (ebk);
  ISBN 978-0-470-89108-7 (ebk); ISBN 978-0-470-89109-4 (ebk)
  1. Rock music—History and criticism. I. Brod, Doug. II. Spin (New York, N.Y.)
  ML3534.S649 2010
  781.66—dc22

                            2010028344

Printed in the United States of America

10 9 8 7 6 5 4 3 2 1

Contents

SIDE 4 **THE RIGHT PROFILE**

SIDE 5 **VOICES CARRY**

Foreword

When SPIN first appeared on newsstands in 1985, it was a revelation. While Lollapalooza's genre-blending was still years away, SPIN boldly put black artists and women on its covers when it was considered commercial suicide for a mainstream "rock" magazine to do so. SPIN was like a mischievous little flashlight illuminating the shadowy edges of the music world. It championed the fledgling art form of hip-hop while giving a national platform to experimental music, outlaw country, and hardcore punk. And the international scene reports! I mean WTF, look how they party in Glasgow! Who knew? Okay, I'll admit that each year when the magazine's Top 40 albums list comes out it's sometimes a little over my head. This year I had only heard of about half the artists named . . . but I got turned on to St. Vincent, Drake, and Miles Benjamin Anthony Robinson, all of whom have been rocking me since. Next year, who knows? Looking forward to finding out.

Oh, and the Rage in Russia article included here is one I wasn't so sure about at the time. I thought it totally missed what was going on in the band/music/Russia—but in retrospect it actually is pretty darn interesting. This book is a collection of unexpected discoveries, trials, and tribulations from the edges. Enjoy.

Tom Morello
*Rage Against the Machine, Audioslave,
the Nightwatchman, Street Sweeper Social Club*

INTRODUCTION

by **DOUG BROD**

IN HIS INTRODUCTORY COLUMN in SPIN's premiere issue, founding editor and publisher Bob Guccione Jr. neatly articulated his vision for the magazine. "From the beginning . . . we were determined to fill every issue with the real excitement of music, wherever it was from and whatever form, from top to muddy bottom," he wrote, adding, "We wanted to say something worth saying, not just add to the unilateral chorus." Yet another objective was to "discover, not just witness (and therefore look, not just wait to be shown)." And that's just what SPIN has done for the past quarter-century, as the authoritative voice of—I'll say it—alternative youth culture.

I've always been a magazine guy. From the early years of my musical education—taping songs off New York area FM stations WPIX, WLIR, and WNYU—I was a voracious reader of *Creem*, *Trouser Press*, *Flipside*, *The Big Takeover*, and the *NME*, among other publications too numerous or obscure to list here. Which is why SPIN's May 1985 debut was such a revelation. Okay, punk and new-wave snob that I was, I didn't much care for the cover subject, some rising pop starlet named Madonna. But inside

I devoured pieces on the Replacements, U2, Jason and the Scorchers (whom I had recently interviewed as a college intern at the now-defunct *International Musician and Recording World*), reviews of Lloyd Cole and Hüsker Dü albums, and a blurb about the immortal Scraping Foetus Off the Wheel. I've never been precious or possessive about the underground or otherwise outré musicians I admired, so the idea of *my* bands getting written up in a large-circulation mainstream magazine was a game-changer. I had—and maybe still have—this naïve notion that the more people who got turned on to this music, the more successful (read: happy) the artists would become, so the longer they'd stay around to make records for me, a true fan. Since taking the editorial reins of SPIN in 2006, I've tried to ensure that this passion comes through on every page.

Some of today's most brilliant cultural critics and music writers honed their skills and shaped their voices in SPIN. And such lit legends as Norman Mailer, William S. Burroughs, William T. Vollman, Nick Tosches, Elizabeth Gilbert, and David Rakoff have all been a part of our legacy, contributing groundbreaking investigations, true-crime narratives, essays, humor, and the uncategorizable stuff no one else would print.

Of course, I wouldn't pretend that this book is the *definitive* collection of the best writing ever to have graced the magazine's pages. Any anthology is subject to the whims and prejudices of its compiler, and I'm nothing if not whimsically prejudiced and prejudicially whimsical. The stories within are not only personal favorites and acknowledged classics among our staffers (and feature brand-new introductions by their authors), but also ones that illuminate larger cultural moments: the commercialization of Charles Manson, the imminent crash and burn of Amy Winehouse. Some are just eye-opening: David Peisner's investigation into the U.S. military's use of music to torture, Tom Sinclair's unearthing of Manhattan's real-life rock'n'roll high school. I've included one non-music-related entry, Elizabeth Gilbert's account of her trip along the Yangtze River during the construction of China's Three Gorges Dam—a rollicking and heartrending travelogue that does what all great magazine writing should: provoke and entertain.

You'll also notice the relative absence of straightforward artist profiles. That's because no matter how well reported and beautifully written, these pieces—usually pegged to some contemporaneous product or other—are often curlicues on a larger career arc, and by design have short shelf lives. But you *will* find a few pieces of outstanding music criticism, which has long been a hallmark of the magazine, as well as selections from our Ultimate List issues (May 2004 and 2005) sprinkled throughout.

It's my hope that with this book, the excitement of the music shines through from top to muddy bottom as we give voice to things worth saying. At the very least, these Greatest Hits are all Great Reads.

A MATTER OF
Life *and* **Death**

6,557
Miles to
NOWHERE

Revisiting the sites of rock'n'roll departures

by **CHUCK KLOSTERMAN**

DECEMBER 2003

*This is the piece that (eventually) became the skeletal structure for
Killing Yourself to Live, a book some people love and many people
hate. The principal reason certain readers dislike that book is that
they feel betrayed—they go into the process assuming it's going to
be about the locations where rock musicians died, and that's not the point.
Killing Yourself to Live is a memoir about all the spaces in between, and
the relationship between the past and the present and the imagined.
Thematically, it's totally different from this original story, which is only
about the places I visited (as opposed to how I got there). I remember
this article as mostly straightforward journalism, except that the para-
graphs are pretty long and I occasionally snort cocaine.*

■ ■ ■

DEATH IS PART OF LIFE. Generally, it's the shortest part of life,
usually occurring near the end. However, this is not necessarily true for rock stars; sometimes rock stars don't
start living until they die.

I want to understand why that is.

I want to find out why the greatest career move any musician can make is to stop breathing. I want to find out why plane crashes and drug overdoses and shotgun suicides turn longhaired guitar players into messianic prophets. I want to walk the blood-soaked streets of rock'n'roll and chat with the survivors as they writhe in the gutter. This is my quest.

Now, to do this, I will need a rental car.

Death rides a pale horse, but I shall merely ride a silver Ford Taurus. I will drive this beast 6,557 miles, guided by a mind-expanding global positioning system that speaks to me in a soothing female voice, vaguely reminiscent of Meredith Baxter. This voice tells me when I need to exit the freeway, how far I am from places like Missoula, and how to locate the nearest Cracker Barrel. I will drive down the eastern seaboard, across the Deep South, up the corn-covered spinal cord of the Midwest, and through the burning foothills of Montana, finally coming to rest on the cusp of the Pacific Ocean, underneath a bridge where Kurt Cobain never lived. In the course of this voyage, I will stand where 112 people have fallen, unwilling victims of rock's glistening scythe. And this will teach me what I already know.

Nancy Spungen, Stabbed to Death, 1978

NEW YORK CITY (WEDNESDAY, JULY 30, 3:46 P.M.): When I walk into the Hotel Chelsea, I can't decide if this place is nicer or crappier than I anticipated. There are two men behind the reception desk: an older man with a beard and a younger man without a beard. I ask the bearded man if anyone is staying in room 100 and if I can see what it looks like.

"There is no room 100," he responds. "They converted it into an apartment 18 years ago. But I know why you're asking."

For the next five minutes, these gentlemen and I have a conversation about drug-addled Sex Pistols bassist Sid Vicious, and mostly about the fact that he was an idiot. However, there are lots of people who disagree: Visitors constantly come to this hotel with the hope of staying in the same place where an unlikable opportunist named Nancy Spungen was stabbed to death. "We hate it when people ask about this," says the younger employee. "Be sure you write that down: We hate it when people ask us about this."

I ask the older man what kind of person aspires to stay in a hotel room that was once a crime scene.

"It tends to be younger people—the kind of people with colored hair," he says. "But we did have one guy come all the way from Japan, only to discover that room 100 doesn't even exist anymore. The thing is, Johnny Rotten was a musician; Sid Vicious was a loser. So maybe his fans want to be losers, too."

While we are having this discussion, an unabashedly annoyed man interrupts us; his name is Stanley Bard, and he has been the manager of the Hotel Chelsea for more than 40 years. He does not want me talking to the hotel staff and orders me into his first-floor office. Bard is swarthy and serious, and he tells me I should not include the Hotel Chelsea in this article.

"I understand what you think you're trying to do, but I do not want the Chelsea associated with this story," says Bard, his arms crossed as he sits behind a cluttered wooden desk. "Sid Vicious didn't die here. It was just his girlfriend, and she was of no consequence. The kind of person who wants to stay in room 100 is just a cultic follower. These are people who have nothing to do. If you want to understand what someone fascinated by Sid Vicious is looking for, go find those people. You will see that they are not serious-minded people. You will see that they are not trying to understand anything about death. They are looking for nothing."

At this point, he politely tells me to leave the hotel. We shake hands, and that is what I do.

100 Great White Fans, Club Fire, 2003

WEST WARWICK, RHODE ISLAND (SATURDAY, AUGUST 2, 5:25 P.M.): For some reason, I assumed the plot of land where dozens of people burned to death during a rock concert would look like a parking lot. I thought it would be leveled and obliterated, with no sign of what happened on February 20, 2003, the night pyrotechnics from blues-metal dinosaurs Great White turned a club called the

Station into a hell mouth. Small towns usually make sure their places of doom disappear. But not this town: In West Warwick, what used to be a tavern is now an ad hoc cemetery—which is the same role taverns play in most small towns, really, but not so obviously.

When I pull into the Station's former parking area, I turn off my engine next to a red F-150 Ford pickup with two dudes inside. They get out, walk through a perimeter of primitive crosses that surround the ruins of the club, and sit on two folding chairs next to a pair of marble gravestones. They are James Farrell and his cousin Glenn Barnett; the two gravestones honor Farrell's uncle, Tommy Barnett, and Tommy's best friend, Jay Morton. The story they tell me is even worse than I would have expected: Farrell's grandfather—Tommy's father—suffered a stroke exactly seven days and five minutes after his son was burned alive.

I realize that this story must sound horribly sad, but it doesn't seem that way when they tell it; Farrell and Barnett are both as happy as any two people I've ever met. Farrell is like a honey-gorged bear, and he reminds me of that guy who starred in *The Tao of Steve.* He's wearing a tie-dyed shirt and a knee brace. He comes here every single day.

"I will remember the night this place burned down forever," Farrell says. "I was in a titty bar in Florida—I was living in Largo at the time. I looked up at the ceiling, and I noticed it was covered with black foam, just like this place was. And I suddenly knew something was wrong. I could just feel it. Then my mom called me, and she told me what happened. I moved up here to help out my grandma. She obviously has been through a lot, what with losing her son and then her husband. The doctor said my grandfather's stroke was completely stress-related. I mean, he stroked out a week after the fire, almost to the very minute. That was fucking spooky."

Farrell is 35, his uncle was just four years older, and they were more like brothers. Tommy, a longtime regular at the Station, didn't even want to see Great White. He referred to them as "Not-So-Great White" and only went because someone gave him free tickets.

Burnt offering: A police officer looks at the Station nightclub's sign the day after a fire claimed 100 lives during a Great White concert. *Douglas McFadd/Getty Images*

A few months after the accident, Farrell, Tommy's daughter and his girlfriend, and two female strangers built all of the Station's crosses in one night. The wood came from the club's surviving floorboards. Originally, the crosses were left blank so anyone could come to the site, pick one, and decorate it however he or she saw fit. There are only about five unmarked crosses remaining, partially because some people have been memorialized multiple times accidentally.

As we talk, I find myself shocked by how jovial Farrell is. "I hide it pretty well," he says. "And between you and me, I just did a line. Do you want to go do some blow?"

It turns out that this kind of behavior is not uncommon here: These grounds have fostered a community of both spirituality and decadence. Almost every night, mourners come to the Station cemetery to get high and talk about how they keep living in the wake of all this death.

"Nothing in West Warwick is the same," Farrell says later, as he paints his uncle's gravestone. "It changed everyone's personality. Everybody immediately started to be friendlier. For weeks after that show, if you wore a concert T-shirt into a gas station, everybody acted real nice to you. If they knew you were a rocker or a head, they immediately treated you better. It's that sense of community. It's kind of like the drug culture."

I ask him what he means.

"I mean, I just met you, but I would give you a ride anywhere in the whole goddamn state of Rhode Island if you asked me, because I know you're a good guy. I have something on you, and you have something on me. It's like that here. The people who hang out here at night—it's definitely a community of people dealing with the same shit. I call it 'the fellowship.'"

A kid pulls into the parking lot and hauls an upright bass out of his vehicle; it's one of those seven-foot monsters like the Stray Cats' bassist used to play. He faces the grave markers, whips out a bow, and begins to play Eccles' Sonata in G Minor. Either I am at the Station at the absolute perfect journalistic moment, or West Warwick is America's new Twilight Zone.

"Oh, I used to play at this club all the time," he says when I wander over. "I was in a band called Hawkins Rise, and I played upright bass through an amp. We were sort of like Zeppelin or the Who." He tells me his name is Jeff Richardson, that he is a 24-year-old jazz fanatic, and that he knew five of the people who died here. He was vaguely familiar with many of the other 95.

"The same people came here every night," Richardson says. "When a band like Great White or Warrant would come into town, all the same people would come out. There was never any pretentiousness at this club. You wouldn't have to worry about some drunk guy yelling about how much your band sucked."

To me, that's what makes the Great White tragedy even sadder than it logically should be: One can safely assume that none of the 100 people who died were hanging out at the Station to be cool. These were blue-collar people trying unironically to experience rock'n'roll that had meant something to their lives when they were teenagers.

Tonight, I will go back to the graveyard at 11 P.M., and lots of the deceased's friends will pull up in Camaro IROC-Zs and Chevy Cavaliers. They'll sit in the vortex of the crosses, smoking menthol cigarettes and marijuana, and they will talk about what happened that night. I will be told that the fire started during the first song ("Desert Moon," off 1991's *Hooked*). I will be told that the Station's ceiling was only ten feet high and covered in synthetic foam and that when the foam ignited, it (supposedly) released cyanide into the air. I will be told it took exactly 58 seconds before the whole building became a fireball. I will be told that a few firemen at the scene compared it to seeing napalm dropped on villages in Vietnam, because that was the only other time they ever saw skin dripping off of bone.

I will also be told (by just about everyone I speak to) that Great White vocalist Jack Russell is a coward and a hypocrite and that they will never forgive him (the fact that his bandmate Ty Longley also died in the blaze doesn't seem to affect their opinion whatsoever). Around 1 A.M., Farrell will read me a poem about how much he despises Russell, and after he finishes, he will stare off into the night sky and say, "I would really like to hit him in the face." But he won't sound intimidating or vengeful when he says this—he will just sound profoundly sad. And it will strike me that this guy is a relentlessly sweet person with a heart like a mastodon, and I would completely trust him to drive me anywhere in the whole goddamn state of Rhode Island, even if he had never offered me drugs.

Three Members of Lynyrd Skynyrd, Plane Crash, 1977

MAGNOLIA, MISSISSIPPI (WEDNESDAY, AUGUST 6, 8:20 P.M.): Despite the GPS, I'm semi-lost in rural Mississippi. And when I say "rural," I mean rural: Ten minutes ago, I almost drove into a cow that had meandered onto the road. This is especially amusing because if I had driven into a cow, I would be only the second person in my immediate family to have done so. When my sister Teresa was in high school, she accidentally plowed into one with our father's Chevy. Teresa hit it at 40 mph, and the old, sleepy-eyed ungulate went down like a tree struck by lightning. Those were good times.

I am hunting for the site of Lynyrd Skynyrd's 1977 plane crash, which killed singer Ronnie Van Zant, guitarist Steve Gaines, and Gaines' sister, backup singer Cassie. This tragedy is the presumed inspiration for the airplane scene in the film *Almost Famous*, although it's a safe bet nobody on the Skynyrd plane came out of the closet just before they collided with the Mississippi dirt.

My initial plan was to ask for directions at the local Magnolia bar, but there doesn't seem to be one. All I find are churches. Near the outskirts of town, I spy a gas station. The auburn-haired woman working behind the counter doesn't know where the crash site is; however, there is a man buying a 12-pack of Bud Light, and he offers to help. "My old lady can probably tell you for certain," he says. "She's waiting in my pickup." We walk out to his extended-cab 4x4 Ford, and his "old lady" (who looks about 25) instructs me to take the interstate southbound until I see a sign for West 568 and then follow that road for ten miles until I see some chicken coops. There's one problem: There are a lot of goddamn chicken coops in Mississippi. It's getting dark, and I'm almost ready to give up. Then I see a sign by a driveway for MOTEFARMS.COM. This is the first time I've ever seen a farm that has its own website, so I suspect it's more than just a chicken ranch. I'm right, and when I pull into the yard, I'm immediately greeted by a shirtless fellow on a Kodiak four-wheeler.

John Daniel Mote is the 21-year-old son of the farm's owner. He is a remarkably handsome dude; he looks and talks like a young John Schneider, patiently waiting for Tom Wopat to get back from the Boar's Nest. "This is the right place," he says. "Follow me." We drive down a dirt road behind the chicken coops. I can hear the underbrush rubbing against the bottom of the Taurus, and it sounds like John Bonham's drum fills from "Achilles Last Stand."

He finally leads me to a landmark that his father constructed years ago. It's dominated by an archway with FREE BIRD painted across the top. There is a Confederate flag, of course, and a statue of an eagle. Mote says that if I were to walk through the free bird arch and 50 yards into the trees, I would find a tiny creek and some random airplane debris.

I start to walk in that direction. He immediately stops me. "You don't want to go in there," he says. I ask him why. "Snakes. Cottonmouths. Very poisonous. Not a good idea." And then young John Daniel Mote drives away.

By now, the sky is as dark as Nick Cave's closet. I am surrounded by fireflies. There is heat lightning to the east. The temperature is easily 100 degrees. It feels like I'm trapped in the penultimate scene of *Raiders of the Lost Ark*, in which Indiana Jones and Marion are tied to a stake while the Nazis try to open the Ark of the Covenant. Or maybe I'm just thinking of that movie because Mote mentioned the snakes.

Still, part of me really wants to see where the plane went down. I feel like an idiot for having driven 547 miles in one day only to be stopped five first downs from pay dirt. I drive the Taurus up to the mouth of the arch and shine the high beams into the blackness. I open the driver's side door and leave it ajar so that I can hear the radio. It's playing "Round and Round" by Ratt. The headlights don't help much; the trees swallow everything. I start to walk into the chasm. I don't make it 50 yards. In fact, I don't even make it 50 feet. I can't see anything, and the cicadas are so loud that they drown out Ratt. I will not find the spot where Ronnie Van Zant was driven into the earth. I turn around, and the cottonmouth snakes gimme three steps toward the door.

Elvis Presley, Drug Overdose, 1977
Jeff Buckley, Drowned, 1997

MEMPHIS, TENNESSEE (FRIDAY, AUGUST 8, 3:14 P.M.): So here is the big question: Is dying good for your career? Memphis offers two key points of investigation for rock'n'roll forensic experts. The first is Graceland, where Elvis Presley overdosed while sitting on a toilet. The second is Mud Island, where the Wolf River meets the Mississippi. This is the spot where singer/songwriter Jeff Buckley went for a swim and never came back. One could argue that both artists have significantly benefited from dying: Presley's life was already collapsing when he passed in 1977, so his death ended that slide and, in all likelihood, kept his legacy from becoming a sad joke (it is virtually impossible to imagine a "noble" 68-year-old Elvis, had Presley lived into the present). Meanwhile, Buckley's death is precisely what turned him into a star. He was a well-regarded but unfamous avant-garde rock musician when he drowned on May 29, 1997. Almost instantly, he became a Christlike figure (and his 1994 album *Grace* evolved from "very good" to "totally classic").

I am typing this paragraph while sitting by the banks of the Wolf River, presumably where Buckley disappeared into the depths. The water is green and calm as a sheet of ice. Buckley's mother once insisted he was too strong a swimmer to die in these waters. I don't know how I feel about this supposition, as I cannot swim at all (I can't even float). The über-placid river looks plenty deadly to me; as far as I'm concerned, it may as well be a river of hydrochloric acid.

But how or why Buckley died really doesn't matter at this point; what matters is how his death is perceived by the world. And as far as I can tell, Buckley's demise is viewed 100 percent positively, at least from an artistic standpoint. There is an entire cult of disciples (led, I believe, by Minnie Driver) who project the knowledge of Buckley's death onto his work, and what they then hear on songs like "Drown in My Own Tears" is something that would not exist if he were alive. It's a simple equation: Buckley is dead, so *Grace* is profound. But this says more about the people who like Buckley than it does about his music. Even when it's an accident, dying somehow proves you weren't kidding.

Robert Johnson, Sold Soul to Devil, 1930

SATAN'S CROSSROADS (FRIDAY, AUGUST 8, 4:33 P.M.): Just north of Clarksdale, Mississippi, at the intersection of Highways 61 and 49, the spirit of rock'n'roll was spawned from Satan's wheeling and dealing. You see, this is the "crossroads" where Robert Johnson sold his soul to the devil in 1930, thereby accepting eternity in hell in exchange for the ability to play the guitar like no man before him. Satan's overpriced guitar lesson became the blood of the blues—and, by extension, the building blocks of every hard-rock song ever written.

Obviously, this never actually happened. Robert Johnson (who was poisoned to death at 27) met the devil about as many times as Jimmy Page, King Diamond, and Marilyn Manson did, which is to say never. But this doesn't mean rock'n'roll wasn't invented here. Rock'n'roll is only superficially about guitar playing—it's really about myth. And the fact that people still like to pretend a young black male could become Lucifer's ninja on the back roads of Coahoma County (and then employ his demonic perversity through music) makes Johnson's bargain as real as his talent.

Unfortunately, these present-day highways to hell don't look like much. They look like (duh) two highways. There is spilled barley on the shoulder of each road, so this must be a thoroughfare for local grain trucks. The only thing marking the site is a billboard promoting "MICROSURGICAL VASECTOMY REVERSAL." Ironically, I was able to find Robert Johnson's crossroads with the Ford's GPS: Somehow, it seems like satellite technology should not allow you to find the soul of America's most organic art form. You'd think the devil would have at least blown up my transmission or something.

CEDAR RAPIDS, IOWA (SATURDAY, AUGUST 9, 11:47 P.M.): Five hours ago, I was looking for a motel. Then I heard something on the radio waves of rural Iowa: 36 miles away, Great White were performing a benefit concert in Cedar Rapids to raise money for the Station Family Fund. Sometimes, you just get lucky.

After turning around and driving to Cedar Rapids, I realize I have no idea where this concert is, and the kind of bars that host Great White shows in 2003 are not exactly downtown establishments. I decide to just walk into a Handy Mart gas station and ask the kid working the Slushee machine if he knows where this show is. He does not. In fact, he hasn't even heard about it. "Well, where do you think a band like Great White would play in Cedar Rapids?" I ask. He guesses the Cabo Sports Bar and Grill, a new place next to the shopping mall. And his guess is absolutely right.

The show is outside on the club's sand volleyball courts; admission is $15. When I arrive, the opening band—Skin Candy—are doing a cover of Tesla's "Modern Day Cowboy." There are maybe

1,000 people waiting for Great White, and it's a rough crowd. When you look into the eyes of this audience, you can see the hardness of these people's lives. More than a few of them are complaining that the 16-ounce Budweisers cost $3.50. This is exactly what the crowd in West Warwick must have looked like.

I go backstage (which is really just the other side of the parking lot) and find Great White vocalist Jack Russell. He's wearing a sleeveless T-shirt and pants with an inordinate number of zippers, and he's got quite the little paunch. Somebody walks by and stealthily hands him some tablets, but it turns out they're merely Halls cough drops.

Arm and the man: Rick Allen performs in London in 2003.

12 Musicians Missing Parts of Their Bodies

1. Def Leppard drummer Rick Allen (arm)

2. Black Sabbath guitarist Tony Iommi (some fingertips)

3. R&B singer Houston (eye)

4. The Geto Boys' Bushwick Bill (eye)

5. The Barbarians' Victor "Moulty" Moulton (hand)

6. '50s and '60s session drummer Sandy Nelson (foot and part of leg)

7. Link Wray (lung)

8. Dr. Hook (eye)

9. Ry Cooder (eye)

10. Jazz-folk singer/songwriter John Martyn (leg)

11. Jerry Garcia (finger)

12. Shane MacGowan (teeth)

I ask him what he remembers about the fire in Rhode Island, but he balks. "I can't talk about any of that stuff, because there is an ongoing investigation, and I don't want to interfere with anything the [Rhode Island] attorney general is doing." This is understandable, but I ask him the question again. "Well, it changed my life. Of course it changed my life," he says. "But I had to make a choice between sitting in my house and moping forever or doing the one thing I know how to do."

Russell tells me he can't discuss this any further. However, guitarist Mark Kendall is less reticent. He's wearing Bono sunglasses and a black 'do rag, and he fingers his ax throughout the duration of our conversation. He seems considerably less concerned about the attorney general. "That night was just really confusing," Kendall says.

"I was totally numb. I didn't know what was going on. I had my sunglasses on, so I really couldn't see what was happening."

I tell him that there are people in Rhode Island who will never forgive him for what happened.

"Oh, I totally understand that," Kendall says. "That is a completely understandable reaction on their behalf. I mean, I've never gotten over losing my grandfather, and he died 15 years ago. On the day of that show, I met five different people who ended up dying that night. I feel really, really bad about what happened. But no blame should be cast."

I ask Kendall how Great White can donate the profits from their tour and still afford to live. "Well, we did sell over 12 million records," he says with mild annoyance. Twenty minutes later, the band opens with "Lady Red Light," and, much to my surprise, they sound pretty great. After the first song, Russell asks for 100 seconds of silence to commemorate the victims. It works for maybe a minute, but then some jackass standing in front of me holds up a Japanese import CD and screams, "Great White rules!"

Bob Stinson, Chronic Substance Abuse, 1995

MINNEAPOLIS (MONDAY, AUGUST 11, 1:30 P.M.): There are a lot of disenfranchised cool kids in downtown Minneapolis, and most of them have a general idea where Replacements guitarist Bob

Stinson drank and drugged himself to death in February 1995. They all seem to think it was the 800 block of West Lake Street, near a bowling alley. They are correct. Stinson died in a dilapidated apartment above a leather shop and directly across the street from the Bryant-Lake Bowl.

I knock on the apartment door. No answer. I knock again. Again, no answer. This is strange, because I know for certain that somebody is in there. While outside, I saw a pudgy white arm ashing a cigarette out of the window. Granted, I don't really have a plan here. I'm not exactly sure what I should ask this person if and when he or she opens the door. But I feel like I should at least see the inside of this apartment (or something), so I keep knocking. And knocking. I knock for ten minutes. No one ever comes out. I try to peep into the window where I witnessed the "cigarette incident," but now the shade is down, and I'm starting to feel like a stalker. I decide to walk away, having learned zero about a dead musician I knew practically nothing about to begin with.

Kurt Cobain, Suicide, 1994

SEATTLE (SATURDAY, AUGUST 16, 2:12 P.M.): Lots of dead people here. If rock musicians were 15-ton ivory-bearing pachyderms, Seattle would be America's elephant graveyard.

First, you have Mia Zapata of the Gits, the female punk who represented liberation and self-reliance before she was raped by a sociopath and strangled to death with the string of her sweatshirt. There is Kristen Pfaff, the Hole bassist and smack addict who overdosed in her bathtub. And one cannot forget the (entirely predictable) demise of Alice in Chains singer Layne Staley, a man who OD'd in perhaps the least rock'n'roll spot in all of Washington: a generic, five-story teal condominium in an area of town widely considered Seattle's least cool neighborhood (it's a block from a Petco).

Perhaps you are wondering how I knew where all these people perished; the truth is that I did not. The guided Seattle death tour was provided by Hannah Levin, a rock writer for the alternative newspaper *The Stranger* and a freewheeling expert on local tragedies. Of course, all the aforementioned demises pale beside the *Citizen Kane* of modern-rock deaths: the mighty K.C. This is what Levin and I discuss as we maneuver the long and winding Lake Washington Boulevard, before finally arriving in what used to be Kurt Cobain's backyard.

"In the weeks before he killed himself, there was this litany of rumors about local singers dying," Levin says. Back in '94, she worked at Planned Parenthood but was immersed in the grunge culture. "There was a rumor that Chris Cornell had died, and then there was a rumor that Eddie Vedder had died. So even though a bunch of my friends called me at work and said Kurt was dead, I didn't believe them. That kind of shit happened constantly. But then I went out to my car at lunch to smoke cigarettes and listen to the radio. My radio was on 107.7 The End, which was Seattle's conventional modern-rock station. And as soon as I turned the ignition key back, I heard the song 'Something in the Way.' That's when I knew it was true, because The End would have never fucking played that song otherwise. It wasn't even a single."

The greenhouse where Cobain swallowed a shotgun blast was torn down in 1996; now it's just a garden. One especially tall sunflower appears to signify where the Nirvana frontman died, but that might be coincidence. When we arrive at the site, there are four guys staring solemnly at the sunflower. One of them is a goateed 24-year-old musician named Brant Colella. He's wearing a Glassjaw sweatshirt, and it has been a long time since I've met someone this earnest. Colella makes Chris Carrabba seem like Jack Black.

"I'm from New York, but I moved to Portland to make music. I'm a solo artist. I used to be in a band, but my band didn't have it in them to go all the way, and that's where I'm going," he says, and then looks longingly toward the sunflower. "His heart is here. My heart is here, too. I wanted to see where Kurt lived and hung out. I wanted to see where he was normal. The night before he died, I had a dream where Kurt came to me and told me that he was passing the torch on to me. Then we played some music together."

Colella was 15 when Cobain died on April 5, 1994. Last night, he and his friends attended a Mariners game—Ichiro Suzuki hit a grand slam to beat the BoSox—but Colella wants to make it very clear that seeing Cobain's house was his primary motivation for visiting Seattle. He also wants to make it very clear that (a) he hates people who wear Abercrombie & Fitch and (b) that Kurt probably didn't kill himself.

"There are some people who assume he was completely suicide-driven, but he wasn't like that," Colella says. "I don't want to stir up waves and get killed myself, but the information that indicates Kurt was murdered actually makes way more sense than the concept of him committing suicide. But I'm not here to point fingers and say Courtney Love did it. Only God knows the answer to this question. And I realize there are people who want to believe Kurt Cobain committed suicide. People are kind of broken into two factions: There are right-wingers who want to use his death to point out that this is what happens when you listen to rock'n'roll, and there are also all his crazy fans who want to glorify depression and have Kurt be their icon forever."

When Colella first said this to me, I thought it was reductionist, simplistic, immature, and—quite frankly—pretty stupid. But the more I think it over, the more I suspect he's completely right. Except for the murder part.

ABERDEEN, WASHINGTON (MONDAY, AUGUST 18, NOON): Kurt Cobain's hometown can be described with one syllable: bleak. Everything appears belted by sea air. The buildings look like they're suffering from hangovers. Just being here makes me feel tired.

In the early 1990s, the suicide rate in Aberdeen was roughly twice as high as the national average. This does not surprise me. It's also a hard-drinking town, and that doesn't surprise me, either: There are actually road signs informing drivers that the Washington DUI limit is .08 (although it would seem that seeing said signs *while you are actually driving your vehicle* is like closing the barn door after the cows are already in the corn).

I notice these roadside markers as I drive around looking for a bridge that does not exist.

What I am looking for is the bridge on the Wishkah River that Kurt Cobain never lived under. He liked to claim that he did. *Nevermind*'s "Something in the Way" is the supposed story of this non-experience. It's quite possible Cobain did hang out down there, since hanging out under bridges is something lots of bored, stoned high school kids are wont to do. But Cobain didn't really live under any bridge; he just said he did to be cool, which is a totally acceptable thing to do, considering what he did for a living. Being cool was pretty much his whole job.

There are a lot of bridges in Aberdeen—this would be a wonderful community for trolls. I walk under several of them, and I come to a striking conclusion: They all pretty much look the same, at least when you're beneath them. And it doesn't matter if Kurt Cobain slept under any of them; what matters is that people believe he did, and that is something they want to believe. Maybe it's something they need to believe, just like they need to believe that a legend's death means something. If they don't, they will be struck with the depressing revelation that dead rock stars are simply dead. Cobain's death was no more remarkable than anyone else's—it was just more "newsworthy," which is something else entirely. All he did was live, sing, and die. Everything else is human construction. Everything else has nothing to do with the individual who died and everything to do with the people who are left behind (and who may even wish those roles were somehow reversed).

As I walk back to my car and prepare to return to the world of the living, I think back to the conversation I had with the unabashedly annoyed man who runs the Hotel Chelsea. It turns out that he was right all along: I am not a serious person. I do not have any understanding of death. And I am looking for nothing.

CHUCK KLOSTERMAN is a writer and journalist in New York. His first article for SPIN was about P.O.D.

2

HANDS
on a
HARDBODY
Fetishizing one's first guitar

by DAVID HAJDU

APRIL 2008

My only big secret as a writer is that when I was starting out, I wrote a couple of romance novels, which were published under a female pseudonym. Since then, the only other love story I've written is this piece, a personal essay about my first guitar. It is also highly unusual for me in that I virtually never write about my own life. After it was published, I got a few hate e-mails from Danelectro buffs who, in the delirium of their fandom, mistook my gushing for ridicule. More significantly, I heard from two guys I had played music with in high school, and we ended up getting together to jam—on the roof of my apartment in New York, naturally. Everything I used to know came back to me, and I played all four chords.

■ ■ ■

IF YOU CAN PLAY PASSABLY, having a really expensive, big-name guitar confers a kind of status that is surpassed only by having a really cheap, crap-name guitar. My first electric, which my parents bought for $24.99—about what my musical talent called for, in their good judgment—was a Danelectro in brown Formica with a wing-shaped white pick-guard. This was some time before Danelectros were rediscovered and reassessed to be so cheesy as to be cool. Then, they were just cheesy. I played mine in a five-boy garage band called the Ryders (after our idols, the Byrds) in a brown Formica town called Phillipsburg, New Jersey, and the instrument contributed significantly to the ridicule I earned among my teenage peers in the cutthroat suburban band scene.

Our lead guitarist, Tootie Ritz, assumed prominence without discussion or dissent, in part because he could play barre chords (he never actually played lead; all three of us guitarists strummed in something close to unison) but mainly because he had a cherry-red Gibson SG, the same model Pete Townshend played.

It is true that Tootie's instrument was secondhand and had a sizable crack in the neck, rendering it impossible to play well but affordable to his dad. To us, the crack—and the mystery of its provenance—only added to the allure of Tootie's Gibson. After all, we knew how Townshend used to smash his guitars at the end of Who shows. Could it be that Pete had broken this very one and sold it to Pettinelli's Musical Instrument Shop?

The image of Townshend unstrapping that exquisite specimen of craftsmanship and hurling it into his speaker cabinet fascinated

Teenager in love: The author at 17 with a Christmas gift from his parents, a Martin D-28. *Courtesy of David Hajdu*

and repelled us. We puzzled over the act, dissected it, debated it like a midrash. We liked to get together on the grounds of our old elementary school, where there was a poured-concrete pool empty most of the year. We would sit on the bottom of the deep part and strum away on our guitars with no amps—E, A, B . . . E, A, B—and the chords would ring around us. We wondered why every rock concert was not held in a pool, and wondered, above all, how Pete could destroy his own instrument. The act seemed sacred and profane in ways we could never fully grasp.

Raised as Catholics, all five of us, we knew from the stories of the saints that sacrifice is the noblest of acts, and so we understood there to be something profoundly holy in the destruction of a Gibson SG. But . . . the saints had given their own lives for a higher cause, for God. What cause could be higher than rock'n'roll? That, we could never figure out.

Before graduation from high school, I got a superb guitar—a Martin D-28 dreadnought acoustic, which my folks were able to buy at a considerable discount with the help of a cousin, an architect who had worked on the Martin family home in Nazareth, Pennsylvania. I did not deserve such an instrument, and I knew it, and I also knew enough not to share that knowledge. I loved the object and fetishized the curves of its rosewood body and the silky patina of its mahogany neck. I modulated up from E, A, B to G, C, D to suit the acoustic—changed what I played, nominally, but played no better than ever. Still, the tone of that Martin was majestic, and it looked so impressive that it elevated my standing in Phillipsburg, especially among nonmusicians, including several girls whose interest was among the main reasons I played guitar to begin with.

It wasn't until I went to college at NYU and started seeing real musicians perform live in the clubs in and around Greenwich Village that I learned the higher physics of instrument ownership, musicianship, and public perception. I saw Talking Heads, early in their career, and David Byrne was playing a Squier—Fender's low-budget version of its own Telecaster. I caught Prince, at the old Academy of Music, and he was using a Hohner imitation of a Telecaster. Later, I noticed the Edge with a Japanese-made Custom starter guitar, Jeff Healy with a Fernandes pseudo Stratocaster, Jack White with a Montgomery Ward Airline plugged into a Sears Silvertone amp. I learned the difference between the make of the guitar and the music the guitar makes, and I discovered that there can be an inverse relationship between the status of an instrument and the stature of its player. To be truly great is to be good enough to use a bad instrument. In that sense, for a musician in a position to buy any instrument he or she wants, choosing a no-brand guitar is not to defy branding, but to brand oneself as superior to the guitar.

Today, I play mostly for myself in the mature knowledge that no one else wants to hear me. I sold the Danelectro and the Martin years ago, idiotically, and I no longer fetishize guitars. Unlike a lot of people I know who play as amateurs, I have only one guitar: a Gibson L-7 acoustic archtop. The other three in my bedroom don't count, because one is a half-size "travel guitar," another needs a neck reset, and the last is a junker I should throw away but just cannot bear to sacrifice.

DAVID HAJDU is the music critic for *The New Republic* and a professor of arts journalism at Columbia University. He is the author of two books on music (*Lush Life* and *Positively 4th Street*), one on comics (*The Ten-Cent Plague*), and an essay collection (*Heroes and Villains*).

3

Summer
of
'69

Exploring the cultural battle between Charles Manson and Woodstock

by **MIKE RUBIN**

SEPTEMBER 1994

I was flattered, of course, when SPIN decided to put my 5,000-word think piece contrasting the 25th anniversaries of Woodstock and the Manson Family murders on the cover of the September 1994 issue (if I recall correctly, I think it bumped off Kate Moss), but also a little embarrassed. After all, my essay culminated in a screed decrying the lazy, persistent use of Charles Manson as a countercultural signifier, and now here was Charlie on the cover of SPIN in bloodcurdling stop-sign red and white, casting his witchy glare from newsstands yet again. Kind of a mixed message, no?

Looking back, the apex of the knee-jerk negativism I was exhorting against was still a few years off, probably cresting with the "Break Stuff" nihilism of Woodstock '99, while the poster child for the cruel kitsch I termed "concentration camp" would ultimately turn out to be Marilyn Manson, then still a neophyte who I actually interviewed for the story but ended up cutting out because he had nothing remotely interesting or original to say (surprising, eh?). Even though my article was published long enough ago that it recently celebrated its own 15th anniversary, Charles Manson remains a durable icon of lurid fascination—on weekends

*he's still the "M" in MSNBC—but does anyone remember who in the
helter skelter Evan Dando was?*

■ ■ ■

WELL IT'S 1969 OK / All across the U.S.A. / It's another
year for me and you / Another year with nothin' to
do . . . ," the Stooges declared in "1969." It's a bit unfair
to use the benefit of hindsight's bifocals to cast doubt on the
Nostradamic abilities of Iggy Stooge, but in retrospect 1969 was
anything but just "another year" for me, you, or anybody.
Although 1968—with its tragic assassinations of Martin Luther
King, Jr. and Robert Kennedy, and violent upheaval in the
streets—is generally considered the most turbulent year in modern American history, 1969, specifically its summer months, has
proven to have had a more lasting resonance among various
streams of popular culture.

Consider these cataclysmic happenings. On June 28, 1969,
a routine harassment raid by police on a gay bar called the
Stonewall Inn in New York City's Greenwich Village touched
off several days of rioting, inaugurating the modern gay-rights
movement. On July 19, on an island off Martha's Vineyard named
Chappaquiddick, Massachusetts, Senator Ted Kennedy deep-
sixed his presidential hopes permanently when his car swerved
off a bridge and into the drink; Kennedy escaped, but his companion, young campaign worker Mary Jo Kopechne, remained
trapped in the car and drowned. Astronaut Neil Armstrong's
stroll on the surface of the moon on July 20 neatly marked the
end of the first era of human progress, as man physically reached
past the confines of the Earth to touch another celestial body. And
somewhere in Canada, Bryan Adams got his first real six-string,
bought at a five-and-dime, and played it till his fingers bled.

The summer of '69, however, is most closely associated in
the collective memory with Woodstock, the legendary concert
festival that has come to symbolize the breakthrough of rock
culture into the mainstream as an unchallenged commercial

force. From August 15 to 17 in Bethel, New York, a sleepy rural hamlet 90 miles north of New York City, a 600-acre dairy farm and alfalfa field was transformed into what was advertised as the "Woodstock Music and Art Fair Presents: An Aquarian Exposition." Organizers planned for a crowd of 100,000 paying $18 each, but when almost 500,000 young people showed up and stormed the gates, the event became a celebration of things free: music, expression, spirit. A million and a half more concertgoers remained in traffic gridlock for 20 miles outside the site, but those who got in braved a steady downpour and a sea of mud to enjoy a lineup of 27 of rock's top acts, including the Who, Creedence Clearwater Revival, Janis Joplin, Crosby, Stills, Nash and Young, and, lest we forget, Sha Na Na, before Jimi Hendrix brought the festival weekend to a close with an electrified rendition of "The Star-Spangled Banner," which for many heralded the dawning of "the Age of Aquarius."

But just how long a cultural moment was this Aquarian Age? Across the country in Los Angeles, less than a week before the festival, on the evening of August 9, intruders snuck into the Benedict Canyon home of filmmaker Roman Polanski and brutally murdered his wife, actress Sharon Tate—eight months pregnant—and her guests: Hollywood hairstylist Jay Sebring, coffee heiress Abigail Folger and her boyfriend, Polish emigre and pharmaceutical enthusiast Voytek Frykowski, and wrong-place-at-wrong-time teenager Steven Parent. The next night in L.A.'s Los Feliz neighborhood, grocery-store owner Leno LaBianca and his wife, Rosemary, were similarly slaughtered. Linking the two crime scenes was the barbarity—a total of 169 stab wounds between the seven victims—and the bizarre messages scrawled on the walls in the victims' own blood.

Three thousand miles apart, the crimes and the concert seemed to have no connection, aside from some festival-goers hearing about the murders on the radio as they drove up through the country toward Bethel. But the subsequent arrests of hippie doppelganger Charles Manson and his confused and drug-addled band of youthful followers proved to be far more sinister and pervasive than any brown acid making the rounds at Max

Yasgur's farm, serving to symbolically bum out all the good vibes that the Woodstock Nation had wrought, and subsequently giving birth to a persistent nihilism and knee-jerk cynicism that dogs rock's underground circles to this day.

Family man: Charles Manson's 1969 police mug shot. *Hulton Archive/ Getty Images*

Twenty-five years later, the anniversary of Woodstock is being marked by a fanfare of media memoirs, CD and movie reissues, and at least two different festivals in the general vicinity of the original show. The anniversary of the Tate and LaBianca murders, however, is being celebrated in its own determined, if less spectacular, fashion, especially by a growing subculture that views Manson as some sort of a misunderstood hero. Mythologized, if not lionized, by the likes of Axl Rose, Evan Dando, and Trent Reznor, among others, Manson is now a familiar figure on album covers, poster art, and T-shirts. As the most enduring symbol of the death of flower power, he's earned a high countercultural Q rating as an unwitting theoretician of punk, exerting an influence on rock's anti-establishment attitude that has yet to be fully measured.

To get to the bottom of the purportedly pessimistic outlook of Generalization X (and then go back to the top of the slide), one has to start with Charles Manson. Approaching the silver anniversary of his crimes, Manson is the only figure who can compete with Malcolm X for the kind of iconic power that attracts disenchanted, disenfranchised, and disaffected white kids. Given the option between Woodstock's and Manson's subtexts—love or hate, peace or war, tastes-great or less-filling— young people are making a surprising choice, perhaps not even fully certain of who Manson is and what he stands for. In the words of graphic artist and subcultural observer Frank Kozik, "Charlie's winning."

■ ■ ■

SORTING OUT ALL its historical significance 25 years down the line, 1969 flickers as a schizophrenic year full of contradictory messages. Of course, the number "69" visually resembles a yin-yang symbol, so a sense of duality does seem implicit. Thus, it's somehow fitting that there will be not just one but two anniversary concerts to mark Woodstock's first quarter-century.

On August 13 and 14, on the original Sullivan County site of Yasgur's farm, a rather modest show with the name of Bethel '94 will take place, featuring Woodstock '69 veterans like John Sebastian, Richie Havens, Melanie, and Country Joe McDonald. Meanwhile, on the same weekend in Saugerties, New York, 50 miles to the northeast, the promoters of the '69 festival will present Woodstock '94, "Two More Days of Peace & Music," with a lineup of over 24 bands including Aerosmith, Metallica, Arrested Development, the Red Hot Chili Peppers, Bob Dylan, Porno for Pyros, and, according to the concert's press release, "the greatest array of 'port-a-johns' in the history of Western civilization." The Saugerties show is planned as a massive affair combining good-ol'-days cause-thumping (excepting the booking of unrepentant homophobe Shabba Ranks) and state-of-the-art technology, with an interactive theme park, food markets, an environmental awareness area, pay-per-view satellite hookup, and a feature film and soundtrack album already in the offing. Virtual utopia, anyone?

All the nostalgic hoopla, of course, is predicated on the notion that Woodstock '69 was an event worth emulating. After all, there were other large music festivals at the time; why doesn't the zeitgeist cry out for "Monterey Pop '92" or "Isle of Wight '95?" According to Woodstock '94 co-producer Joel Rosenman, Woodstock ushered in an understanding of "Aquarian qualities," which he defines as "a heightened sense of importance placed on the attributes of community, neighborliness, love for other people, respect for the planet . . . and tolerance for diversity.

"It seemed like the dawn of a new age," says Rosenman. "Kids who had previously been convinced by the establishment that they were aberrations stood up, looked around, and saw half a million of themselves as far as the eye could see, and suddenly realized that they were not weirdos, that they were the new generation."

"It was the high-water mark of people's ideals actually coinciding with their behavior," says Atlantic Records' president, Danny Goldberg, who covered the '69 fest for *Billboard*. "It became a symbol of what people can do as a community, even if most of the time we don't."

"It was the first time so many people were together without it being a demonstration," muses Rick Danko of the Band, who performed at Woodstock '69 and may also play at the Saugerties show.

"The goal," says satirist Paul Krassner, who watched the show from the press tent, "was to try to bring the feelings that you had at Woodstock into the real world."

Back in the real world, not every observer among the countercultural critics present was so enamored of what they had witnessed. Ellen Willis, reviewing the festival for the *New Yorker*, warned that "before history is completely rewritten . . . [it should be noted that] the cooperative spirit did not stem from solidarity in an emergency . . . so much as from a general refusal to adopt any sort of emergency psychology," adding that "by Sunday I couldn't help suspecting that some of the beautiful, transcendent acceptance going around was just plain old passivity."

"Had helicopters not airlifted food and doctors, had water purifiers not been hastily installed, had the locals not caught the sharing spirit, Woodstock would have become *Lord of the Flies*," remembers underground journalist Abe Peck in his book *Uncovering the Sixties*.

"'I left one thing out of my Woodstock article,'" critic Robert Christgau quotes writer Tom Smucker as saying. "'I left out how boring it was.'"

Musician, poet, and journalist Ed Sanders remembers that even shortly after the fact, Woodstock seemed of little significance to the bohemians on New York's Lower East Side. "The light from Woodstock did not reach 12th Street and Avenue A." The ex-Fug attributes Woodstock's eventual media rhapsodization to "the visual gestalt of it, you know, two naked kids in a pond washing each other."

At some point after the festival, however, history was indeed rewritten, and the concert became WOODSTOCK in bold capital letters, something approaching paradise on earth for those hip enough and old enough to have been there (or claim that they were). And the proof that there was a nation of millions (or at least 500,000) ready and able to gather and peacefully partake of this crazy rock'n'roll music also meant there was a substantial new market to be catered to and exploited. Everyone wanted to get a piece of the Woodstock mystique, and it was sold in millions of units. There was a feature film, a three-record soundtrack, then another double album of music left off the first soundtrack. Woodstock lent its name not only to a generation but to the inscrutable yellow bird in Charles Schulz's *Peanuts*, who in turn became a fowl-feathered shill for MetLife. This summer, Hendrix's "Star-Spangled Banner" has been appropriated by Budweiser to hype the World Cup. Somewhere in the translation, Woodstock's idealism got stuck in the mud.

Young people have been force-fed Woodstock's monumental importance—its hipness, its bigness, its wowness, its nowness—until it has become an official gospel of the rock'n'roll church, to be swallowed like an Owsley blotter communion wafer. You either jealously wish you had been there to partake in history, or you deny it was anything more than a rustic version of a weekend at MTV's *Beach House*. What's more, the age schism, which in the '60s pitted young against old, is still with us, albeit in a more benign manifestation. The generation gap may have been replaced by the Gap Generation, but kids and their parents still march to the beat of a different drum machine.

Bassist Mike Inez, who will perform with his band Alice in Chains at Woodstock '94, experienced Woodstock like most of his peers, through the soundtrack albums and the movie. "With all those heavyweight musicians thrown into one place at one time, it was kind of magical," says Inez. While he's honored that his band was chosen to play at Saugerties, Inez feels that ticket prices—$135, a considerable leap from the $18 that was charged (and rarely paid) in 1969—are "pretty steep." Inez adds, "It would be really unfortunate if kids went down to experience Woodstock and got this corporate jerk-off money-making thing."

Many observers fear that's just what the Saugerties show has become; with a projected cost of $30 million, about $20 million underwritten by PolyGram, some locals have taken to calling the event "Greedstock." The product of extensive market research, Woodstock '94 has been meticulously plotted, with regard to transportation, security, and concessions. The concert's TV ads trumpet the show as a "convergence of generations," but it's more a convergence of corporations; even the commercial itself features the familiar dove of peace sitting on a guitar neck, now cloned into two birds, intertwined with a Pepsi logo. "It's just a gig, except that they're putting 'Woodstock, Inc.' on it," remarks Henry Rollins, also scheduled to play Saugerties.

The "gig" is expected to draw a sellout crowd of 250,000, partly a result of the strength of the lineup, and partly due to nostalgia and mystique. The power of the myth of the shared rite is so strong that people are willing to pay the hundred-dollar-plus initiation fee to experience the "magic," even if it's a prepackaged simulacrum of the Woodstock vibe. "The idea wasn't to go to a shopping mall and buy and consume," says Michael Wadleigh, director of *Woodstock*, the Academy Award–winning documentary of the original festival. "I have passed on being involved in any of these Woodstock events because all they are trying to do is cash in and make money. . . . We do this to everything—Mom, apple pie, the flag. I guess that's the American way."

Many people I know in Los Angeles believe that the '60s ended abruptly on August 9, 1969, ended at the exact moment when word of the murders on Cielo Drive traveled like brushfire through the community, and in a sense this is true.

—Joan Didion, *The White Album*

DESPITE 25 YEARS of celebrated killers with flashier stats and higher body counts, America's hate affair with Charles Manson continues unabated. He's done the talk-show circuit from Tom Snyder to Geraldo, all without leaving the prison grounds. Comedian Ben Stiller turned him into a gibberish-spouting but lovable Lassie surrogate on his now-defunct Fox sketch series. When ABC wanted to inaugurate Diane Sawyer's new *Turning Point* series this past March, they sent their camera crews behind bars to stage a Family reunion, and the result was the highest rated debut of a newsmagazine show ever. Manson's Nielsen following is longstanding; when the made-for-TV docudrama *Helter Skelter* aired back in April 1976, it earned the top ratings ever for any television show up to that point.

"It's the most bizarre murder case that we have ever had in America," says Vincent Bugliosi, the former L.A. deputy district attorney who prosecuted Manson and later went on to write about the case in *Helter Skelter*, still No. 1 among True Crime books, with over six million copies sold. "If you compare the Manson Family's lifestyle to other mass murderers, it's certainly much more appealing to kids who want to drop out." Poster artist (and societal dropout) Frank Kozik agrees: "Most people would like to be Charlie for a day; have a bunch of fine hippie chicks sucking your dick all day long, taking acid, getting off on the system. It has its appeal." (Ironically, Manson owes a great deal of his durability to the forces of liberal humanitarianism; Manson and his female disciples were all sentenced to be executed, but California repealed the death penalty less than a year after the guilty verdicts. Instead of getting the chair, Manson receives four letters a day in prison.)

Still, all hedonistic fantasies aside, Manson makes for an unlikely role model. At five feet two inches, he was nasty, brutish, and short; a con man, pimp, and car thief who spent most of his formative years buried within the penal system. Released in 1967 after spending 17 of his 32 years behind bars, he headed straight to San Francisco's Haight-Ashbury district, where he quickly donned the costume of a Summer of Love casualty and began recruiting the middle-class cast-offs who, in L.A., would become the bedrock of his Family. Through a combination of prolific psychedelics and even more prolific sex, Manson built a loyal posse of lotus eaters who were willing to do his bidding, whatever the whim; unlike his co-defendants/co-dependents Susan Atkins, Patricia Krenwinkel, Leslie Van Houten, and Tex Watson, Manson was charged and convicted not for taking part in the actual slayings, but for masterminding the murders through mind control.

Although their messages were antithetical, Manson and Woodstock are inextricably linked, with Manson considered the Grim Reaper of the Woodstock dream. If the murders and their portrayal in the press didn't end the Aquarian Age, they at least splattered blood on the moon in the seventh house—one for each of the victims in the Polanski and LaBianca homes.

"It was horror on parade," remembers Ed Sanders, who headed out from New York to L.A. to cover the trial, with his reportage later becoming the basis for his book *The Family*. "The right wing couldn't have bought with a trillion dollars a better death to the '60s scenario." After the murders, recalls Paul Krassner, "people stopped picking up hitchhikers, police raided communes." Older folks who already didn't trust anyone under 30 now had their worst fears made flesh. "Your whole system is a game," shouted Van Houten after hearing her guilty verdict. "Your children will turn against you." It was youth subculture on trial, and President Nixon—elected with a mandate to "restore law and order"—was only too eager to pronounce a nation of defendants guilty.

Manson and the other Family members were indicted in the first week of December, the same week that concert promoter Bill Graham attempted to out-Woodstock Woodstock at a racetrack southeast of San Francisco called Altamont. When Hell's Angels, acting as security, beat the life out of a young black fan at the front of the stage, it was the spirit of Manson all over again; those observers who weren't yet convinced that Charlie Company had offed the '60s now settled on Altamont as the cause of death. An anecdotal story in Christopher Andersen's 1993 Mick Jagger biography even places Manson backstage at Altamont, smoking a joint and telling Mick what a big Stones fan he is. While totally spurious—Manson was in jail, after all—it is wishful allegorical thinking to place prime suspect Manson right there at the murder site.

Manson, though, was hardly a newcomer to the music scene; his has always been a rock'n'roll saga. In 1968, Manson was linked to Beach Boys drummer Dennis Wilson—the two shared a mutual taste for controlled substances, wild orgies, and good vibrations—with Charlie even living out of Wilson's pad for some months. Manson tried to use Wilson to jump-start his own career, and one Manson composition, "Cease to Exist," was indeed rewritten and recorded by the Beach Boys, appearing on their 1968 album *20/20* as "Never Learn Not to Love."

But Manson's troubadourial endeavors were basically a bust. Manson's "debut album," *Lie*, seems less the work of a twisted, criminal mind than that of someone who doesn't know how to tune. "Kids buy it thinking they're going to get devil-worship music," says Stephen Kaplan of New Jersey's Performance Records, the distributor of *Lie* for the last ten years. "But when they get home and find they have an album of mediocre folk songs, a lot of them are disappointed." *Charles Manson Live at San Quentin*, a bootleg on the British label Grey Matter packaged as a parody of the Beach Boys' *Pet Sounds*, has none of the cellblock charm of, say, Johnny Cash live at the same venue. In 1970, the Family even recorded its own album, imaginatively titled *The Manson Family Sings the Songs of Charles Manson*, a collection of lightweight campfire sing-alongs occasionally punctuated by demonic laughter. These records have some merit as artifact, but are eminently forgettable as art.

Except that rock'n'roll never forgets. Over the years, performers have consistently stepped forward to perform Manson's songs, invariably for some reason that has little to do with the music itself. Last December, most notably, came the fallout from Guns N' Roses "secret" cover of Manson's 1968 "Look at Your Game Girl" at the end of *The Spaghetti Incident?* As "Charliegate" unfolded, it was unclear which the media found more repellent: the idea of Manson earning an estimated $62,000 in royalties for every one million *Spaghettis* sold, or Rose's recommendation to "do yourself a favor and go find the originals." Although *Spaghetti* eventually sold 1.1 million copies, the royalties issue ended up a bust: A 1971 federal court judgment diverts all of Manson's mechanical royalties to Bartek Frykowski, son of murder victim Voytek Frykowski.

More than likely, it was Manson's punk-rock street cred that brought Rose to perform the song in the first place. Since punk's inception, Manson's image has retained a powerful presence in no-future circles. As Johnny Rotten snorted, "The only good hippie is a dead hippie," so what better poster boy than the man who had symbolically laid waste to them all en masse? "If you think about it, punk rock is about no rules: making your own culture, making your own thing," suggests Kozik. "Well, he did that." Oppositional, confrontational, and violent, Manson's story is a classic punk-rock text.

Not surprisingly then, Manson references abound in the underground. Redd Kross, then still teenagers who could spell Red Cross, cut a version of Manson's "Cease to Exist" on its 1982 debut album, *Born Innocent*, as well as its own irony-driven Tate-house tribute called "Charlie" ("Flag on the couch / Lady on the floor / Baby in the gut / Widdle biddy boy"). British proto-industrial pranksters Psychic TV recorded a 1983 cover of Manson's "I'll Never Say Never to Always" retitled "Always Is Always." Sonic Youth, with Lydia Lunch along for the ride, explored the taboo territory in "Death Valley 69" on 1985's *Bad Moon Rising*. SST Records was rumored to be releasing an album of Manson's prison recordings in the mid-'80s, from tapes that Manson had sent to pen pal Henry Rollins, but according to Boston lawyer David Grossack, who was trying to find Manson a deal, the label got cold feet. (A spokesperson for SST denies any such project.)

On a different front, the avant-garde composer John Moran, a protégé of Philip Glass, staged his *The Manson Family: An Opera* at Lincoln Center in 1990. George Clinton has a Manson skeleton in his closet: Both Funkadelic's 1971 *Maggot Brain* and 1972 *America Eats Its Young* include liner note essays adapted from writings by the Process Church of the Final Judgment, a Satanic cult with reputed links to Manson that flourished in the late '60s and early '70s. Mansonmania might even be emigrating to the hip-hop nation: The name of the upcoming collaboration between Dr. Dre and Ice Cube is *Helter Skelter.*

But few performers have worked as hard at cornering the market on Manson name checks as the Lemonheads' Evan Dando. The band's 1988 album, *Creator,* includes a cover version of Manson's "Your Home Is Where You're Happy," a photo of Dando posing in front of a picture of Manson, and CD booklet thank yous to family members "Susan; Lynette; Gypsy; Katie; Mary; Sandra; Leslie; Snake; Ouish; little Paul; of course, Charlie," as well as the note "Evan would like to thank No Name Maddox a.k.a. Jesus Christ a.k.a. Soul"—all pseudonyms of Manson. More recently, Dando discussed Manson on "Ballarat" on 1990's *Lovey* and, last year, posed with a copy of Manson's *Lie* in a promo spot for MTV's *120 Minutes.* Dando refused to comment for this article, but in a December 1993 interview with *Request* he explained his fascination. "Charlie is just like really, really good black humor," he declared. "I was born in 1967, and it was, like, Manson and Altamont . . . the one-two punch. It was the first image I saw . . . of America that really stuck with me."

Despite Dando's best efforts, however, first prize in the Man(son) of the Year competition goes to Nine Inch Nails' Trent Reznor. In 1992, Reznor rented the Tate house on 10050 Cielo Drive where the first night of murders took place, building a portable studio there named "Le Pig," where most of *The Downward Spiral* was recorded, including the songs "Piggy" and "March of the Pigs." "PIG," of course, was the message written on the front door in Sharon Tate's blood. Not content with realizing the '90s version of Jimmy Page renting Aleister Crowley's mansion, Reznor started but never completed shooting the video for "Gave Up," from the 1992 EP, *Broken,* in the house. "It had bad karma all around," says a crew member who worked on the aborted shoot. Moreover, in order to keep his, ahem, stranglehold on the title, one of Reznor's first signings to his own Nothing Records label is the South Florida group Marilyn Manson, whose debut album, *Portrait of an American Family,* includes the song "My Monkey," which borrows four lines of lyrics from Charles Manson's "Mechanical Man."

More and more, Manson's mug is turning up in the unlikeliest places, as the now familiar image of him from the cover of *Life*—the mushroom cloud of hair, the A-bomb stare that follows you across a room—has creepy-crawled out of the fringes and onto a variety of "Mansonia" memorabilia. "That's one of the most charismatic photos of the fucking century," says Kozik. "For good or bad, people react to it." Manson turns up as a frequent muse in Kozik's poster art, as well as in the work of artists like Joe Coleman and Raymond Pettibon, best known for his work on early Black Flag record sleeves. Rise Records, an Austin, Texas, label, uses Manson's eyes as their logo ("Rise" was one of the "witchy" messages painted in blood on the living room wall of the LaBianca home).

Perhaps the entrepreneurs most responsible for boosting Manson's product placement are the Lemmons Brothers of Zooport Riot Gear in Newport Beach, California. For two and a half years, Zooport has been plastering Manson's face on the front of T-shirts with messages like "Charlie Don't Surf," "Support Family Values," and "The Original Punk" on the back. They've sold more than 30,000 Manson shirts, over 20,000 since Axl Rose wore a shirt throughout GNR's 1993 tour and their "Estranged" video. Zooport's edge on the competition is that it's the only Manson merchandising company with a signed royalty agreement with Charlie. The brothers got their share of bad press last year when they sent over $600 to Manson in prison, before Bartek Frykowski's lawyers interceded. "Why should we give money to a drug dealer's son?" protests Dan Lemmons. The brothers, who are fundamentalist Christians, instead donate the proceeds to the anti-abortion group Operation Rescue.

The support Manson enjoys from right-wingers should come as no surprise. Manson's white-power agenda was hardly a secret. Helter Skelter, Manson's concept of an impending race war based on messages he thought the Beatles were transmitting to him through *The White Album*, would be frightening if it weren't so harebrained. He forbade his followers to listen to Jimi Hendrix, calling him "black slave music." "He hates women, hates blacks, hates Jews, likes guns," says Sanders. "He's a guy, a real guy." Manson's Aryan vision thing is a big hook for folks on the racialist fringe, where he's a mascot for neo-Nazi groups like the Universal Order.

Meanwhile, in the world of mass murderer bubblegum trading cards, Manson is a Mickey Mantle rookie card. Serial killers are big business these days, not just in the cultural margins but in literature (Bret Easton Ellis' *American Psycho*, Stephen Wright's *Going Native*) and film (*The Silence of the Lambs, Kalifornia, Natural Born Killers*). Manson's name recognition makes him the spiritual figurehead of serial killer chic espoused in such au courant white-rage hate zines as *Answer Me!* Romanticizing killers such as Manson is a way for these pomo rednecks to lash back against the perceived "marginalization" of white men, asserting their manhood against women, gays, and minorities.

One would assume that Manson fandom tests the limits of irony, to say nothing of good taste; for most people, especially the victims' families, Manson's legacy is only viciousness and dread, not a cheap laugh. But in a milieu where John Wayne Gacy is the next Jasper Johns and "political correctness" is portrayed as the greatest threat since the Red Menace, there are no longer any sacred cows. Anything that society would likely find repellent is exalted as a kind of cruel kitsch—call it "concentration camp." In this mindset, nothing is too touchy to be a potential target for humor, from child molestation to murder. But while making sport of tragedy may seem to rob it of the ability to hurt, it also robs one of the ability to feel at all, not only for others, but for oneself. And that theft takes away something much greater—our humanity.

FOR A SOCIETY that thrives on violence as entertainment, Charles Manson is a centerfold pinup. He's a defective product of the system whose own fallibility enables him to spit society's hypocrisy right back at it: You don't like me? Well, you made me what I am. And the more authority figures or the media cluck disapprovingly at him, the more his taboo appeal grows. He's been chosen by a jury of his peers to be America's bogeyman, and he plays the role to the hilt. (Ed Sanders calls him a "performance artist" who "probably polishes the swastika on his forehead" when he knows that Barbara Walters is coming.)

Rock has had a rich tradition of collaboration with the devil since Robert Johnson made his fateful deal back in the '20s, but in an age where authenticity is key, a "realer" devil is needed. Not some abstract horned figure of lore and legend, or a mystical object of gobbledygook incantations and incense burning, but an actual, live devil in the flesh. We may not have Nixon to kick around anymore, but we still have Manson, an original gangsta.

The question of how Manson resonates in the culture as compared to Woodstock tends to break down along generational lines. Baby boomers cling to Woodstock like the Holy Grail, the defining sociocultural statement of their leafy-green salad days, while younger folks in general reluctantly cast their metaphorical vote with negative creeps like Manson. Invoking Manson is a way for young people to exert their displeasure at boomer co-optation of countercultural milestones, at the fact that their very identity is measured in terms of their parents' anniversaries.

However, the fact that Woodstock is widely considered hippie counterculture's peak means that everything has been downhill from there—and it has been, at varying rates of velocity, depending on personal perspective or organizational allegiance. Today's wet-behind-the-ears Mansonites are fueled by the spirit of betrayal, the sense that somewhere along the line the Woodstock generation copped out. For some, hitching their wagon to Manson is not merely wallowing in shock value or patented post-adolescent rebellion, but a reaction against those who are presumed to have dropped the ball. After all, if everything were still at the pristine natural state of the Aquarian Exposition, a new set of young turks would feel no need to disrupt the bliss.

"Look around you," demands Kozik. "Do you see, like, love and togetherness and positive growth, or do you see everything fucking disintegrating at an exponential rate? You tell me. The empire is crumbling, buddy." One wishes that this view were wrong, that the Woodstock ideal were the rule, but reality would seem to hold that violence and antipathy are more the norm.

Crime and intolerance are on the rise. Nation rises up against nation. Nine Inch Nails is performing at Woodstock '94.

But just because everything is coming down fast doesn't make Charlie the winner. Anomie may seem to have carried the day, but that's hardly cause for rejoicing; it's tragedy. Even as a figure of righteous resistance to boomer oligarchy, even acknowledging the stuff that makes intellectual and emotional sense, Manson's nihilistic equation only adds up to weak-ass shit. In the end, everything he stands for is abhorrent and bankrupt; everything he endorses bitter, empty, reactionary. Is that all there is? Is that the best we can offer as a revolutionary warrior soul? The hippies may have failed, but there's no bigger failure than Manson himself. He may be put forward as a symbol of insurrectionary power, of getting the fear, but ultimately he's the very embodiment of cowardice. The Manson saga is fascinating, but only to a point. No matter how it's retold, he's still a convicted murderer, still a bigot, still a zero. He's a loser, baby. So, if only figuratively, why can't we kill him?"

MIKE RUBIN was a SPIN senior contributing writer from 1994 to 2003. His work has also appeared in *The New York Times*, *GQ*, and *Rolling Stone*, among other publications, and he was one of the learned elders behind *Motorbooty* magazine. He is currently at work on his first book.

4

My Bloody
VALENTINE

Breaking up with a letter composed of lyrics from 69 breakup songs

by **DANA ADAM SHAPIRO**

FEBRUARY 2008

■ ■ ■

"Real Talk." It was R. Kelly's "vérité" video about "just how real shit gets when you're arguing with your girl" (check YouTube) that inspired this valentine. Lines like "They don't eat with us, they don't sleep with us . . . besides, what they eat don't make us shit" made me think of all the other too true (and blue) breakup lyrics. It was a cathartic, wintery walk down a memory lane strewn with little black clouds, old crumb cakes, chrome hearts, and pork swords.

■ ■ ■

DEAR _____,
Your picture is still on my wall. A little black cloud in a dress, with your chrome heart shining in the sun—so pretty when you're unfaithful to me. You don't look different but you have changed.

It's coming on Christmas. They're cutting down trees, they're putting up reindeer. It's so cold in this house. I can't stand the rain against my window. The bed's too big without you. I'll be sleeping with the television on, talking to the shadows from one o'clock 'til four, thinking how it used to be. It's a desperate situation. All I perceive is wasted and broken. Yeah, we still go to dinner sometimes, but we don't sneak a kiss when the waitress turns around. I've been forgotten. You don't love me and I know now. Nothing hurts like someone who knows everything about you leaving you behind.

Everybody's high on consolation. Who would've thought that a boy like me could come to this? I go walkin' after midnight, doing anything just to get you off of my mind. Confidentially, I never had much pride. But now I rock a bar stool and I drink for two. And then the jukebox plays a song I used to know:

> "I used to fart under the covers and she'd just laugh.
> She even cleaned my balls when we would take a bath."

There's always something there to remind me. I saw two shooting stars last night—I wished on them but they were only satellites. Is it wrong to wish on space hardware? It's not a question, but a lesson learned in time. Did you stand by me? No, not at all. Tell me, where did you sleep last night?

Oh shit.

Don't speak.

Shut up, 'cause I know all about it. You keep lyin' when you oughta be truthin'. Heard it from a friend who heard it from a friend who heard it from another you been messin' around. Your cheatin' heart, headed for the cheatin' side of town. Kind of evil make me wanna grab my submachine.

You thought you could keep this shit from me? Into the arms of Mr. Rebound—that alley-cat-coat-wearin' crumbcake, like a matador with his pork sword. You swallow his kids? Lookee here, honey—you don't need to be coy. Why'd ya do it? What'cha gonna say now? Lift me up, hold me, just like you told me you was gonna do. That's what I thought—you're pitiful.

I wish I was as mellow as, for instance, Jackson Browne, but "Fountain of Sorrow" my ass, motherfucker. I've lost my equilibrium, my car keys, and my pride. There's only so much wine you can drink in one life, but it will never be enough to save you from the bottom of your glass. I'm glad that you're sorry, but it's too late, baby, now it's too late. Cry me a river. Here's a quarter, call someone who cares.

Wait. Give me my money back, you bitch. And don't forget to give me back my black T-shirt. Take my picture off the wall. Give back my TV. I don't wanna walk around with you. I don't like a thing about your mother and I hate your daddy's guts too. You can tell your dog to bite my leg. I wish that for just one time you could stand inside my shoes—you'd know what a drag it is to see you. You're just . . . a fuck. I can't explain it 'cause I think you suck. I'm taking pride in telling you to fuck off and die. Die, die, my darling. Just shut your pretty mouth. Don't call me anymore. And the next time your ass gets horny, go fuck one of your funky-ass friends.

I'd show you everywhere you're wrong but I'm never talking to you again. If the phone doesn't ring, you'll know that it's me.

Loveless,

Song Index

1. "Your picture is still on my wall" (Daniel Johnston, "Some Things Last a Long Time")
2. "A little black cloud in a dress" (Billy Bragg, "Must I Paint You a Picture")
3. "With your chrome heart shining in the sun" (Neil Young, "Long May You Run")
4. "So pretty when you're unfaithful to me" (Pixies, "Bone Machine")
5. "You don't look different but you have changed" (the Beatles, "I'm Looking Through You")
6. "It's coming on Christmas. They're cutting down trees, they're putting up reindeer" (Joni Mitchell, "River")
7. "It's so cold in this house" (Bloc Party, "Like Eating Glass")
8. "I can't stand the rain against my window" (Ann Peebles, "I Can't Stand the Rain")
9. "The bed's too big without you" (the Police, "The Bed's Too Big Without You")

10. "I'll be sleeping with the television on" (Billy Joel, "Sleeping With the Television On")
11. "Talking to the shadows from one o'clock 'til four" (Sarah Vaughan, Peggy Lee, Tricky, et al., "Black Coffee")
12. "Thinking how it used to be" (Led Zeppelin, "Tangerine")
13. "It's a desperate situation" (Marvin Gaye, "It's a Desperate Situation")
14. "All I perceive is wasted and broken" (Neutral Milk Hotel, "Where You'll Find Me Now")
15. "Yeah, we still go to dinner sometimes, but we don't sneak a kiss when the waitress turns around" (Bright Eyes, "It's Cool, We Can Still Be Friends")
16. "I've been forgotten" (Bobby Vinton, "Mr. Lonely")
17. "You don't love me and I know now" (Dawn Penn, "You Don't Love Me [No, No, No]")
18. "Nothing hurts like someone who knows everything about you leaving you behind" (Eels, "Last Time We Spoke")
19. "Everybody's high on consolation" (Hall & Oates, "She's Gone")
20. "Who would've thought that a boy like me could come to this?" (Cutting Crew, "[I Just] Died in Your Arms")
21. "I go walkin' after midnight" (Patsy Cline, "Walkin' After Midnight")
22. "Doing anything just to get you off of my mind" (Player, "Baby Come Back")
23. "Confidentially, I never had much pride. But now I rock a bar stool and I drink for two" (They Might Be Giants, "Lucky Ball and Chain")
24. "And then the jukebox plays a song I used to know" (the Greg Kihn Band, "The Break-Up Song [They Don't Write 'Em]")
25. "I used to fart under the covers and she'd just laugh. She even cleaned my balls when we would take a bath" (Devin the Dude, "She's Gone")
26. "There's always something there to remind me" (Sandie Shaw, Dionne Warwick, Naked Eyes, et al., "[There's] Always Something There to Remind Me")

27. "I saw two shooting stars last night—I wished on them but they were only satellites. Is it wrong to wish on space hardware?" (Billy Bragg, "A New England")
28. "It's not a question, but a lesson learned in time" (Green Day, "Good Riddance [Time of Your Life]")
29. "Did you stand by me? No, not at all" (the Clash, "Train in Vain")
30. "Tell me, where did you sleep last night?" (Lead Belly, Bill Monroe, Nirvana, et al., "Where Did You Sleep Last Night")
31. "Oh shit" (Buzzcocks, "Oh Shit")
32. "Don't speak" (No Doubt, "Don't Speak")
33. "Shut up" (Sunset Rubdown, "Shut Up, I'm Dreaming of Places Where Lovers Have Wings")
34. "'Cause I know all about it" (John Lee Hooker, "No Substitute")
35. "You keep lyin' when you oughta be truthin'" (Nancy Sinatra, "These Boots Are Made for Walking")
36. "Heard it from a friend who heard it from a friend who heard it from another you been messin' around" (REO Speedwagon, "Take It on the Run")
37. "Your cheatin' heart" (Hank Williams, "Your Cheatin' Heart")
38. "Headed for the cheatin' side of town" (the Eagles, "Lyin' Eyes")
39. "Kind of evil make me wanna grab my submachine" (Johnny Cash, "Delia's Gone")
40. "You thought you could keep this shit from me?" (Eamon, "Fuck It [I Don't Want You Back]")
41. "Into the arms of Mr. Rebound" (Richard Thompson, "Mr. Rebound")
42. "That alley-cat-coat-wearin' . . . crumbcake" (Oran "Juice" Jones, "The Rain")
43. "Like a matador with his pork sword" (Elvis Costello, "I Hope You're Happy Now")
44. "You swallow his kids?" (Ghostface Killah, feat. Ne-Yo, "Back Like That")

45. "Lookee here, honey" (Son House, "I Ain't Gonna Cry No More")
46. "You don't need to be coy" (Paul Simon, "50 Ways to Leave Your Lover")
47. "Why'd ya do it?" (Marianne Faithfull, "Why'd Ya Do It")
48. "What'cha gonna say now?" (the Magic Numbers, "Forever Lost")
49. "Lift me up, hold me, just like you told me you was gonna do. That's what I thought—you're pitiful" (Eminem, "Go to Sleep")
50. "I wish I was as mellow as, for instance, Jackson Browne, but 'Fountain of Sorrow' my ass, motherfucker" (Tonio K., "H-A-T-R-E-D")
51. "I've lost my equilibrium, my car keys and my pride" (Tom Waits, "The One That Got Away")
52. "There's only so much wine you can drink in one life, but it will never be enough to save you from the bottom of your glass" (the Handsome Family, "So Much Wine")
53. "I'm glad that you're sorry" (Connie Francis, "Who's Sorry Now")
54. "But it's too late, baby, now it's too late" (Carole King, "It's Too Late")
55. "Cry me a river" (Justin Timberlake, "Cry Me a River")
56. "Here's a quarter, call someone who cares" (Travis Tritt, "Here's a Quarter [Call Someone Who Cares]")
57. "Wait" (White Lion, "Wait")
58. "Give me my money back, you bitch. . . . And don't forget to give me back my black T-shirt" (Ben Folds Five, "Song for the Dumped")
59. "Take my picture off the wall. . . . Give back my TV" (Uncle Tupelo, "Give Back the Key to My Heart")
60. "I don't wanna walk around with you" (Ramones, "I Don't Wanna Walk Around With You")
61. "I don't like a thing about your mother and I hate your daddy's guts, too" (Ugly Kid Joe, "Everything About You")
62. "You can tell your dog to bite my leg" (Billy Ray Cyrus, "Achy Breaky Heart")

63. "I wish that for just one time you could stand inside my shoes—you'd know what a drag it is to see you" (Bob Dylan, "Positively 4th Street")

64. "You're just . . . a fuck. I can't explain it 'cause I think you suck. I'm taking pride in telling you to fuck off and die" (Green Day, "F.O.D. [Fuck Off and Die]")

65. "Die, die, my darling. Just shut your pretty mouth" (the Misfits, "Die, Die My Darling")

66. "Don't call me anymore" (Megadeth, "1000 Times Goodbye")

67. "And the next time your ass gets horny, go fuck one of your funky-ass friends" (R. Kelly, "Real Talk")

68. "I'd show you everywhere you're wrong, but I'm never talking to you again" (Hüsker Dü, "Never Talking to You Again")

69. "If the phone doesn't ring, you'll know that it's me" (Jimmy Buffett, "If the Phone Doesn't Ring It's Me")

DANA ADAM SHAPIRO is a former senior editor at SPIN, the codirector/producer of the Oscar-nominated *Murderball*, and the author of *The Every Boy*. His latest film, *Monogamy*, stars Chris Messina and Rashida Jones.

MORRISSEY

Vauxhall and I

Sire/Warner Bros.

APRIL 1994

by **ROB SHEFFIELD**

I finally got to inhale Morrissey's sweat in 1992. The man played my local high-school auditorium with his flashy new glam-rockabilly band and, aside from being the most excellent night of my entire life, it was a really good show, eliciting squeals from the gladiola-clutching kids swarming around me. Onstage, the guitarists circled Morrissey with wreaths of feedback as he gave voice unto the undulations within his very soul while ripping off his gold lamé shirt. A friend managed to snag a shred of Morrissey's frock and let me sniff it, so I can tell you authoritatively that even the Mozzer's sweat bears the aroma of genius. And just a few months ago I spent a weekend's food money on an import CD called *Beethoven Was Deaf*, which only contained near identical live versions of songs I already knew by heart. It sounds sub-*fuckin'*-lime.

Ten years of mindless devotion to a compulsively ironic rock star with flabby pectorals and an Oscar Wilde fetish makes no sense, I know. But then, Morrissey makes no sense. He's rock'n'roll's untamed shrew, frivolous and coy, heterosexually unintelligible, our prodigal prince of frippery and froppery. Long before pop culture fixated on cyberspace and virtual reality, Morrissey took you through the looking glass with a shamelessly excessive vocal style, a fey parody of all the contradictions and illusions built into the human voice. These days, of course, there are Morrissey newsgroups in cyberspace on the Internet—just what his fans need, another reason never to leave the apartment—but it's still more vertiginous to listen in on his musical tea party. He serves fiber-optic cables coiled around cucumber sandwiches and hashish fudge.

The new *Vauxhall and I* takes a big step away from the frantic guitar havoc of 1992's *Your Arsenal,* which guitarists Boz Boorer and Alain Whyte made the most exuberantly gorgeous album of Moz's career. Although Boorer and Whyte are still on hand, producer Steve Lillywhite has muted their roar until *Vauxhall* sounds soft and dreamy, more like the early Smiths than a Morrissey solo album. Although I wish there were a single track as instantly stunning as "Certain People I Know" or "We Hate It When Our Friends Become Successful," the overall flow is powerful. Delicate acoustic textures weave through haunting drones and synthesized strings. The sweetest tune here, "Why Don't You Find Out for Yourself," warns about "The glass / Hidden in the grass," gloating over all the traps you'll fall into following in Morrissey's foolsteps. "Speedway" could be Oscar Wilde singing on the witness stand and flirting with the judge: "All of the rumors / Keeping me grounded / I never said that they were / Completely unfounded." Although the draggy tempos and lush settings make *Vauxhall* sound unbecomingly mellow on the surface, Morrissey does his best to get on your nerves.

Because it sounds so much like his earlier work with the Smiths, *Vauxhall and I* maps how far Morrissey has come since then. The early Smiths were merely tolerable; every couple of years I pull their 1984 debut LP off the shelf and admire the morose grace of "Still Ill," "This Charming Man," and "Reel Around the Fountain." Then I file it again and go back to *The Queen Is Dead*, their endlessly playable 1986 classic wherein Morrissey decided verbal plumage was a musical end in itself, and that he'd "rather be famous / Than righteous or holy." Some fans miss the Smiths, but Morrissey has come to outshine his former band, and it's not because he gets wiser with age. Even on the new album he makes silly complaints against smokers and sunbathers. Now, however, he really sings, and even as he's pledging his sincerity, he's fabricating new verbal and vocal devices for what Baudelaire called *les paradis artificiels*.

American critics will probably never forgive the Mozzer for his vocal overreacting. Minimalist he's not, and his modifier-to-noun ratio is still over the legal limit in many states. He doesn't fit in with the terse, tight-lipped diction of more sensible songwriters, what Lester Bangs called "the Lou Reed 'I walked to the chair / Then I sat in it' school of lyrics." British critics slam Morrissey for hanging around too long, associating him with their other adolescent miseries: scurvy, rickets, mutton, getting caned, not being chosen head prefect because they played cricket with Socialists, etc. But the Morrissey audience is now big enough to support a music business of its own, as insular and self-sufficient as the Christian Contemporary or Spanish-speaking industries: Suede is our own hard rock, the Auteurs are our own roots music, Stereolab is our own New Age, and so on. Even noise-rock kings Pavement quoted a stray

Morrissey lyric in the *Slanted and Enchanted* CD booklet: "I'm the end of the family line." The irony is that Morrissey's line isn't ending at all, merely recombining and mutating into new strains of personality. If by chance you get your own fatal taste of it, don't blame me if you're still tuning in ten years after *you're* old enough to know better.

ROB SHEFFIELD is a writer for *Rolling Stone* and the author of *Love Is a Mix Tape* and *Talking to Girls About Duran Duran.* He first wrote for SPIN in February 1989, reviewing the second Tiffany album.

REBEL YELL

5

Chinese
WATER TORTURE

Visiting the Yangtze River's controversial Three Gorges Dam

by ELIZABETH GILBERT

APRIL 1996

I had no business, at the age of 27, going to China for an undercover investigation into the construction of the Three Gorges Dam. I had no proper journalistic credibility (my previous feature for SPIN, I'm pretty sure, had been about Renaissance Faires), and I was certainly no expert on China. Moreover, this was a high-risk expedition: Chinese authorities were arresting Western journalists they caught investigating the dam operation. But did that daunt me? No, it did not! For I had an airtight alibi: I would pretend to be a tourist! A hydroenergy-fascinated tourist! Brilliant!

    Looking back on it now, the whole trip seems capricious at best, dangerous at worst. But editor/publisher Bob Guccione Jr. let me go anyhow—and that's what I loved about those years I worked for SPIN: the casual trust (the almost reckless trust) that was placed in me (and others like me) by adults who really should have known better. I am staggered sometimes by what we were allowed to attempt. I will always consider myself enormously lucky to have been part of that generation . . . and enormously lucky never to have been arrested.

■ ■ ■

N THE EARLY **1950s**, the Chinese government began building a network of 62 dams along the Yangtze River. It was an act of savage ambition, even during this era of proud, happy dams. America had Hoover, Egypt had Aswan, but this 62-dam Chinese whim was something else altogether, particularly considering that the Yangtze is the third-largest river in the world, a muddy brute and an unpredictable killer. But China persisted, and the dams were completed successfully. The whole system performed perfectly until August 4, 1975. That was the morning it started to rain.

The rain turned into a typhoon, which caused a flood. On the night of August 7, all 62 beautiful new dams broke, one after another. They let loose in a fast row, like buttons on the Incredible Hulk's shirt—pop! pop! pop! pop!—all the way down the river.

The last dam to fall that night was a monster called Banqiao, the pride of the fleet. Banqiao had been constructed under Soviet supervision, and was called the Iron Dam because it was officially indestructible. When the flood wave reached Banqiao, it crumbled in a pathetic instant—taking down with it a string of workmen who had just been sent out across its crest (in the dark! in waist-deep water!) to build with sandbags a last line of defense against the river. Tens of thousands of people died in the next hour. Several hundred thousand more died in the following months from famine and disease.

That's what happened the first time China tried to dam the Yangtze River. It was so much fun they just had to try it again.

REMEMBER WHAT JAY COCHRANE once said: "My goal is to be the most celebrated, most talked-about wire-walker who ever lived."

Jay Cochrane lives down in Florida. Professionally he's known as "the Skywalker." The Skywalker recently executed the longest and tallest successful high-wire walk in history, crossing China's Yangtze River at a dramatic place called the Three Gorges. This would be very much like crossing the Colorado River at a dramatic place called the Grand Canyon.

It was a very exciting stunt, and despite the fact that the Skywalker didn't plummet to his death, several hundred million Chinese watched the event hopefully on live television. This was exactly what the Chinese government had anticipated, which is why they paid the Skywalker "a large fee up to six figures" for his trouble.

China's hope was to bring international attention to their pet construction project, a little something they're building across the Yangtze River called the Three Gorges Dam. Actually, they needn't have bothered, because the project's been getting a lot of free international attention already. Partially, this is because China is building the world's biggest dam right on top of an earthquake fault line. That's always a headline-grabber.

But there's more. The Three Gorges Dam will be the biggest dam ever built, stretching more than a mile across. It will be the largest concrete structure on the planet: It will create a reservoir

Dam shame: Trucks dump rocks into the Yangtze to close a dike designed to reroute the river, at the Three Gorges construction site. *AP Photo/Xinhua*

on the Yangtze River nearly 400 miles long. (On the Mississippi River, this would be like stretching a lake from New Orleans to St. Louis, sinking everything—and everyone—in between.) It will submerge 800 ancient sites, including temples and unexcavated archaeological ruins. It will fill the famous and scenic Three Gorges area like a bathtub. It will exterminate a few rare and endangered Yangtze River species, including the river dolphin and the finless porpoise. It will destroy seven counties and 770 villages. Before it's all finished, at least 1.5 million Chinese citizens will have been forcibly relocated from their homes. Just to add insult to injury, any citizen who refuses to move can be arrested, tossed into a labor camp, and forced to build the fucking dam.

All this excitement has created an interesting paradox: While Chinese citizens are leaving the Yangtze River in droves, foreigners are running toward it in herds. By the time I went to China, I was following a beaten path. All the biggest, sluttiest public-works whores were already there: German structural engineers, French geologists, South American metals experts, Hong Kong financiers, Danish hydroelectricians, Canadian bulldozer salesmen.

I met a drunken Brazilian seismologist one night in a Chongqing bar who said, "So what if they build this dam on a fault line? There are fault lines everywhere! Anyway, I only give advice. If the dam collapses, not my problem!"

It follows naturally that every decent tour agent in the Western Hemisphere has a package deal for a "Farewell to the Treasures of the Yangtze River" boat excursion. *Travel & Leisure* magazine strongly recommended a Yangtze trip in a recent column called "Take a Cruise, Darling." A travel agent in New York told me, "Visit China now, honey. A lot of that old cultural stuff will be gone in a few years."

"Perfect," I said. "I want to be the last kid on my block to see China before it's destroyed."

She said, "So does everyone else, sweetheart. Book your trip today."

A month later, I was in China.

■ ■ ■

"IMPOSSIBLE," MY GUIDE INSISTED.

"Must be possible," I said.

"Impossible," she repeated. "The Three Gorges Dam is China's highest-security top-secret priority! American tourists cannot see this dam."

"But I've come so far," I protested.

This much was true.

I'd been given only four days to infiltrate the dam's construction site. I was staying in the nearby city of Yichang—a sad, toxic industrial town on the banks of the Yangtze River, whose entire population has upper respiratory diseases. The roads to the construction site were guarded by Chinese soldiers, who recognize foreign journalists for what they actually are (dirty spies) and handle them accordingly (deportation/organ-harvesting).

But I am wily and cunning. I disguised myself as a tourist. This was particularly inspired, because no actual tourist would ever travel 13,000 miles expressly to visit Yichang, China. This would be like traveling 13,000 miles expressly to visit Camden, New Jersey.

Yichang isn't terribly used to visitors, so I had a bit of trouble blending in. For instance, I was the only guest in a ten-story luxury hotel. Also, when I walked down the streets of Yichang, women would point me out to their children, as if I were an escaped zoo animal. Then the children would hide behind their mothers, screaming in spasms of terror. It was fun for all of us.

I got the celebrated Yichang chest infection, and I sat in my hotel room for hours, reading my Chinese phrase book, trying to memorize the "Visit to the Doctor" section. I practiced saying: "It's . . . dull/sharp/throbbing/constant/broken/sprained/torn."

After three days, I still hadn't infiltrated the dam. So I hired an official guide. Her name was Miss Sally, and she was a lovely and fragile girl. A delicate little water lily. I tried persuading her to show me the dam's construction site, careful not to offend her vulnerable sensibilities. I begged and flattered her.

"Impossible," she kept saying.

I was desperate. Understanding the traditional Chinese respect for filial loyalty, I finally spun a beautiful lie about my father.

"Miss Sally," I said. "My father is a hydroelectric engineer. When I was very young, he took me to see the great dams of America. Now he is very old. He sent me to China to see its glorious dam while it is under construction. Please, Miss Sally. For the sake of my beloved old father, I must see this dam."

I was near tears. Miss Sally herself was deeply moved.

"Impossible," she said.

Then we were silent for a long time. In fact, it was almost an hour before I finally had the thought.

And that thought was, "Duh."

I said, "Listen, Sally. I would pay money to see that dam. A lot of money."

And she said, "American dollars?"

LET'S MOVE FORWARD a few days. I met an American tourist named Florence. She was from Dallas, and she had just taken a cruise down the Yangtze River on a luxury boat. She recommended that I do the same.

"It's very nice," she said. "Expensive, but nice. They show you every single one of the important temples and cities that is going to be destroyed."

"Gosh," I said. "That didn't bother you?"

"I'll tell you what bothers me," Florence said. "My video camera broke down in Fuling. That whole city is going to be flooded soon, and I don't have a single goddamn picture of it. That's very depressing."

I booked a trip up the river. My boat was called the *Princess Sheena*. Secretly, I was praying it would be filled with goofball American tourists like Florence. Wrong boat. I was the only goofball American tourist on the *Princess Sheena*. The rest were rich, expatriate Chinese, quite a slick crowd. They'd all escaped China during various revolutions, to resettle in places like Malaysia, Hong Kong, Taiwan, and Toronto. They were big-shot, high-rolling business mavens.

A woman from Singapore with diamond earrings the size of ashtrays bragged, "We are proof of how successful Chinese can be when we don't have to live in stupid China!"

These swingers were all visiting China with stacks of newly made cash, eager to view the fated—and expensive—temples of the Three Gorges. This would seem like a solemn event for people of Chinese descent, but nobody on the *Princess Sheena* was in mourning.

"This dam will only affect peasants and farmers," one Taiwanese industrialist told me. "1.5 million people may seem like a lot to you, but it's nothing in China. I believe these people are—what's the word?"

"Expendable?" I offered.

"Yes! Expendable."

I asked another Taiwanese businessman, "Is this a happy trip or a sad trip for you?"

He shrugged. "I understand they are flooding the most beautiful part of China. This is my homeland, of course. I am sorry for the lost temples, but not so sorry for the people. What did China ever do for me?"

"Killed your family in the street?" I guessed.

"Exactly," he said. "This dam is no big deal to me."

"So why did you come?"

He smiled widely. "Because I can afford it."

The *Princess Sheena* was their perfect vehicle. It had a sauna, a sun deck, room service, and a cruise director who looked like a high-end Thai prostitute.

"Welcome to Sheena," she whispered breathlessly, as each tourist boarded. "Welcome to luxury pleasure cruise."

I told the cruise director, "I'm a student. I'm interested in understanding the history and culture of the Three Gorges. I want to learn as much as I can on this trip."

"Come to the lounge tonight after dinner," she breathed. "We will have educational program, especially for you."

I went to the lounge that night, expecting a sparsely attended lecture from an eminent local anthropologist. Instead, the joint was packed. They were watching a variety show performed by the staff. Mostly, this meant watching the ship's housemaids singing karaoke. Cocktails were served. The educational part was at the end of the night, when the sexy cruise director came out onstage in a leopard-print dress.

She said, "The Yangtze River is very old, important river in Chinese history. But soon the river will become a lake. To honor the Yangtze, we have created this American-style educational dance. It is interpretation tribute of Yangtze. The dance is called Yangtze! It is special gift to our American guest."

That was me. Everyone in the room nodded and smiled at me, and I nodded and smiled back.

The lights went down, and six young Chinese men ran onstage, shirtless. I recognized them as busboys from the dining room. They were wearing purple silk shorts and nylon tights. When the music started, they began rolling on the floor, chanting, "Yangtze! Yangtze!" Some of them made rowing gestures, and some made swimming gestures. One of them pretended to be a fish, and another one seemed to be drowning. Then one of the busboys started spinning awkwardly on his back. He was supposed to be a whirlpool.

"Oh my God," I said to the woman next to me. "He's break dancing."

She didn't speak English, but she smiled and nodded at me. The other dancing busboys pranced around the spinning whirlpool boy, chanting "Yangtze! Yangtze!" and the audience also chanted "Yangtze! Yangtze!" When the break dancer finally staggered up from his whirlpool act, his purple shorts were twisted painfully around his genitals and he was sweating. There was driving applause.

"Thank you!" the cruise director proclaimed. "This is how we honor the Yangtze River in modern China!"

"Modern China is in big trouble," I said to the woman next to me.

She nodded vigorously and happily.

INTERNATIONAL ENVIRONMENTALISTS and human-rights activists have great hopes that the Three Gorges Dam can still be stopped, but I wouldn't be too optimistic. China has been considering this project since 1944. Its motivation here is twofold. The dam's primary function will be flood control, which has been a pressing issue for centuries. The Yangtze River floods every year out of habit and every few years out of malice, taking thousands of lives and—more compelling in this era of economic enhancement—destroying factories and farms. Ideally, the dam's reservoir would contain and carefully release massive quantities of this flood water, although there is a substantial concern that the dam will be better suited for containing massive quantities of silt. (In the famous 62-dam-wrecking Yangtze flood, for instance, engineers tried to open Banqiao's floodgates, and found them completely blocked with mud and gravel.)

The other purpose of the Three Gorges Dam, of course, is to provide clean, safe hydroelectric power to the region. This is a pretty irresistible argument. China currently has a dirty little habit of burning 1.2 billion tons of coal a year, and—for the sake of all the world's air—could seriously use a better source of power. Between 1970 and 1990, China's energy consumption rose 208 percent, compared with a 28 percent average rise in already developed nations. Existing resources are understandably strained. Chinese factories often have to shut down three days a week due to electricity shortages, and many villages are without power of any kind. Chinese engineers insist that the Three Gorges Dam will produce the electrical equivalent of 10 nuclear-power plants, and angrily accuse Western environmentalists of plotting to keep the world's largest nation locked in the Stone Age.

So the dilemma is this: Will the Three Gorges Dam save China, or merely sink it? The current World's Biggest Dam is Itaipu, built by Brazil for the same needs and reasons China has expressed. Expensive, dangerous, environmentally nightmarish Itaipu has never produced the electricity it promised. Brazil borrowed up to the eyeballs to build the thing, and was left with a foreign debt so outrageous that the country's inflation rate grew to over 300 percent a year. Compare that to America's three percent, and see what this project actually did to save Brazil's economy.

Big dams are out of favor these days. The more sensible alternative would be to build several smaller dams along the Yangtze's many tributaries, yielding a safer, more efficient return on a lesser investment. But there's no glory in that, is there? That wouldn't be the second Great Wall of China. That wouldn't be an eternal monument to a mighty empire. So forget it, there isn't even any debate. The Chinese are good at building real big things real fast—if there's one thing they've got, it's labor—and their goals here are especially grand. Work began two years ago, and the latest push is to start actually damming the river's flow by 1997. This is a political decision, accompanied by this catchy slogan: "Complete the work of blocking the river a year in advance and make it coincide with the year of Hong Kong's return to the motherland so as to turn 1997 into a year of double celebration!" I'm sure the jingle is on everyone's lips.

The World Bank, the United Nations, and the United States government have all made it clear that they do not approve. Opposition to the dam within China itself has been huge and unprecedented—although it quieted down somewhat after a few outspoken journalists and engineers were arrested for treason. Work goes on. This shouldn't be surprising. An elderly Chinese official named Madame Zhengying is in charge of the dam project. A few decades ago, she was also in charge of building the 62 dams that all broke in one night.

Madame Zhengying really wants this dam.

She recently said, "If I am kept from damming the Three Gorges, I will not rest—even in death!"

Madame Zhengying is just a little bit relentless.

THE CHINESE TOURIST SERVICE has a gentle euphemism for the villages and cities that will be flooded by the dam. They call these places "affected areas."

One morning on the *Princess Sheena*, I made the sexy cruise director sit down with me and a map of the Yangtze River. I asked her to confirm all the affected areas in the Three Gorges. The sexy cruise director was beginning to hate me.

"What will happen to Zigui City?" I asked.

"Gone," she said, bored.

"Badong?"

"Gone."

"Wanxian?"

"Gone."

"Fengjie?"

"Gone."

She liked the other guests better, since they were more relaxed about all this upcoming destruction. In the afternoons, for instance, the Malaysian ladies would sit on the deck, sunning themselves contentedly while doomed villages floated by.

"It's so serene!" they would say. Sometimes they would fall asleep, and make a sound like purring.

Each day, the *Princess Sheena* would stop at the docks of some particularly interesting "affected area," and let the passengers tour the city. The local villagers took advantage of these visits to make a little money. They would crowd around the cruise ships, calling the tourists by the names of whatever product they were selling.

"Hello, silk!" they would yell. "Hello, jade! Hello, Kodak film!"

The Malaysian ladies from the *Princess Sheena* would hire local Chinese men with sedan chairs, and then be carried through the town on the shoulders of these peasants. They seemed absolutely comfortable this way, being treated like ancient Chinese royalty. One afternoon I overheard one of the fancy Malaysian ladies berating her sedan-chair carriers in Chinese. Her voice was so scornful it sounded like something sizzling in oil.

"What did you tell that man?" I asked her later.

She said lightly, "I told him that if he stumbled again, I would have him killed."

"Excuse me?"

She laughed. "Of course, I could not actually have him killed, but he doesn't know that. He was much more careful after I scared him."

On these day trips, we would always cross paths with tourists from other boats. In the ancient city of Fengjie, I met a retired

American couple resting on a bench. His name was Ed, and she was Sheila. They were taking a trip up the river too. Her sister had talked her into it, in order to see "all the old stuff."

"What do you think of it?" I asked her.

"There are steps everywhere in this darn country," she moaned. "My ankles are so darn swollen from climbing the darn steps!"

She lifted her caftan and showed me her ankles, which were indeed very swollen.

Then she said, "And another thing! The food here is so bad, I wouldn't soak my feet in it."

This brought an awkward silence.

Sheila's husband asked, "Is that really an expression, honey?"

Sheila and Ed didn't like China. They were planning a trip to Thailand next year, where there would be "more creature comforts."

"They do have great creature comforts in Thailand," I said.

"And great creatures," Ed growled, winking at me with greasy lust.

In the meantime, Sheila and Ed had hired a local guide who called himself Mr. Keith. He was very good, and they let me tag along.

"I love tourists!" Mr. Keith said graciously. "I take your money from you!" He showed us around his city of Fengjie, and shared some brilliant statements about the dam.

"There are many ancient temples in the Three Gorges area," Mr. Keith explained. "Some of them are very high in the mountains, and tourists have to walk up many steps to visit. After the reservoir is filled, the tourists can just float by these temples on comfortable boats!"

Swollen-ankled Sheila liked this.

Later, Mr. Keith took us to a stone marker 175 meters above the town of Fengjie. He explained that everything below the marker would be submerged. The entire city, carved delicately into the side of the mountain, was below us. An ancient Buddhist monastery was also below us. And a handsome new suspension bridge spanned the river below us.

"What will happen to that bridge?" I asked.

"It's in an affected area," Mr. Keith said. "It will be destroyed with dynamite and then submerged."

"But it looks brand new!" Sheila said.

"Yes. It was just finished last year."

"And when will it be destroyed?"

"Next year," Mr. Keith said casually.

"Why build a bridge if you have to tear it down the next year?" Ed asked.

Mr. Keith shrugged. "It is a very nice bridge."

(I remembered something a Canadian engineer had told me. "In China, when it comes to construction, the right chopstick doesn't know what the left chopstick is doing.")

Mr. Keith also said, "Do not be sad about the dam. Geologists have proven that this area was under water millions of years ago. So it is natural for this area to be under water again."

"Where will you go when the water comes?" I asked him.

He smiled, as innocent as a turkey on November 20.

"The government is building a beautiful new city for me," he said.

Of all China's lies, this one is the cruelest. There ain't gonna be no beautiful new city. Although thousands of people have been relocated already, a Hong Kong newspaper reported that "not a single family has moved into new, permanent housing, because of slow progress and lack of funds." At least 5,000 citizens were evicted from Hubei Province last February and forced to spend the winter in shoddy temporary buildings. In many cases, farmers are moved from economically rich agricultural floodplains to overcrowded industrial cities, where the per capita income is less than half that of rural areas.

Peasants who object to the move are kindly reminded to "take more good ideology with them, and less old furniture." Reluctance to relocate is a crime against the state, and legislation hastily passed in 1994 allows "threats to state security" to be punished by death.

"The people of the Yangtze are very proud to make sacrifices for the good of the country," one Chinese official said. "They have been waiting all their life to make such a sacrifice."

"Chinese peasants have an unhealthy attachment to the land of their ancestors," one Chinese hotel manager told me. "They make the relocation process difficult. These peasants often do not understand what is good for them."

In 1992, some students from Kai County didn't know what was good for them, either. Because 179 of them protested the Three Gorges Dam's relocation policies. They were arrested as counterrevolutionaries, and nobody has heard from them since. People wait all their lives to make such a sacrifice.

WHICH REMINDS ME of something that happened back in the stinky city of Yichang.

"I like your President Clinton," Miss Sally told me one day. "He doesn't care so much about human rights. He leaves us alone about it, and makes much trade instead."

"Thanks," I said. "We can all be proud of that."

We were driving through Yichang. We'd been talking about politics, and Miss Sally had been telling me how much China valued its citizens. Then she wanted to show me how much China valued its endangered species, so she took me to the Chinese Sturgeon Research Institute.

The Yangtze River sturgeon is an endangered fish about the length of a Volvo. It has a scary fin like a shark's, and a mouth like a Frisbee. The sturgeon is approximately 14 million years old, and has that spooky, dreadful-ancient-knowledge look of all prehistoric creatures.

For the last 14-or-so million years, the Yangtze River sturgeon has spawned by swimming 3,000 miles up the Yangtze, from the East China Sea to the flood plains of Tibet. This was a pretty good system until dams on the river stopped the fish like this: THUD.

Now the Chinese are trying to keep river sturgeons alive in captivity. In the middle of the Research Institute was a tiny, above-ground swimming pool, the kind you see in suburban backyards. And in this pool was a Yangtze River sturgeon almost 15 feet long. He was swimming around and around in a slow circle. Chinese schoolchildren on field trips tried to grab his dorsal fin.

We watched him. Finally, Miss Sally said, "Poor river sturgeon. He used to have to swim up the whole Yangtze River. Three thousand miles! Very frustrating swimming trip! But not anymore. Thanks to Chinese scientists, today the river sturgeon swims in a safe and comfortable swimming pool instead."

"Interesting theory," I said.

"Yes," Miss Sally agreed. "Very lucky ending for this venerable fish."

WHEN WE LEFT the conservation center, I asked Miss Sally to take me to the national archaeological museum in Yichang. I'd read an article in the *New York Times* about the director of this museum. The story said he was an archaeological hero, almost single-handedly trying to excavate 8,000 years of Chinese history before the dam floods it all forever. His name was Yao Ying Qin. He'd been photographed in his crowded Yichang Museum, looking tired, holding an ancient clay pot. In the article, he was quoted gently criticizing the dam project.

I'd heard that Yao Ying Qin had "gotten into some trouble" after that story ran. So when I was in Yichang, I decided to check on him. But when we got to the museum, the gates were all locked.

Miss Sally found the custodian limping around the grounds. For a small bribe, he let us into the museum for the Big Surprise: The museum was empty.

"The museum business is not so booming," Miss Sally observed.

But the museum was booming—that is, making great booming echoes from our voices and footsteps. It was an impressive stone building, three stories tall, with vast ceilings and long hallways, and it had been completely sacked. Every cubicle was empty; every display case was empty, every creepy hallway was empty.

"Where are the exhibits?" I asked the custodian.

The custodian said he didn't know.

"Where are the Yangtze River artifacts?"

The custodian didn't know that, either.

"Where is the curator of this museum?"

The custodian didn't know this word, "curator."

"Where is Yao Ying Qin?" I asked instead.

The custodian looked down at his hands, and said something in Chinese.

Miss Sally translated. "He does not know where is Yao Ying Qin. He wonders why you ask such questions."

THAT NIGHT, I MET a man in the lobby of my hotel. His name was Derrick and he was a British-born citizen of Hong Kong. He was currently the primary agent for an Asian company that manufactured and sold bulldozers. He was erudite and aging, with a thick chest, white hair, and fat, pink fingers. He was sitting with his Bangladeshi manservant, a small, quiet individual called Comjhi, who spoke eight languages, and was "indispensable." In the movie, Orson Welles would play Derrick, and Peter Lorre would play Comjhi. Together, they'd spent the last 25 years traveling through Asia, dealing in heavy machinery, and making quite a bit of money for their assorted employers.

Derrick knows how to make money in foreign lands. He and Comjhi are partners easily placed anywhere throughout history, a classical pair of figures who pre-date capitalism, and even colonialism. They are traders. You can find them anywhere, in any century: smuggling spices out of Ceylon, or diamonds out of the Belgian Congo, or rum out of Barbados. When I met them, they happened to be in China, selling bulldozers to the good people at the Three Gorges Dam.

"As for the dam itself," Derrick speculated casually, "it will collapse. Every project in China is underfunded, and this is the most underfunded of all. It's a disaster, guaranteed. The construction site would make you sick."

"And your name shall be upon it, Derrick!" I pronounced.

Derrick laughed. "I don't want my fucking name on it. And if they do put my name on it, be sure to put it above the water line, if anyone is to ever see it."

"What's your best prediction for the dam?" I asked.

"Several million people will die the day it breaks. It will drown everyone from here to Shanghai. It will cause the worst flood since Noah."

There were some very somber cocktails after that statement.

Much later, Derrick told Comjhi and me a story. It dated back to 1993, when the initial construction was just beginning on the dam. Derrick had secured the contract to deliver some of the first bulldozers for the project, and he was bringing them up the rough mountain roads on a flatbed truck. He was with the dam's major construction overseer, a very important Chinese official. They were stopped by soldiers at a roadblock, and had to wait hours in the truck for the appropriate authorization to continue.

"We were hungry," Derrick said. "So my big-shot Chinese companion pulls out a bag of ricebirds."

"What are ricebirds?" I asked.

"Ricebirds are these tiny little sparrows which used to fly around China in flocks of thousands. They land in rice paddies. You toss a net out, and catch the entire flock. Then the birds are boiled alive in oil—whole, with bones, feathers, eyeballs—and sold in huge sacks. It's always been a delicacy. They aren't much bigger than chestnuts, and very pretty. You just pop the ricebird into your mouth, and eat the whole thing—crunch, crunch, crunch."

"You snack on another species like it's popcorn?" I said.

"Sort of, except for one thing. Just before you swallow, you spit out whatever bones you can find. That day, we ate the whole sack of ricebirds, spitting out the bones and waiting for the approval to go in and start building the dam. By the end of the afternoon, the floor of the cab was piled with thousands of tiny little bones."

"Did they taste good?" I asked.

"Oh, you don't understand," Derrick said, exasperated. He was tired of my questions, and it was late.

"Good or bad doesn't matter," Comjhi explained gently, speaking for the first time that night. "It is just a way that powerful men will pass the time in China. It is simply what is done, Miss. My friend is simply telling you that it has always been this way."

■ ■ ■

AS IT TURNED OUT, of course, Miss Sally did take me to see the top-secret, highest-security Three Gorges Dam. It cost me 100 American dollars. China is for sale, and that's how much it costs.

"I will be an excellent guide for you today," Miss Sally said. "I have many entertaining facts about this dam!"

"I love entertaining facts," I said.

"Okay," she laughed. She had just gotten her cash, and was acting pretty sassy. "Did you know that this dam will be four times the size of your American Hoover Dam?"

She translated this entertaining fact into Chinese for the benefit of our driver, who laughed in my face for having such a puny-ass dam in my country. I also laughed. Nothing is funnier than a dam four times the size of Hoover.

It was a two-hour drive out of Yichang. The road was a single-lane dirt road of mountain switchbacks, following the muddy Yangtze River. We were among a caravan of trucks packed with rubble, bricks, sand, and steel. Flatbeds behind us carried cement mixers, backhoes, cranes, and other machines you wouldn't be able to name unless you'd grown up around a well-stocked sandbox. Along the slight shoulder of the road, workers with more modest tools—hoes, shovels, pickaxes—walked in the dust. This traffic of trucks and men began two years ago, and will continue, unbroken, until the year 2013.

The construction site itself was impossibly random. It looked like workers and machinery had been dropped down from the sky, and that everyone just started digging where they fell. Sometimes the single-lane dirt road turned into a beautiful four-lane concrete highway, but only for a few hundred yards. Here was half a bridge, there was half a tunnel. There were tall cranes everywhere that seemed to be picking structures apart, not creating them.

At one point, a worker walked in the road before us and vaguely gestured for our car to stop.

"We must wait," Miss Sally explained, as the man talked to our driver. "Because of dynamite."

As she spoke, the side of the mountain wall just ahead of us blew out in a gut-shaking explosion. A blast of boulders spat across the stretch of road we'd just intended to cross. More explosions followed, and rocks the size of dinner rolls pelted our car, as well as the heads of the workers in the area. There were no barricades, no hard-hats, nobody supervising this.

It's difficult to express how little this explosion seemed to concern anyone else. My driver and the workman chatted casually throughout it. When the blasting was finished, someone cleared a path through the rubble for us. On the shoulder of the road, a young man was bleeding down his cheek.

"Very good," Miss Sally announced. "Now they are finished breaking the mountain. We shall continue."

"How many people are working on this project?" I asked.

"More than 10,000," Miss Sally answered.

"Where do they live?"

"They will live at the dam for the next 19 years. Nobody will leave until the dam is finished. The government has built lovely housing for them."

As we approached the site, though, it became clear that whatever housing existed had been cobbled together by the workers themselves, using stolen moments and borrowed objects. Cardboard was the most popular roofing material, held down by hunks of rock. It snows up there, by the way.

The workers' children were everywhere, climbing like squirrels under machinery and over piles of bricks. No schools or hospitals appeared at the dam site, although several luxury hotels were being built for visiting dignitaries. The children will live scattered in this place of work until they get big enough to work themselves. In the meantime, their hair and faces were already coated white with cement dust, giving them the creepy looks of miniature old people: tottering, gap-toothed, lost.

We continued driving through the construction site, to the center of the realm, where a watchtower stood on the highest point. The cement dust was so thick it was barely possible to see the river in question.

In a massive cavity below us, laborers were digging what will someday be the world's biggest ship-lock. So far, this consisted of a hole you could easily use for burying the great cathedrals of Europe. Bulldozers floated around the rim like corks. Miss Sally took out a sheet of notebook paper and sketched the planned design for me. Even on that tiny scale, it looked absurd: a six-part hydraulic lock, capable of lifting several 10,000-ton shipping vessels over a 600-foot wall. She explained how the dam would be able to perfectly control flooding on the Yangtze, and bragged about the electricity it would produce for all Chinese people.

After a long silence, she said without looking at me, "Miss Liz, there is a question I have been wanting to ask you for three days."

"Go ahead," I said, sure that I had been found out.

"In your country, I believe you have many modern electrical conveniences. Do you have an oven in your house?"

"Yes, Miss Sally, I do."

"We do not have many ovens in China. It is very primitive. Here, we still must cook over fire."

Suddenly, she was shy.

"Excuse me, Miss Liz," she ventured. "But what do you bake in your oven?"

I didn't have the heart to tell her that I use my oven to warm up take-out food that some Chinese person cooked over a fire.

"Cakes?" she suggested, when I didn't answer right away.

"Yes," I lied. "I bake cakes."

Her look was triumphal.

"That is exactly what I shall do when I receive my modern electrical oven," she announced, folding up her sketch of the Three Gorges Dam. "I shall bake a cake every day."

ELIZABETH GILBERT wrote for SPIN for four years. She's the author of five books of fiction and nonfiction, including *Eat, Pray, Love* and, most recently, *Committed: A Skeptic Makes Peace With Marriage.*

6

WAR

is

LOUD

Investigating the U.S. military's use of music as an instrument of torture

by **DAVID PEISNER**

DECEMBER 2006

I first began thinking about music and interrogation in 2005. With two wars raging overseas and civil liberties being trampled at home, it was hard not to feel a little irrelevant spending your days weighing the relative merits of the new Strokes album.

Armed with both outsized ambition and naiveté, I set off on what I imagined to be a noble quest to get to the bottom of this practice: Why were the military and the CIA blaring Metallica at detainees in overseas prisons? Whose idea was it? Did it even work?

I had never done much real reporting in my life, but I muddled through, got lucky more than a few times, and after three months of diligent work was so filled with a sense of my own self-importance, I was certain the story would be greeted upon publication like a bombshell. Instead, the silence was deafening: no letters to the editor, no angry e-mails, no bookings on Charlie Rose. *Oh, well.*

As time went by, though, people slowly starting noticing. Nine months after the story came out, I did an interview about it for NPR. Six months after that, I was invited to speak at a university, followed by another public radio interview, and another college speaking gig. This taught me something valuable: If you can find a subject that nobody else knows anything about, by default you become a leading authority on it. I doubt the story had any real impact on the insular world it discussed, but if it made anyone consider the idea of blaring music at prisoners as something other than a joke, I'd consider it a resounding success.

■   ■   ■

N MAY 2003, Shafiq Rasul was led from his cell at the Camp Delta detention facility in Guantanamo Bay, Cuba, to a small, drab interrogation booth. He sat down and a military police officer chained his leg irons to a metal ring in the center of the linoleum floor. Rasul had grown accustomed to this procedure since his arrival in Cuba nearly 18 months earlier. Every few weeks he'd be brought into the booth and questioned about people he knew, places he'd been, and what he and two friends, Ruhal Ahmed and Asif Iqbal—all English citizens in their 20s—were doing in Afghanistan in late 2001.

This time was different. An interrogator walked into the booth, pressed play on a nearby stereo, and walked out. Rasul immediately recognized the sound coming from the speakers: It was Eminem's "Kim." "It was weird because I'd heard it before," he says. "I've probably got the album at home somewhere. [They] just put Eminem on and left, and I thought, 'What the hell is going on here?'"

Rasul sat in the room with "Kim" on repeat. He wasn't particularly bothered ("It was just like playing music at home, but chained to the floor"), and after a few hours MPs returned him to his cell.

It wasn't long before he was back in the booth. This time, the room was pitch black except for the irregular flashes of a strobe light. Eminem had been replaced by loud, menacing heavy metal. The air-conditioning had been cranked way up, and Rasul was short-shackled—his wrists fastened to his ankles, then shackled to the ring in the floor in what is known as a "stress position." He was left there for hours. "Being in that position is really stressful

Incoming!: U.S. Army MPs accompany a detainee in March 2002 at Camp X-Ray in Guantanamo Bay, Cuba. *Corbis/Reuters/Marc Serota*

on your back," he says. "If you try to move, the chains start digging into your feet and wrists."

Rasul endured such "interrogation sessions" every day, sometimes twice a day, for nearly three weeks. Often, there was little or no interrogation taking place. After up to 12 hours in the booth with raging metal as his only companion, he'd just be marched back to his cell—now on the prison's isolation block.

Rasul, Ahmed, and Iqbal had been captured in Afghanistan in November 2001 by a Northern Alliance militia, and then transferred to U.S. custody. U.S. intelligence seemed to lose interest in Rasul after his first few months in Guantanamo. Even if they doubted his story—that he and his friends had traveled to Pakistan for a wedding, then entered Afghanistan after the U.S. invasion to do humanitarian work—he seemed to know next to nothing about Al Qaeda and was interrogated infrequently. But in 2003, U.S. agents found what they believed was a smoking gun: a videotape apparently showing the three men sitting in on an August 2000 meeting with Osama bin Laden and lead 9/11 hijacker Mohammed Atta. The increasing harshness of Rasul's treatment directly corresponded to this discovery and soon began having its desired effect. "It just starts playing with you," he says. "Even if you were shouting, the music was too loud—nobody would be able to hear you. You're there for hours and hours, and they're constantly playing the same music. All that builds up. You start hallucinating."

Rasul's interrogators showed him the video and pressed him to admit he was at the meeting. After he initially denied the charge, the weeks-long barrage of metal, extreme cold, and strobe lights did its job and Rasul confessed.

There was only one problem: In August 2000, Shafiq Rasul couldn't have been breaking bread with bin Laden because, as investigators would soon confirm, he was attending university and working at the electronics store Curry's back in England. In early 2004, Rasul, Ahmed, and Iqbal were released without charges.

RASUL'S ORDEAL MAY SEEM bizarre and disturbing, but it's hardly unique. Over the last five years, loud music has quietly become a valued tool in the Bush administration's war on terror. The list of artists reportedly drafted to help break down prisoners for interrogation reads like an eclectic iPod playlist, heavy on rap (2Pac, Dr. Dre) and hard rock and metal (Metallica, Marilyn Manson, Rage Against the Machine), but also sprinkled with pop (Britney Spears, Matchbox Twenty), classic rock (Aerosmith, Meat Loaf), and the odd head-scratcher (Stanley Brothers, Barney the dinosaur).

Music isn't a new military weapon. Probably the first commander to order its use was, perhaps not coincidentally, the same one often viewed as the architect of the Bush administration's Middle East policy. According to the Old Testament, during the siege of Jericho by the Israelites, God tells Joshua to have priests march around the city blowing trumpets for seven days. On the seventh day, "at the blast of the rams' horns, when you hear the trumpet sound . . . the city wall will collapse, and the army will advance" (Joshua 6:5). Joshua follows his orders, Jericho's walls crumble, and the Israelites rush in to slaughter every single resident, save a prostitute and her family.

The Jericho model has more or less persevered into modern times. U.S. psychological operations (PsyOp) units began experimenting with blasting music at enemies in Vietnam and infamously rocked a 1989 standoff with Panamanian dictator Manuel Noriega. But it's only been in the past few decades that music and other sounds began turning up during interrogations. The British blared white noise at Irish Republican Army suspects in the '70s but swore off the practice after the European Court of Human Rights ruled in 1977 that it was "degrading and inhuman." Israel's military employed loud music until 1999, when an Israeli Supreme Court judged that this exposure "causes the suspect suffering. It does not fall within the scope of . . . a fair and effective interrogation."

Perhaps the first example of music being used by the U.S. for interrogations came post-9/11, in spring 2002, during the questioning of suspected Al Qaeda operative Abu Zubaydah. According to *The New York Times*, while in custody at a secret CIA facility in Thailand, Zubaydah was subjected to "deafening blasts of music by groups like Red Hot Chili Peppers."

Nobody in the U.S. government seems eager to take credit for this innovation. Loud music isn't among the standard interrogation tactics described in the Army Field Manual. It's never mentioned in any of the declassified memos to and from Defense Secretary Donald Rumsfeld's office concerning the authorization of special "enhanced" techniques for use against particularly resistant detainees. It's not taught at the U.S. Army Intelligence School at Fort Huachuca, Arizona, where military interrogators are trained. And the CIA refuses to comment at all on its interrogation practices.

Yet it's clear that music has been employed repeatedly to help set conditions for fruitful interrogations. What's far less clear is how it came to be used, if it's legal, if it's effective, and whether the practice will continue. The answers to those questions are hardly straightforward but offer a window into the kind of war we've been fighting since 9/11 and the kind of war we're willing to continue fighting five years after.

MAMDOUH HABIB, AN EGYPT-BORN Australian citizen, was hauled off a bus by Pakistani police in Karachi in early October 2001, weeks before the U.S. invasion of neighboring Afghanistan. He was soon transferred, allegedly by U.S. agents, to Egypt, where he endured beatings, electric shock, and sonically enhanced interrogation methods. "What surprised me is they used English[-language] music," Habib says. "They put headphones on me, then put on the music very loud." After six months in Egypt, Habib was transferred to a U.S. facility in Afghanistan, then flown to Guantanamo. He was in such bad shape at that point that he has almost no memory of his first year in Cuba. Habib says his interrogators asked him about his treatment in Egypt, and after learning the things that troubled him most (threats to his family, loud music), they proceeded to apply them themselves. "They were trying to make me crazy," he says. "They try to take your mind away from you." To some extent it worked. "Even today, when I hear any loud noise, I get disturbed."

Dr. Stephen Xenakis, a psychiatrist, retired brigadier general, and former commander of the Southeast Regional Army Medical Command, says this sort of musical bombardment can indeed cause permanent damage. "It's really traumatizing to the brain," he says. "It will lead to anxiety and the kind of symptoms you get with post-traumatic stress disorder."

Habib, who the U.S. had said admitted to having prior knowledge of the 9/11 attacks and training some of the hijackers—confessions Habib says were made only under duress—was released without charges in January 2005.

Tom, who requested his last name be withheld for security reasons, began working as an interrogator in the late '80s. He served in a senior position at Guantanamo in early 2002 and in a similar capacity in Afghanistan. After leaving the military, he worked for a government agency he's not permitted to name, both in Iraq and at secret prisons around the world, often dealing with those considered "high value" prisoners. He cautions against taking ex-detainees at their word, noting that they've learned to "exploit the media." In particular, he calls Shafiq Rasul, whom he interrogated in Guantanamo, "a lying sack of shit." (The episode Rasul described concerning Eminem and heavy metal occurred more than a year after Tom had left Guantanamo.) It's nearly impossible to confirm the details of many ex-detainees' allegations, but the incidents Rasul, Habib, and others describe fit a pattern consistent not only with one another's stories, but also with the U.S. government's own investigations into reported abuse.

That said, Tom and other interrogators I spoke to maintain that the use of music in interrogations was anything but standard operating procedure. "It was definitely not part of military doctrine," Tom says. The music itself would usually be chosen by the interrogators either from CDs or downloaded off a file-sharing service. Boom boxes or iPod speakers might be borrowed from a soldier or purchased at the military PX or in a nearby town. Occasionally, music would be broadcast over the prison's public-address system.

Shortly after Tom arrived at Guantanamo, some PsyOp soldiers convinced the guards to play Neil Diamond's "America" over the loudspeakers. "It was to try to keep the prisoners agitated and from talking to one another," he explains. "We wanted to prevent them from keeping each others' spirits up and emboldening one another to resist interrogation." The results were disastrous. "It just about caused an all-out riot. Strict interpreters of Islam are forbidden from listening to music. The whole place basically erupted."

Tom makes an ethical distinction between blasting music for the purposes of interrogation and using it to disorient a recent capture. "If [the detainee] is accustomed to his surroundings and you force him to listen to Limp Bizkit, that's clearly an interrogation tactic," he says. "That would only be used in very rare situations, to annoy someone to the point where their only way out is you. To me, the only purpose of that is to drive somebody nuts, and that constitutes torture.

"When we use it at remote facilities, it's to maintain what we call 'the shock of capture,'" Tom continues. "The hardest cases to break are those guys that sit there and smugly smile because they know we're not going to beat them up or rip their fingernails out. So we use music to keep them from knowing what time it is, from communicating with others or hearing sounds that would help orient them."

For better or worse, these were distinctions Tom and others made on the fly. The agency had trained him in the use of white noise on prisoners. Switching to music was simply an innovation made on the ground. He also says the agency authorized all the techniques he employed at these secret sites. But the standard often used to determine how far interrogators could go was rather haphazard. "You couldn't keep somebody up while you went to bed," he explains. "If you can stay up, they can stay up. If you could take the music, they can take the music."

MARK HADSELL IS A 41-YEAR-OLD mechanical engineer and, until recently, an Army Reservist with the 361st Psychological Operations Unit. From February 2003 until April 2004, he led a mobile, three-man PsyOp team in Iraq. He says he blasted music when assisting interrogators in the questioning of insurgents in al-Qa'im, a town near the Syrian border. "We had key prisoners that had information we knew would be useful in finding their counterparts who were ambushing us," he explains. "So we [played] Metallica's 'Enter Sandman' on repeat for a 24-hour period as sleep deprivation. You wanted to get [the prisoners] emotionally exhausted. Say you're up for 24 hours straight, music pounding in the background—nine times out of ten you'll just answer a question without thinking."

Hadsell says he had authorization to try this technique from his commanders but claims the idea was his own, as were the details of its use: "I wanted to see if it would actually work. I just picked music I knew they didn't like."

One interrogator who served in several prisons in Iraq, and spoke on the condition of anonymity, says the commanding officer at one facility ordered the use of music on some prisoners along with other techniques, including strobe lights, stress positions, and air-conditioning set to hypothermia-inducing levels. The choice of songs, though, was the interrogator's. "I was the guy out there all night, sitting with the [detainee], so I was the DJ," he says. "We started out playing stuff we'd gotten from the MPs, which was, like, unlistenable death metal. But we had to sit there and listen, too, so after a while, I'd play whatever I wanted." That included James Taylor, and Janeane Garofalo and Ben Stiller reading an audiobook about their friendship. "They hated Janeane Garofalo."

The purpose, he confirms, was to keep detainees from thinking. "The way we talked about it was 'prolonging the shock of capture,'" he says. "Frankly, it wasn't terribly effective, but that's what our leaders were coming up with over there." This interrogator says he'd heard about such techniques at the Army Intelligence School but was never trained to use them. "We were told these methods were illegal because we were following the Geneva Conventions. But when we got to Iraq, it was decided these guys weren't covered by the Geneva Conventions."

In actuality, the Bush administration's selective interpretation and application of the Geneva Conventions makes it less than clear if, when, and for whom the rules' protections against abusive treatment and torture were deemed applicable in Iraq. From the beginning of the conflict, the administration asserted that the Geneva Conventions would apply to all Iraqi detainees but left a loophole open for foreigners captured on Iraqi soil. In this obtuse legal environment—an environment, it's worth noting, in which MPs at a prison in Abu Ghraib would brazenly photograph prisoners being sexually humiliated and threatened with dogs—it's hardly surprising interrogators would assume playing Metallica at ear-splitting volume would be inbounds. And a September 14, 2003, memo from the commander in Iraq, Lieutenant General Ricardo Sanchez, hardly clarified things. In the document, Sanchez authorized a host of techniques that human rights groups claimed violated not only the Geneva Conventions, but also the United Nations Convention Against Torture and Other Cruel, Inhuman and Degrading Treatment, which the U.S. ratified in 1994. Among these techniques (many of which would be rescinded in a new memo a month later) were "yelling, loud music, and light control: used to create fear, disorient detainee, and prolong capture shock."

According to Pentagon spokesman Lieutenant Colonel Mark Ballesteros, music was only sanctioned on a case-by-case basis with specific approval by Sanchez, and Sanchez never actually gave this personal authorization, which means any soldier in Iraq blasting a detainee with music (or any commander who gave such an order) was, apparently, violating military policy. Nonetheless, the Sanchez memo is significant: Of all the unearthed documents and orders concerning detainee treatment passed between the White House, the Pentagon, the Justice Department, the CIA, and various military commanders, it appears it's the only one that mentions music specifically. Additionally, the Sanchez memo was written after consultation with Major General Geoffrey Miller, then the joint task force commander at Guantanamo. Miller had been charged with bringing the Iraq interrogation programs up to the level of Guantanamo's.

"Everything Sanchez wrote he got from Miller," says Alfred McCoy, author of the book *A Question of Torture: CIA Interrogation, From the Cold War to the War on Terror*. "Miller came and delivered the manual with everything they'd learned at Guantanamo." McCoy traces the coercive interrogation practices back to psychological experiments the CIA cofunded at Montreal's McGill University in the early 1950s. In one, subjects were played three recordings: "Four repetitions of 16 bars from 'Home on the Range'; a five-minute extract from a harsh atonal piece of music; and an excerpt from an essay instructing and exhorting young children on the methods and desirability of attaining purity of soul." This was part of a series of tests dealing with sensory deprivation and overload. The results were unequivocal.

"A changing sensory environment is absolutely essential to the good health of the mind," a report by the Canadian government on the experiments concluded. "Without it, the brain ceases to function in an adequate way, and abnormalities of behavior develop; for example, the subject quickly begins to hallucinate. By 'softening up' a prisoner through the use of sensory isolation techniques, a captor is indeed able to bring about a state of mind in which the prisoner is receptive to the implantation of ideas contrary to previously held beliefs."

THE CIA MAY HAVE BEEN working with music for the past 50-plus years, but it's not the only one. The SERE program, now headquartered in Fort Bragg, North Carolina, was created after the Korean War to train American soldiers to survive capture by enemy forces and resist interrogation. (The program's acronym stands for Survival, Evasion, Resistance, and Escape.) Its curriculum is based on tactics employed by foreign governments and is, in the words of Greg Hartley, an ex-Army interrogator who went through SERE, "nasty, physically violent, and harsh with intent."

Hartley has worked training interrogators and also as a SERE instructor. He says music by avant-gardists like Diamanda Galás and Throbbing Gristle is a vital part of SERE's interrogation-resistance training. Hartley is convinced music found its way into U.S. interrogation rooms after soldiers who had been subjected to music at SERE simply flipped the tactic for use against detainees. "Someone decided, 'If [music] works that well at SERE, why wouldn't it work on prisoners?'" he says. The problem, says Hartley, is SERE was never intended as interrogation training. "Just because someone gives you a good blowjob doesn't mean you're going to be able to give one, too. You go through SERE and someone does something horrible to you and you don't understand the reasoning behind it. If that's all you're exposed to, you think that's interrogation."

A spokesperson for Special Operations Command, which oversees the SERE program, insists that Special Operations doesn't train interrogators. But there's ample evidence to the contrary. SERE's chief psychologist advised Behavioral Science Consultation Teams at Guantanamo on interrogation strategies. And Tom, the former interrogator, says that, while there, he recommended through the chain of command that SERE instructors come to Cuba to teach counterresistance techniques. "But," he says, "it didn't happen while I was there."

Eventually it did. A sworn statement taken in March 2005 from Guantanamo's interrogations chief says as much: "My predecessor arranged for SERE instructors to teach their techniques to the interrogators at [Guantanamo]." The statement was taken during an investigation into the questioning of Mohammed al-Kahtani. A log of al-Kahtani's interrogation reveals frequent blasting of loud music, notably Christina Aguilera.

IF THE MILITARY HAD its own People's Choice Awards, Drowning Pool would win top honors. Nearly every interrogator and soldier I spoke to mentioned the aggro-metal outfit's 2001 hit "Bodies"— with its wild-eyed chorus, "Let the bodies hit the floor!"—as a favorite for both psyching up U.S. soldiers and psyching out enemies and captives. Some might view this as a dubious distinction, but Drowning Pool bassist Stevie Benton isn't among them. "People assume we should be offended that somebody in the military thinks our song is annoying enough that, played over and over, it can psychologically break someone down," he says. "I take it as an honor to think that perhaps our song could be used to quell another 9/11 attack or something like that."

Others in Benton's position feel no such pride.

"The fact that our music has been co-opted in this barbaric way is really disgusting," says Tom Morello, whose recordings with his former band Rage Against the Machine were employed by Guantanamo interrogators, according to one intelligence officer who served there. "That particular kind of interrogation has rightly been cited by Amnesty International as torture. If you're at all familiar with the ideological leanings of the band and its support for human rights, that's really hard to stand."

Morello says Rage Against the Machine have gone as far as to send cease-and-desist orders to the State Department, the Army, and various intelligence agencies in an effort to halt the use of the band's tunes, but so far have been stonewalled. Lars Ulrich and Kirk Hammett of Metallica have also expressed displeasure with the use of their music, but as Ulrich asked rhetorically in a 2003 interview, "What am I supposed to do about it? Get George Bush on the phone and tell him to get his generals to play some Venom [instead]?"

The options for artists in Morello's or Ulrich's shoes are extremely limited. One prominent human rights lawyer is currently petitioning songwriters to make claims against the government for unpaid royalties in an effort to embarrass the Bush administration into stopping the practice. But two separate intellectual-property experts said such claims would face massive practical and legal obstacles.

To Drowning Pool's Benton, the whole issue just needs to be put in perspective. "If they detain these people and the worst thing that happens is they have to sit through a few hours of loud music—some kids in America pay for that," he says. "It doesn't seem all that bad to me."

UNDERSTANDING THE REAL CONCERNS with this practice is about understanding the context. For detainees raised according to the strictest Islamic doctrine, repeated blasts of "Enter Sandman" are often their first exposure to Western music and simply compound the misery of an existence marked by exhaustive interrogations, indefinite confinement, and brutish treatment.

According to Captain James Yee, the Army's Muslim chaplain at Guantanamo from November 2002 until September 2003, interrogators sometimes played recordings of the Koran, then drowned them out with louder music. "That's offensive to Islam," says Yee, who was dismissed from his position and himself held in solitary confinement for 76 days on suspicion of espionage, before all charges were eventually dropped. "When the Koran is played, because it's the word of God in the eye of Muslims, it should be respected."

The legality of blasting music at detainees is murky. National, international, and military law provides a dizzying array of statutes, treaties, and legal opinions governing treatment of enemy captives, and these standards are still being fought over. According to A. John Radsan, a professor at Minnesota's William Mitchell College of Law who was assistant general counsel at the CIA until 2004, music may have been a legal interrogation tool during the time that many of the reported incidents took place. But once Congress passed the Detainee Treatment Act of 2005 (also known as the McCain Amendment), which prohibited not only torture but also "cruel, inhuman, and degrading treatment" of anyone in U.S. custody, and the Supreme Court ruled in *Hamdan v. Rumsfeld* that all detainees in U.S. custody were protected by the Geneva Conventions, any legal justification appeared to be swept away. "Common Article 3 of Geneva includes things like, 'outrages upon personal dignity,'" says Radsan. "Even if loud music isn't prohibited by [the] McCain [Amendment], it's prohibited by Common Article 3. That would be considered an 'outrage.'"

Michael Ratner, a human rights lawyer and coauthor of *Guantanamo: What the World Should Know*, says such delicate legal parsing is unnecessary. "These practices have been unlawful since 1949 and the ratification of the Geneva Conventions," he says. "Whether it's loud music, chaining to the floor, or temperature control, it's utterly illegal."

The debate may be moot anyway. In late September, Congress passed legislation that upheld the Geneva Conventions in name but likely undercut them in practice, by allowing President Bush to define what constitutes certain breaches of Common Article 3 under U.S. law. Administration officials themselves argue this effectively enshrines a set of "alternative interrogation techniques" as acceptable. According to a recent *Newsweek* report, these alternative techniques include "sound and light manipulation."

Regardless of the outcome of the legal and political wrangling, music seems likely to continue being employed in interrogations, at least selectively. On a very basic level, some interrogators

I spoke to questioned the tactic's efficacy, but Hartley, the former SERE instructor, claims that when used correctly, music can be extremely productive, albeit as a shortcut that a more talented interrogator wouldn't need to employ. Government officials would likely vouch for music's usefulness; they've already insisted that Abu Zubaydah, who was blasted with Red Hot Chili Peppers, provided valuable intelligence on key Al Qaeda operatives. But even Hartley concedes that the tactic's effectiveness may not be the most important issue. "When you start to ask whether I think music's appropriate, that's a tough call," he says. "Do I think it's inhuman? If it's too loud, absolutely it's inhuman. It's physical torture. If you're using it to isolate a person so they don't know what's going on around them? That's a tough call. And that's a call for Americans to make, not some general."

Radsan, the former CIA lawyer, believes the nature of the threat demands serious discussion about what the country is willing to do about it. "There are people out there that want to kill us," he says. "I think the human rights people forget that we have to play mind games to get suspects to talk. If you don't want to ratchet it up, you're not going to get information.

"Most people will say you can't drill into a guy's teeth, but they agree you might have to do something more than establish rapport," he continues. "That gets you into that messy area: What kind of stuff, short of torture, are we willing to accept as a democracy?"

This is a question as important as it is radioactive. Those who take a hard line against any forms of coercive interrogation are seen as coddling terrorists or failing to comprehend the gravity of the threat. Those who endorse more aggressive techniques—be it blasting Eminem, short-shackling detainees, or menacing them with dogs—are accused of justifying torture. And many would surely prefer all these discussions take place far from public light, not simply to keep our enemies from learning our tactics, but also to avoid owning up to the fear that makes behaviors many would call morally repugnant tacitly acceptable. To Michael Ratner, it's this fear that has caused us to, as a nation, lose perspective on this issue. "I think in five or ten years," he says, "people will be appalled by what happened with music and dogs and all that. People will say we overreacted. They'll look at it like what happened with the Japanese internment camps during World War II.

"But right now," he adds, "we're in the heat of it."

DAVID PEISNER is a freelance writer based in Decatur, Georgia. His work has also appeared in *The New York Times, Rolling Stone, Blender, Vibe, Playboy, The Atlanta Journal-Constitution*, and many other publications he's far less proud of.

7

FEARLESS BOUNCERS, CRITICAL BEAT-DOWNS, and INSANE POSSES at
America's
CRAZIEST CLUB

Enjoying Detroit's alarming nightlife

by CHRIS NORRIS

NOVEMBER 2002

Six months after I visited St. Andrew's Hall, the Detroit nightclub made its movie debut as the Shelter, proving ground for white rapper B-Rabbit, his dreadlocked buddy Future, and the other hip-hop strivers in 2002's 8 Mile. Astute music fans can probably ID at least the leads' real-life counterparts (that is, Eminem and his best friend Proof), but it took the venue's security staff to show me how others bring their personal battles to a place like St. Andrew's, and how reality sometimes doesn't make it into songs or films. Proof himself factored into a few of the less appealing accounts I got from the club bouncers, who recalled a beef-seeking troublemaker that didn't sound at all like the funny, diplomatic guy I'd met doing SPIN pieces on Eminem. I thought about their stories four years later, when I learned that Proof (né Deshaun Holden) had been shot to death—after a brawl with a bouncer at a Detroit nightclub. To me, this story is about hip-hop.

■ ■ ■

ANDREW SCHUSTER is a very good worker: responsible, efficient, attentive to detail. He even does well on surprise job
tests. He got one about three years ago, when he was patting
down patrons at St. Andrew's Hall, a storied Detroit nightclub that
is surrounded by possibly the worst slums in America. The club
hosts some of the country's more thug-oriented hip-hop nights and
mosh-intensive rock nights. Weapons checks are, shall we say, an
important part of the process. Staffers rely on frisking rather than
metal detectors, which miss plastic shivs, fiberglass knuckles, and
other popular accessories.

"I mean, you don't cup their junk or anything," Schuster says
of crotch detail. "You just kinda put your forearm up there."

This night, he felt a telltale rigidness—"The guy had jocked his
gun." So Schuster responded accordingly: He punched the guy in
the face. "I was swingin' on him, and he was like, 'I work here!
I work here!'" Turns out the guy was a former head of security, checking to see if new staffers were following procedure. They were.

"Any time there's a gun or a knife, we start swingin'."

There's no macho bluster in Schuster's voice. In fact, he
sounds like a machinist explaining the drill press. A robust 6'1",
the 25-year-old Air fan and amateur photographer is far from the
bouncer ideal (typically, a steroid-amped linebacker with ties
to motorcycle gangs). He's more like a hip camp counselor, earrings and tattoos offset by short brown hair and a dimpled smile.
Schuster was raised the only child of a special-education teacher
mom and Vietnam vet/credit union CEO dad in the cluster of
Detroit suburbs called Downriver. But like most of his friends,
he really grew up at St. Andrew's punk rock shows. Over time,
the place became a home away from home. By 1999, it had also
become his job.

Schuster didn't get into fights as a kid. He's not a football player,
boxer, or martial artist. Says coworker Eric Leidlein: "Dude, Andy
was so passive." Then he laughs. "Until he worked at the Hall."

THE TRIP TO DETROIT along I-75 takes you between the dense gray
spires of an oil refinery and the old petrochemical facility Zug
Island, a lump of toxins that ranks among the most polluted spots

in the U.S. Downtown, the train station on Michigan Avenue is a giant shell of concrete and broken glass. The clock on the CPA Building has been stuck at 10:55 for years. Fifteen hundred properties are officially designated for destruction, with nearly 10,000 more abandoned and deemed "dangerous," looming ruins from the most notorious white flight of the last century. It's as close to a ghost town as any American city gets. In other words, it's *fucking* cool.

"I love it down here," says Schuster, driving the streets one night. "My friends and I used to walk around all the time, meet people, hang out. You see the best shit." A recent sighting was the "wheelchair gang"—a group of wheelchair-bound homeless men towed by a leader in a motorized chair. "It was like a little train!" he marvels. "*So* good."

On one corner of this surreal landscape stands the brick-faced former home of the Scottish St. Andrew's Society. Built in 1907, the building is now a 1,400-capacity, three-story nightclub institution. It has been Detroit's hottest music space for years, presenting acts like Nirvana and Red Hot Chili Peppers, along

Back in action: A St. Andrew's bouncer gets busy. © *Scott Houston*

with thousands of local bands. It has also hosted the club night Three Floors of Fun, with a mixed crowd dancing to rock, techno, and hip-hop. As an integrated center in a crumbling, segregated city, the club has been a strange social experiment, offering melting pots or floating ghettos, depending on the night. Yet the bouncers were mostly from one side of the tracks.

"We all grew up hardcore punk kids," says Chris Holland, 24, another St. Andrew's bouncer. At 6'2" and a weight-lifter-buff 230 pounds, Holland has short dark hair, a pierced lower lip, and nickel-size plugs in his earlobes. His upright bearing and black-eyed stare give him the look of a Delta Force member gone goth. Like Schuster, he first saw the light at St. Andrew's, obsessing on early-'90s bands Gorilla Biscuits, Civ, and Quicksand. "That shit made my skin crawl," he says.

Holland wanted to be an EMS worker or firefighter, but bouncing seems more in line with his experience. The all-ages shows he attended at small Detroit clubs were full of flying elbows, ass-kicking Dr. Martens, and that Michigan specialty, genuine racist skinheads, which inspired a pastime the kids called "Nazi boxing." It's a simple game, really. You stand near a skinhead and wait to see if he gives the *Sieg heil!* arm salute. If he does, you punch him in the face.

This is how Holland met 17-year-old punk (and future St. Andrew's bouncer) Jeremy Nadolsky. Six feet two and 400 pounds, Nadolsky, now 21, looks like a shaved-head, overgrown version of Jack Osbourne—horn-rimmed glasses, pierced lower lip, and tattoos running up his neck. He has a giddy, nervous energy, gesturing with fleshy, tattooed forearms. He goes by the childhood nickname Worm and, like many Detroit punks, has a vaguely sallow, mutt ethnicity that he wears with attitude. "I'm a Po'billy [i.e. Polish hillbilly], dude," says Worm, sitting on a threadbare sofa in Schuster's suburban Wyandotte walk-up. "My ma's straight out the sticks. Summertown, Tennessee."

Worm dropped out of high school his junior year to take a job in the post office. "They put me on this 3 a.m. shift and worked us like slaves," he says, cradling a pellet gun shaped like a Tec-9 handgun. "I so understand why people go crazy from working there." Literally a disgruntled postal employee, he found himself well suited for bouncing. "I won't lie. I love it," he says. "You get to see shows for free. You get to fight and not get in trouble. There's just a lot of benefits."

There are also a few drawbacks. Pay is low, turnover is high, and the job carries no prestige. Far from the glitzy, VIP clubland of velvet ropes and tiny earpieces, security here is an entry-level position, one rung down from barback. While many venues require police-approved training courses, the education at St. Andrew's is informal. "After a couple of nights, you understand that if you bend an arm this way, it hurts," says Schuster. "If you rake the side of your foot down a person's shin, they'll go down. If you cut off somebody's windpipe, they'll go unconscious."

Physically and temperamentally, the effective St. Andrew's bouncer often resembles the *Trainspotting* character Begbie, a smallish, wiry sort who happens to have a screw loose. Schuster points to Eric Leidlein, a bony, 5'10", 140-pound punk standing by the bar. "Eric can toss guys out as fast as anyone," says Schuster. "He just knows what to do." He's also pretty demonstrably nuts. With spiky hair and a pierced lip, Leidlein recalls *one* of the nights he was knocked out—this time by five skinheads from the bands Hatebreed and Madball.

"I was pulling a guy away from a fight, and I turned my back for a second," he says. Leidlein caught a fist in what doctors refer to as the occipital region (the back of the skull) and collapsed. He started convulsing on his way to the emergency room. "I got a CAT scan, an MRI," he says, twirling a lollipop in his mouth. "I had bruised ribs, concussion, broken nose." He was back at work in a week.

The physical activity at St. Andrew's is both unpredictable and orchestrated. As the lights fall on a recent May night, patrons trickle into the main room: eyes alight, fists clenched, arms raised, yelling "Whooo!" Soon, nü-metal heroes Papa Roach take the stage. Dressed in the dark work clothes of a NASCAR pit crew, they run through their set efficiently. Midway, singer Jacoby Shaddix stops to instruct the crowd. "You guys take five steps that way," he huffs, pointing at the right side of the pit.

Then, shouting to the left and gesturing wildly: "You guys take five steps that way. This shit's called 'the Braveheart.' When I say 'Go,' fuckin' Braveheart-style, lunatic—the biggest pit ever!" When the band begins its next song, "Born With Nothing, Die With Everything," Shaddix yells, "Go!" Bodies fly and faces contort as both sides crash into each other.

Two bouncers stand at barriers enclosing the pit, charged with catching bodies and depositing them safely to the side. Relatively speaking, it's light work. On other nights, security is more like infantry duty—with a correspondingly high casualty rate. "Lots of people get fired quick or quit," says Schuster. "They get scared."

IF AMERICAN YOUTH CULTURE has entered a crazier, more violent phase, Detroit is the logical vanguard. An urban economic failure, the city has, in a sense, a tradition to uphold—a legacy of working-class toughness, drunken sick kicks, and black humor. St. Andrew's is a temple to that tradition. The main floor still feels like an old men's club, with burnished blond molding and a cigarette machine that looks like it's left over from the '40s. Rimmed by a beaux arts balcony, the central hardwood floor forms a dramatic rotunda straight out of the famous battle royal scene in Ralph Ellison's *Invisible Man*—in which cigar-chomping fat cats throw bills at blindfolded victims beating each other senseless.

"There's something about Detroit, man," says Darius Gordon, 31, a St. Andrew's bouncer who grew up in various low-income sectors of the city. "Out in the street, there's all these gangs and stuff around you. Detroit feels like it's gotta put its chest out."

"Detroit has to fight harder," says Sergeant Marcus Harper, a police officer at the First Precinct downtown. "It's like, 'I'm the damn underdog. I take two steps up, you kick me three down.'"

Even if you're courageous, even if you possess the skills to disable large, angry, wasted patrons, even if you're dedicated to preserving order, there are situations that even the most capable bouncer cannot handle. And recently, St. Andrew's—a focal point for Detroit's long-ignored, now notorious rap scene—has specialized in them.

"When I started working the Three Floors of Fun, the main floor was hip-hop, downstairs was rock'n'roll or industrial, and the top floor was techno," says Schuster. "If a fight broke out, you could stop it pretty quick." Then, in 2000, St. Andrew's started all-hip-hop Fridays, which were advertised across the entire region via live broadcasts on a local rap radio station. "The first night we got, like, 1,600 people," says Holland. "Ninety-eight percent black." Around this time, security at St. Andrew's became less like a job and more like a war.

Now, a young black crowd isn't all that different from a young white crowd. Both want to hang out, hear music, get laid, have fun. But there are complicating factors for the mostly white bouncers at St. Andrew's. "For some reason, everybody in Detroit thinks they're harder than the next person," says Darius Gordon. "They felt like they had to let [staff] know 'I ain't no sucker.'"

According to Sergeant Harper, violence at the club has been constant ever since. "There's always a fight going on," he says. "I hate working down here [downtown], because the only people we deal with are the ones with negative attitudes from the clubs."

On hip-hop nights, haggling over ticket prices is common. There is no tipping at the bar. A tap or nudge is likely to provoke a fight, especially if the bouncer is white. "You ask someone to move, and they're like, 'You ain't got shit to say to me, white boy,'" says Holland. Worm gets similar treatment on the front steps. "When I'm checking IDs, they rag on me all night," he says. "'Look at this white boy out here; he ain't shit.' They see white and think I'm a punk-ass." Schuster has learned to laugh off such epithets. "When you're kicking somebody out and they're calling you 'white devil,' it's just funny. If you take it any other way, it'll make you bitter and angry."

To be fair, primarily white rave crowds often pose bigger security threats, due to the lucrative, cutthroat drug trade involved. "It's just a ton of kids hopped up on the drug of the week, in an abandoned warehouse," says Schuster. "This one guy [a bouncer] who worked at the Hall, he got shot, like, three times in the chest at a rave." And racial tension at St. Andrew's has diminished drastically as the bouncer crew has become fully integrated—largely due to changes in hiring practices by Detroit scenester Mike "Mike D" Danner, who started managing the club's hip-hop night in June 2000.

The *real* problems at St. Andrew's began when club altercations started to take on a professional edge. At first it was little things, like party promoters showing up in flak jackets. "When it's known that they have [bulletproof] vests, but we don't, it kinda sends the wrong message," says Schuster. Then rap groups started bringing their own security—leg-breakers willing to fight the house staff to impose their posse's will. By 1999, it was obvious that the mafia-enthralled muscle of big-time hip-hop had finally reached Detroit.

"The whole rap mentality is they wanna be gangstas," says Sergeant Harper, who is African-American and distinguishes between rap and hip-hop. "Hip-hop is just an urban crowd. But rappers want to live out the persona that 'You have to fear me; I'm a gangsta.'"

Explains Schuster: "Some guy will be like, 'I'm ballin' this week. I'm gonna rent out St. Andrew's for my boys.' And there'll be a mob of 500 people out front—everybody's on the list, and there is no list." Disagreements get dire fast. "Let's say some guy keeps coming up to the bar, ordering shitloads of drinks, and he doesn't have enough money to pay—*every time*. When I refuse to serve him, he's like, 'I'm gonna get my boys to shoot you.' It's that style of crowd, customers saying that they're going to their cars to get their guns."

AS IT HAPPENS, it was a marginalized Detroit white boy from the other side of the bouncer line who ushered in Detroit hip-hop's crazier, more high-profile era. With his weapons charges and inflammatory lyrics, Eminem brought the extremity of his hometown into an already extreme rap culture. Slim Shady and his crew, D12, put the city on the map; money and attention flowed toward the Midwest. St. Andrew's benefited mightily. The club's bouncers did not.

Says Gordon, "Suddenly, everybody [at the club] wanted to battle Eminem. I'd see him in the middle of the dance floor with eight guys around him waiting for their chance. I think that's why he started to bring security." In any case, massive rent-a-terminators soon became a consistent presence at St. Andrew's—and not just with Eminem. "The people who should be patted down get in without it," says Holland. "'Cause they're a performer or famous. Like D12 and their entourage. They blatantly walk through the pat-down. And they make sure everyone sees them."

On one Friday night in 1999, revered hip-hop elder Afrika Bambaataa was booked at the Hall, but as he started to take the stage, Eminem jumped up and had the DJ throw on his sky-rocketing hit "My Name Is." Upset when the event's promoter asked him to leave the stage, Eminem tussled with the promoter, sparking a near-riot. "All of a sudden, beer bottles started getting thrown, and the whole place was fighting," Schuster recalls. "It was straight out of a movie."

The verbal feud between Eminem and former House of Pain rapper Everlast had been going on for several months by the time Everlast took his show to St. Andrew's in February of 2001, challenging his rival to step forward. News organizations reported the ensuing incident as an altercation led by several D12 fans. But according to the bouncers, the aggressors were not typical fans.

"It was about 14 gigantic guys," recalls Schuster. "Dressed in black—sweatshirts, boots, jackets, everything. At first, I thought they were part of the act, because it was so professional, you know? It was like [Public Enemy's drill team] the S1Ws." But after assaulting two security guards at the front door, the ninjalike posse rushed the stage. Nathan Keeler, 24, the band's house-assigned gofer for the day, quickly evacuated Everlast to a walk-in freezer downstairs. The intruders formed a circle around two staff members and began beating them into oblivion. Schuster, who was tending bar, grabbed a fellow bartender and breached the circle. "We got Brandon out, but we couldn't get Arrick Lanier," Schuster says. "He was unconscious." Lanier had been bashed in the skull with the iron base of a mic stand; he

9 of America's Least Livable Cities, as Suggested by Rock Songs

Slam dunk: Fear promote chaos at Reseda, California's Country Club in 1982.

1. Olympia, Washington: Everything there is the same, including the methods of sexual intercourse. ("Rock Star," Hole)

2. Rockville, Maryland: Local citizens want to bring you down and waste your time. ("Don't Go Back to Rockville," R.E.M.)

3. Big Sur, California: You will be disappointed by this community's inability to satisfy expectations. ("Big Sur," the Thrills)

4. Los Angeles: Grifters and hustlers will make you promises, but then they'll fuck you over. ("Welcome to the Jungle," Guns N' Roses)

5. Detroit: The highways are filled with drunken, stoned drivers. ("Detroit Rock City," Kiss)

6. San Francisco: The community is overrun with unwashed hippies. ("San Francisco [Be Sure to Wear Some Flowers in Your Hair]," Scott McKenzie)

7. Toledo, Ohio: Though the problems with this city are vague, it is nonetheless the ultimate affront to be sent here. ("Expecting," the White Stripes)

8. El Paso, Texas: Women can't be trusted and gunplay is the norm. ("El Paso," Marty Robbins)

9. New York City: It's actually an okay place to live, provided you don't mind freezing to death, having tuberculosis, or getting mugged or murdered. ("New York's Alright If You Like Saxophones," Fear)

was carried out on a blood-soaked stretcher. When staffer Ryan Murphy entered the fray, one of the assailants revealed a pistol in his waist-band, warning him off. Then, at some invisible signal, the goons stopped, turned, and left.

Detroit police finally showed up and took statements from the woozy bouncers. No one could directly implicate D12, who were on tour in Europe at the time. St. Andrew's general manager Mike Danner, who arranged a police escort out of town for Everlast, says he knows the assailants' identities but will refer to them only as "diehard fans of D12, the people they grew up with." He adds: "When you talk shit about them, they will come and get you. It could be a year later, in your own town; they will get you." D12 were unavailable for comment.

ON A RECENT FRIDAY NIGHT out on Congress Street, a parked truck bears a Remy Martin–sponsored ad for a local rap radio station: WJLB—GET WITH THE CRU. The front stairs of St. Andrew's are mobbed with young black men chatting, calling out to cruising cars. "Yo, yo, yo, yo, yo," one yells, tugging the elbow of a large, fleshy white bouncer checking IDs. Inside, Schuster greets an enormous black bouncer in a staff T-shirt who wears his nickname (and height), "Six Eight," on a platinum chain. They exchange a hip-hop-ish bear hug. Schuster walks on and steps into the main room. The place is utterly transformed from the Papa Roach moshfest of two nights ago; it's now a ghetto-fabulous soiree shimmering with disco lights and hormones. The main floor is shoulder-to-shoulder with people dancing, mingling, and drinking—the most popular beverages are the "Blue Motherfucker" (a Long Island iced tea plus blue Curaçao liqueur) and Moet ($100 a bottle at the bar; $37.50 at the corner store).

Downstairs in the section of the club called Shelter, things are rawer. A DJ in a barred cage spins DJ Assault's underground hit "Hoes Get Naked" (Assault developed the fast and filthy Detroit style of booty rap called "ghetto tech"). A bleached-blonde woman gyrates suggestively in skintight, acid-washed shorts, copious flesh spilling out above and below. A petite black girl sipping a cocktail wears a turquoise shirt that reads FUCK MOBY.

Female patrons like these are also frisked—surrendering the occasional switchblade or even kitchen knife—by one of the club's five women bouncers. "I've been a fighter all my life," says Violet Edwards, a devout Christian white girl who is 5'4" and 127 pounds, "I'm not too much afraid of nothin'." Raised in a mostly male family in southwest Detroit, she got into her first fight in elementary school. A boy pulled her hair and she broke his nose. She became a St. Andrew's bouncer after her talents were discovered in a spectacular clash with a soon-to-be-ex-boyfriend in the club's lobby.

As a new Ludacris joint drops, the crowd roars and jumps up. Opening verse: "The fight's out / I'ma 'bout to punch yo' lights out." Later, there's a promise to "beat up security for stopping a fight." A few songs later, the DJ mixes into Eminem's "Without Me," and the crowd again erupts. Just miles away, the angry blond himself shot the loosely autobiographical *8 Mile*, with *L.A. Confidential* director Curtis Hanson. The set featured a full-scale reproduction of St. Andrew's, called "Shelter" in the film.

Outside, Holland guards the rear entrance alone, standing below graffiti that reads ASS MUNCH and DISEMBOWLMOVEMENT. He sips bottled water and looks down a dark alley. "I get a gun pulled on me every Friday," he says. "It's fucked." Shortly after he says this, a low-riding Cougar with tinted windows rolls down the alley for its third pass. The driver gives a cold stare, while Holland muses about why he keeps his job. "I guess the only reason I stay is because I've been here so long," he says. "Because I fuckin' love this place, and I don't know why."

It's not too hard to imagine the addiction of being a St. Andrew's bouncer, of being a member of a real fight club—with its own rules, fellowship, and mainline doses of adrenaline. But there's obviously some other primal instinct at work here that keeps people like Holland, Worm, Gordon, and Schuster in the fray.

"This place is our house," says Gordon. "It's a camaraderie—punks, hip-hop heads. There's so many different culture blends here; it's crazy, but it's a good thing."

"I've never seen a work environment where there's such a bond," adds Edwards.

With the patrons gone, the bouncers gather in a circle on the trash-strewn, alcohol-soaked main floor. Co–security head John Monier II leads them in a prayer of thanks—for having survived another night. Schuster watches from the doorway leading to the main floor. He has moved on from security head to the higher-paying post of bartender but still jumps the bar to break up fights. "The point is just to get everybody out," he says. "Who cares if they're fighting on the street? It's not in our club. Nobody that we know is getting hurt."

It was at this very dividing line, right here in the entryway, that Schuster performed his first act as a bouncer. He instinctively jumped into a tussle between two large thugs and a staffer. "I saw one of my coworkers getting hurt," he says. "So I broke it up." He also popped a thug's head through some drywall. This may have been the moment when Schuster discovered what his law-student girlfriend Marcy calls "a love and aptitude" for fighting.

I ask Schuster how he felt after that first time, after his first successful bounce. "I don't know," he says, rubbing his neck and thinking. "It was weird, I guess. My adrenaline was pumping, and I was really worked up." He looks out the doors into the desolate night. "Mostly, I just remember feeling like everyone was safe."

CHRIS NORRIS was a SPIN staff writer from 1998 to 2004 and a wedding DJ for one night in 2006 when he was arrested for an ill-timed N.W.A cut. In 2009, he coauthored *The Tao of Wu* with Wu-Tang Clan mastermind RZA, who calls him "a student of philosophy."

RED, HOT,
and
Bothered

Moshing with Rage Against the Machine in Moscow

by RJ SMITH

OCTOBER 1996

To watch a combustible band at the peak of their powers in a combustible country discovering its powers was a rare excitement. Rage Against the Machine were at war with the administration and the Man, but watching them up close on the road in Russia, it was clear how much they were at war with one another, too—and to imagine that this was what gave them their power.

I reported on the life of singer Zack de la Rocha, and what I learned, and what comes across in this story, only makes me more impressed by what he has been able to achieve. Not that Zack was so thrilled to have me peer into his backstory. I see him from time to time in the Eastside L.A. neighborhoods we both frequent, and I don't think he's said yo since this story hit the stands. Oh well. The band were incredible, the vodka was great, and the hookers in the hallways of our businessmen's hotel were unforgettable. Not long after this trip, the band more or less ground to a creative halt. Fans still hope the parts will find new noise, grooves, things worth fighting about and for.

■ ■ ■

THE RUSSIAN REVOLUTION was supposed to lead to a higher human species, an evolutionary role model for the rest of the world: *Homo sovieticus.* But the downfall of communism instead suggests that the future may be more Beavis and Butt-head than Brezhnev and Bukharin.

In the lobby of the huge DK Gorbunova cultural center, where Rage Against the Machine will play tonight in Moscow, black-leather-jacketed teens are pounding each other on the shoulders, mouthing Rage lyrics like they're memorizing English-language tapes. Outside, truly scary skinheads are robbing grunge kids. Beer cans dot the sidewalk, and the kids are scalping tickets at black-market prices for the sold-out show. We have defeated the Evil Empire!

Backstage, in halls twisty and windowless, you can smell about seven decades of damp funk. A Russian interviewer quizzes Rage guitarist Tom Morello: "Can you explain your attitude toward modern social reality?" Yes, he can. Because while the USSR invented agitprop, the 31-year-old Morello's making sure the term at least survives. The interviewer asks him about his political mentors, and you can practically see Morello, good left-leaner, trying to come up with an answer that will be both pro-revolution, yet not seem, well, defcon-four bonkers in a country not really in the market for a revolution right this very moment.

He smoothly offers the names of Emma Goldman and Rosa Luxemburg—revolutionaries who thrived outside of Russia, and thus without the taint of the gulag. Asked what he thinks of the Russian Revolution today, Morello deftly notes that today is the Fourth of July, and ties the original hopes of the Russian Revolution to those of America's Revolutionary War. He brings it up to the present, observing, "There's a permanent culture of resistance here in Russia, and I feel pretty comfortable with that," before cautioning Russians fleeing the authoritarian past to not adopt the modern excesses of the West. "I would warn all your listeners to closely watch Boris Yeltsin and his masters on Wall Street," he finishes.

As the interviewer pads away, Morello looks quite pleased with himself. "Doing interviews is a lot like freestyling," he says. I dare you to ask Nas about modern social reality.

Elsewhere, the members of Rage are suiting up for battle. Tim Bob, 27, tall bassist with a shaved head, has a good scowl on. Drummer Brad Wilk, 27, is chatting with friends, scoping out the boxer shorts the band has put on the contract rider; sometimes, free underwear is easier than doing laundry.

Mostly the room is filled with relaxed banter, but in one chair sits 26-year-old singer Zack de la Rocha, staring a hole through his sneakers. He's got his show T-shirt on, with two comic-book eyes staring out at you intensely from behind a mask. But you can't read de la Rocha's eyes: He looks far-away possessed, zoned way low . . . until he starts hopping like mad.

The band meets up in the hallway behind the stage, nobody making eye contact. "We're going to teach these kids some iron discipline," says Morello.

He means it. "People of the Sun," the latest single from their second album, *Evil Empire*, starts the show. De la Rocha cannonballs from bass-drum level high into the air as he raps a fast-forward history of cowboys and Indians, this time with

Frying the flag: Rage Against the Machine in 1996. *Niels Van Iperen/Retna*

the Indians returning for blood. Dreadlocks shooting out like sunbeams, he's railing about gut-eaters, and suddenly 2,000 Russians are also hopping . . . well, not as one, but as 2,000 individuals. Many are literally figuring this rock stuff out for the first time; they are slamming, twirling, hair-whipping, pogoing—pogoing!—doing everything but the Patty Duke. Rage follow with "Bullet in the Head," a rant against blindly accepting your gang or your nation. "They say jump, you say how high," de la Rocha shouts mockingly—to Russians! After which the crowd shouts back, "Inside Out," the name of de la Rocha's first group. Nobody back in Orange County even remembers them. This is love. This is a little bit crazy.

And when "Vietnow" begins, everybody elevates. Morello's deck of guitar effects is out of control; he's part Fripp and part Flipper, Robin Trower sent to reeducation camp. Wilk seems to backshade the beat a touch more live; you wait for his bass drum like you wait for that bead of sweat to roll down your neck. And Bob, stripped to the waist and jumping up and down, he's a Stakhanovite dream, an unfaltering man-machine. "Fear is your only God!" screams de la Rocha, but it ain't fear the Russkies are registering.

"The main thing with Rage Against the Machine is that when it comes to rocking a crowd, no way can you beat them," says Morello's friend, Beastie Boy Mike D, when the Russian trip is over. He knows, because weeks before Moscow, Rage played at Adam Yauch's Tibetan Freedom Concert in San Francisco, and promptly made everybody forget that the Dalai Lama is a man of peace. How undeniable were they? Standing at the edge of the stage between Dave Grohl and Krist Novoselic as Rage rocked 50,000 people, San Francisco Mayor Willie Brown looked like he'd found Buddha. "I love them!" Brown beamed. "I love the spirit, and I love the energy—I think it's just beautiful." As he shouted this, Rage was blasting "Killing in the Name," a James Brown groove with fused vertebrae.

"I mean," the mayor said incredulously, gesturing to the sea of slammers, the cloud of dust hanging over the crowd, "do you see that scene out there?"

If Rage are a band of many ideas, live they are a juggernaut. And if the juggernaut has any ideas, it has only one: Knock it down. They will rock revolution's children, machine politicians, and everyone in between.

SINCE THE FALL OF COMMUNISM in 1991, much has been learned about the former Soviet Union. One small thing we now know is that hundreds of feet beneath Lenin's Tomb, a decades-old chamber equipped with bar and buffet was kept for the needs of visiting Communist Party dignitaries. Red banquets might be too much to hope for, but surely there was wine—perhaps the sweet Georgian reds that Stalin so prized—and even song.

The time has come to take the party above ground.

Today, Russia wants to rock. Its political candidates camp it up with pop groups in Red Square. That should make musicians visiting from the West very, very happy. But several hundred feet above the Politburo's private martini lounge and currently eye to eye with Lenin, Rage Against the Machine seem only very, very confused.

"I want to put my hand on him and see him spin," de la Rocha says half-jokingly. He's wearing a T-shirt with pictures of Malcolm X and Emiliano Zapata, which says ¡REVOLUCIÓN X Y Z! Lenin, on the other hand, sports a traditional dark suit and a bold print tie, set off by his bright yellow fingers.

After exiting the mausoleum, Morello blinks in the bright sun and readjusts his Harvard baseball cap, merchandise from his alma mater. He's momentarily lost in thought. Finally, he utters a regret that seems to sum up the bittersweetness of the band's whole trip to Russia. "I ate soggy McDonald's french fries in the very shadow of the monument to the 1905 uprising," he laments. "A double scoop of shame."

"Hey buddy, the party's over," de la Rocha taunts.

The band preaching "the party's over" to millions of teenage capitalists has come to a place where it's barely gotten started, and the contradictions are piling up in drifts at our feet. After Tim Bob departs Lenin's Tomb, he does his Alanis Morissette impression, singing, "Isn't it ironic?"

"I don't know, I didn't read a lot of books about it, I haven't studied Marxism," he says. "But a lot of people died, and a lot of people killed them. And I don't think anything improved after Communism.

"It's the Morello Irony. I know he's down with Communism and stuff, but Rage wouldn't be playing here if Communism was still kicking." Just days ago, the band's Russian promoter nervously faxed Rage's manager in Los Angeles to say it might not be a good idea for Morello to wear one of his favorite baseball caps, the one that says COMMIE, because, well, kids in Moscow don't like Communists these days.

At a time when critics justly bemoan the disappearance of politics not just from the pop charts but even from the fringes, here is a platinum act brazenly craving paybacks from all kinds of worthy villains—Ollie North, violent West Bank settlers, mainstream radio, Pete Wilson, agribusiness. Here are lyrics that plead for class war: on "Bulls on Parade," de la Rocha tells the Pentagon that "tha triggers cold empty ya purse." It's Independence Day, and the aliens have come to free Leonard Peltier. ARM THE HOMELESS, it says on one of Tom Morello's guitars. Another reads SENDER O LUMINOSO (the Shining Path).

Plenty of populist acts have made great popular music (the Clash, Merle Haggard, Ruben Blades), and radicals have long tied their ideas to radical sounds (Linton Kwesi Johnson, Gang of Four, Boogie Down Productions). But Rage's music and politics cross at right angles, they work in very different ways. And while Rage's words are aimed through a laser scope, their hybrid of hip-hop and metal strikes like a paintball—splat—right between the clavicles. It's fun as hell, a head rush you walk away from.

It's happened fast as a head rush, too. In 1991, they played their first public show. A year later they had signed with Epic. They released *Rage Against the Machine* that year, and industry approval was instant. *Billboard* editor in chief Timothy White and *Los Angeles Times* pop-music critic Robert Hilburn, critical biz barometers, wrote paeans. They landed a Lollapalooza slot. If the Black Panthers, to cite one of their heroes, had packed this much industry heat, today we'd all be eating free lunches.

As it is, Rage have an amazing way of having their free lunch and eating it too. In 1993 they appeared naked at a Lollapalooza stop in Philly, standing motionless for 15 very long minutes with their mouths duct-taped, a silent protest of the PMRC. They blasted an important Los Angeles radio station from stage because the station was editing a four-letter word out of a Rage song. And then there was this year's *Saturday Night Live* debacle, when the band got the boot for disrespecting the American flag. Nobody regrets taping flags upside down to their amps, which outraged *SNL* brass.

"It would have been another thing if that show had been really funny," says Wilk. "But I could eat a bowl of alphabet soup with orange juice and shit out better skits than I saw that night." Ironically, Rage got more publicity for their eviction than if they'd just played the damn show.

Give 'em enough rope and they'll hang who?

IT WAS THREE YEARS since Rage's 1992 debut, and a rumor was circulating in Los Angeles. De la Rocha had been interested in the Zapatistas, a.k.a. the EZLN, from the moment the indigenous group rose up against the Mexican government in the southern state of Chiapas on New Year's Day, 1994. It seemed that de la Rocha had been visiting Chiapas so often, and the label was so desperate for a sequel, that Epic executives flew down to the south of Mexico with a suitcase full of money to entice de la Rocha to return home.

De la Rocha laughs and dismisses the story, but even as a fable it reveals a pair of truths.

One is how badly Epic hungered for a follow-up. They'd already talked the band into renting a house in the neutral territory of Atlanta, provided them with a single car (the better to tie them down), and requested that they stay put until a record emerged. It didn't. Instead, Atlanta put a whole lot of disagreements, musical and personal, on the living room couch.

"I wish I could say there were a lot of positive things that came out of it, but there weren't," says de la Rocha. "Look, I don't particularly care for [Black] Sabbath, and Tom doesn't particularly care for a lot of the hip-hop riffs that I come up with. But the two, when fused together, makes something unique."

Beyond their jazzbo tendencies—de la Rocha touts Wayne Shorter's *The All Seeing Eye*, Wilk admires drummer Elvin Jones, and Bob, who owns three stand-up basses, wants to be Christian McBride—there may be few bands with members who have so little in common. This is not a crew that hangs out when they're off the road. The differences among them are fixed most clearly by comparing de la Rocha and Morello, the two most responsible for the songs; de la Rocha writes most of the lyrics, and together they hammer out the basics of the sound.

De la Rocha is explosive and evasive, capable of disappearing for days. Ask him the question Morello swatted over the fences, the one about the fate of the Revolution, and he's endearingly self-conscious. "Because I had such difficulty getting through high school, Marx is difficult for me to understand. I've got the basic principles down, but . . ."

Morello talks about issues with self-confident detachment, enjoys turning political talk into collegiate talkathons. He's the Rage member most concerned with the band's image and its business. Buttoned-down about much of his personal life, Morello's far more comfortable answering questions about Mumia Abu-Jamal than about the last book he read for pleasure (*Watership Down*). On the subject of band tensions he sounds like Warren Christopher trying to smother a flare-up, but impolitic de la Rocha comes clean.

"I think throughout the last few years we've all gone through a series of ego explosions, and it's been very difficult to resolve them," de la Rocha admits. "The band has gotten very big. It's often really difficult for me. I haven't fared very well with the band's popularity, with the position that I've found myself in. I'm at constant odds with it."

One more thing about the suitcase story: It also hints at de la Rocha's sense of divided obligations. He'd rather talk about the Zapatistas than about himself or the band. And sometimes it seems like Rage matters most to him as a vehicle for aiding and promoting the Zapatistas, whom he's visited four times. He's just returned from his most recent trip, where he shot some footage he's hoping MTV will air.

Once while he was down there, de la Rocha, who speaks only English, was asked to teach school so that the teachers could work in the fields.

"I couldn't really call it a classroom, it was more like a boarded tomb. It had a dirt floor, and was very poorly constructed out of wood, very desolate in there," he says.

"The classroom was stuffed with 40 children, all the way from kindergarten to sixth grade. We taught basic math to these kids. The supplies we had were minimal; we had to break pencils several times and sharpen them so everybody had something to write with." The lesson began, but de la Rocha had to step out of the shack and steady himself.

"I realized that the Mexican government had been spending hundreds of thousands of dollars a week just to keep the military force in those communities, while there was nothing these kids had to write with. That shook me. It was a haunting reminder."

De la Rocha traces his interest in Chiapas, as well as his entire political sensitivity, back to his father. Beto de la Rocha was part of Los Four, an artist collective who in 1974 became the first Chicanos to exhibit in the L.A. County Museum of Art. Their art, full of Mexican folk icons and references to the Chicano political movement, was crucial to a thriving East Side cultural scene.

"At home, my father often reminded me about who we were as a people, that we were indigenous," says de la Rocha. "My father helped me understand . . . the devastation that the Mexican people felt under the Spanish conquest in the early 1500s. I began to draw a sense of how that particular struggle and resistance affected my life. The slaughter of it is just so amazing and hidden. Seeing it through my father, in his artwork, had a profound effect on me.

"So when the uprising happened in Chiapas and unmasked the conditions down there, I was drawn to it in a way that I can't fully explain."

De la Rocha's parents divorced when he was 13, and he lived mostly with his mother, an Irish-German-Chicana studying anthropology in Orange County. But on weekends, Zack stayed with Beto in East L.A. About that time, Beto began a downward slide, triggered by a severe nervous breakdown in 1981. Zack's father drew the drapes, put huge locks on the door, and spent day after day reading a dog-eared Bible. He'd go on 40-day fasts, and when Zack came to stay, Beto forced his son to take part in his delusions. Beto would deprive his son of food, and keep him under close guard while wandering the house interpreting the Bible.

"I'd spend three weekends out of the month at my father's house, eat on Friday night, and not eat again until Monday morning when I'd get back to my mother," Zack says, his hands making the smallest of movements.

"I was so young at the time that I didn't really question it too much. I love my father, dearly, and didn't understand the level of abuse that was happening. I'm not sure that he did, either."

During one visit, Zack pointed to a painting on the wall and asked, "Daddy, can I have that?" "Hey, that's mine," Beto snapped. And then, flushed with guilt for denying his son, Beto began pulling down all his artwork—paintings, prints, drawings—and shredding them all. The frames he smashed. Then he took his paint and brushes and hurled them into a trash can that he set on fire.

"He burned over 60 percent of his artwork," says Zack. The art that had given Zack a sense of identity was going up in flames. "It was very, very, very difficult, and at one point he forced me to burn it for him. These were paintings that I grew up around and loved and admired him for creating. I had no clue why he'd want to destroy them.

"I am not anywhere near as self-destructive as he is," says Zack. "Although I'm very critical of some things I've written, I value them very much.

"I worry more just about what that experience did to me, how it affected my way of thinking. I think it affected me in good ways too, because I feel like at this point what could anyone possibly to do to me that could hurt me more?"

Hours after he tells me this in Moscow, de la Rocha says he wants to talk more tomorrow, that he was pretty nervous about the interview and wants to expand on some answers. After weeks trying to get him to sit down and talk, now it seemed he didn't want to stop. And so the next day we talked for another hour and a half. Completely about Chiapas: Everything else was off the table.

When I'd ask him about his father, he'd talk about Chiapas. But ask him about Chiapas or his poetry or who his heroes were growing up, and he'd talk about his father. Come to think of it, there may be a third lesson to be learned from that story about the suitcase full of money: Chiapas is de la Rocha's release. It's a place he goes when he wants to get away from everything that's pressing down on him—the label, fame, his past.

THANKS FOR THE INSPIRATION BETO (YOUR STRUGGLE I WILL NEVER FORGET) it says in the notes to *Rage Against the Machine*. In recent years, Beto has returned to painting. Limping around a small studio in Highland Park, the Los Angeles neighborhood where father and son, by L.A. standards, live virtually next door to one another, Beto de la Rocha shows impressive paintings and collages in a variety of styles lining his walls. When he sits down, a portrait of Zack peeks out just above his right shoulder. The resemblance—most of all in the curly hair—is unmistakable. Today Beto says, "I took [the Bible] too literally." He refers to the commandment against making graven images. "It says, 'Make no image.'. . . I was an image maker and so I said, 'Okay, I quit.' I quit being an artist and destroyed my work. Which was good, because I was being so possessive."

Beto acknowledges that he'd make his son fast along with him. "Wrongfully, and on occasion. He was too young for that." I ask if he's talked with Zack about how those years of darkness affected him. "I only heard he had remembered this through other sources," Beto says. "We've never talked about it. He'll come around when he's older, like I did," he chuckles. Of what Zack went through, Beto says, "I don't regret it. It's a learning experience."

When Zack was a teenager, neither Mom's student housing in Orange County nor Dad's East L.A. felt like home—the only Chicanos he saw in Orange County were mostly pushing brooms or picking strawberries. And in his pop's largely Latino neighborhood, a Minor Threat–loving skateboarder didn't have much in common with the homeboys on the block. He was in high school then, perfecting break-dancing moves at lunchtime, rummaging through subcultures, looking for an identity. And it's that subcultural signage—the skate-shop clothes, and the traces of Dischord-label hardcore and Public Enemy hip-hop—that he brings to Rage Against the Machine. They've helped him cobble out a sense of himself. Then Chiapas came along and brought it all back home.

"He identifies with the indigenous people of the Americas," his father says, a faint touch of worry in his voice. "That has him in quite a grip." I feel like saying something that may not reassure Beto: Actually, it seems that working for the Zapatistas had freed Zack from some kind of grip. It's brought part of him, unknown even to himself, to life.

WITH TOM MORELLO'S GENES, perhaps he was born to be the band's diplomat without portfolio: Morello's father was Kenya's first representative to the United Nations. Before that he was a warrior in the Mau Mau rebellion that freed the country from British rule. When his parents divorced a year after Morello was born (Morello just met his dad two years ago), Tom left Harlem with his mom, a white high school teacher, and moved to Libertyville, a town outside of Chicago.

Perhaps being the very first black kid in a place called Libertyville is enough right there to insure a lifetime of dissidence. On one hand, Morello had plenty of friends, and thrived in the drama club (he starred in *How to Succeed in Business Without Really Trying*). On the other hand, he'd go out to his garage to ride his bike, and he'd discover a noose.

"Often in interviews people will ask, 'When did you become politicized?'" Morello says. "Well, the second you have brown skin and you walk out on an interracial playground, your political education begins."

Having a progressive mom helped. Today Mary Morello heads the Parents for Rock and Rap, the anti-PMRC. "She's the coolest mother that anybody could imagine having," raves Brian Grillo, singer for Los Angeles band Extra Fancy. Grillo and Morello played together in Lock Up, a leftish, flashy funk group that put out an interesting record on Geffen five years ago. "When we were on the road, his mom would send him copies of *The Nation* in the mail instead of clean underwear."

Morello grew up on Alice Cooper and Black Sabbath, his first concert was Kiss—there is a shopping mall deep within him. The recognition of it made him desperate to leave. "You have to understand the area—it's a place where if you're under 18, you don't really have rights," explains John Rory Eastburg, a student at Libertyville High School. "Bill Clinton's call for teenage curfews at eight might go over well here." Eastburg is the first recipient of the Freedom in Libertyville award, a $500 scholarship Morello and a few other battered suburban survivors pledged to freethinking graduates of their alma mater. (Eastburg protested the cancellation of the school's spring play due to pressure from a conservative Christian group.)

"I've felt lines my entire life. And it's not just being African-American," says Morello. "Obviously growing up, that was one which kind of set me apart. Then as my political views traveled leftward, that set me very much apart. Then being at Harvard with the aspiration of being a rock musician set me apart. Then being a rock musician with a Harvard degree, which is, surprisingly, incredibly alienating. . . ."

The Harvard connection (graduate with honors, social studies degree, Class of '86) is not his favorite subject; he rattles off other bands with alums in them (Trip Shakespeare, Weezer, uh, Trip Shakespeare) to show it isn't such a big deal, let alone a contradiction, for a guy who calls public school "publicly funded bullshit."

But then, some dissidents are born, and others are made—a personal turning point came after college, when he moved to Los Angeles to get a band together. He landed a day job as scheduling secretary for California Senator Alan Cranston. Morello was the guy who would get off the phone and write down CHARLES KEATING, APPOINTMENT, 6–9. He'd see the Senator, a dependable liberal, spend all his time dialing contributors for money. "The underlying principles are lost in the wash of sucking up to power," he says disgustedly. He quit his day job, with a fresh understanding of how money runs the show.

Morello's absorbed the writings of linguist/anti-imperialist Noam Chomsky, and shares with Chomsky an abiding belief in a monolithic conspiracy among big business, the media, and elected officials. Whatever his shortcomings, Chomsky does a useful job producing tons of circumstantial evidence documenting the American juggernaut's involvement in evils around the world. And Morello does a great job of disseminating the information. With a few thousand more Rage Against the Machines and Noam Chomskys to even the score, we'd at least have a fair fight.

That's what I generally think. But then I specifically ask Morello, over lunch one day in a Los Angeles Chinese restaurant, who his heroes are today. For starters, he mentions the EZLN. "And in Peru there's a revolutionary struggle as well, which is also . . ."

"You're referring to the Shining Path?" I ask. Or, as these millenarian extremists are known in their native Peru and on Morello's guitar, *Sendero Luminoso.*

"Yeah."

"You feel no qualms about identifying yourself with the Shining Path? Pretty murderous people."

"It's not uncommon that the U.S. press will take a group which is so threatening to its interests and demonize them, vilify them," Morello begins. "You see it happen every day. To use a Chomsky quote, 'The greatest acts of international terrorism are planned in Washington.'"

"C'mon," I respond, "a lot of reports—not just from right-wing media—indicate that those people in villages are told that if they want to eat, if they want to not be shot, they better do what they are told by Shining Path people."

"I think you should take those [reports] with a grain of salt," counters Morello. "Consider the source. And I'm not disputing the fact that in liberation struggles there's often an enormous amount of violence. The centuries of deprivation and brutality that have been heaped upon people sometimes have a boomerang effect. There's been insanely genocidal U.S.-paid-for behavior on the part of the Peruvian government. When the mostly indigenous rural poor finally stand up for themselves and take up arms against their oppressors, suddenly Uncle Sam starts whining, 'Terrorist! Terrorist! Terrorist!'"

The restaurant was getting dark, the fortune cookies had arrived. The late-afternoon quiet just made the strangeness of what was being said even stranger.

The truth about the Shining Path won't fit on a guitar. They are led not by indigenous people but by light-skinned Maoist urban intellectuals. They in no way resemble your average liberation movement. "We reject and condemn human rights because they are bourgeois rights, reactionary, counterrevolutionary," their leader, Abimael Guzmán, has decreed, and he's backed it up, too. *Sojourners* magazine has called them "one of the most brutal and violent movements in the world today." "The Shining Path, for its part, frequently murders civilian noncombatants, including engineers, priests, teachers, peasants and journalists," *The Nation* has reported. Leftists who agree on nothing else acknowledge the atrocities of the Shining Path.

A few weeks later, at a photo shoot, Morello urges me to check out a BBC documentary that will change my understanding of what's happening in Peru. He sends me to a small bookstore in downtown L.A. which—surprise—is to all appearances run by fringe Maoists the Revolutionary Communist Party. At the front counter there's a display promoting RCP confreres Refuse and Resist, which has had great good luck duping well-meaning musicians into playing benefits that seem to benefit only the party. (Rage's *Evil Empire* booklet gives R&R a free plug.) Tables are piled with the numerous pronouncements of Bob Avakian (sort of the Robyn Hitchcock of indie politics—been around forever, nobody understands him), as well as works by Mao and Guzmán.

Maybe Morello just gets off playing air guitar for the last Maoists on earth. But something about the way he's talking reminds me of other animated conversations I've had outside the music world. Who does he remind me of? I wonder. Comic-book-store clerks? No, Morello's far too self-possessed, more driven, smarter. Flying saucer enthusiasts? Closer, but still not quite right. Fringe political sect members?

Who knows. All I can say is, they sure grill you in that bookstore. How did I hear about them? What was my name? Looking for anything in particular? And when they asked who sent me and I answered, "Tom from Rage Against the Machine," a clerk said, "We usually agree with Rage, but we take issue with some of their statements regarding human rights in Tibet," and then tried to interest me in a bunch of anti–Dalai Lama literature. All I know is, I got the hell out of there.

THE MOSCOW SHOW has ended. No encore—none necessary. There's a stack of socialist realist pizzas backstage, curdled and imposing, ready to be hauled back to the hotel. In the hall outside the dressing room, teenager Vasya Gavrilov, guitarist in a local band called Against the Stream, leans against a wall.

"I have no papers, you know," he says in broken English with a big smile on his face. No backstage pass. "To get here I was being like a tomcat."

While he waits for the group to come out, Gavrilov asks me, "Do they really like Communism?" He says it the way kids once asked if Ozzy really bit the head off bats. "If they lived here for 70 years, they would not play this kind of music. Only patriotic songs."

A joke circulated in Moscow punk rock circles just before the election, he says—the Communist candidate Gennady Zyuganov was down in the polls, so he asked Rage to come to town and help him campaign.

"My friends, we have a joke. It goes that everything rules or everything sucks." Thanks, but I think I've heard that joke somewhere before. "Zyuganov sucks."

Just then, Morello comes out of the dressing room, wearing his cap that says COMMIE, and Gavrilov buttonholes him for an autograph. While he runs up to the band, I ask him, if he's so unsure of Rage's politics, why is he here? He just shoots me a look that says forget the contradictions, dude. It says: Because they rule.

RJ SMITH is a former SPIN contributing writer. Based in Los Angeles, he is currently writing a biography of James Brown.

SLEATER-KINNEY

Dig Me Out

Kill Rock Stars

JUNE 1997

by **ANN POWERS**

Nobody wants to be radical anymore. On the right, radicals blow up family planning clinics; on the left, they're shaggy '60s relics and fat, hairy man-haters who destroyed feminism for ordinary women. Even as slang, "radical" seems about as fresh as Pauly Shore in a pair of Bongo shorts.

Until you hear Sleater-Kinney. "Dig me out!" hollers Corin Tucker on the title track of the band's new album. "Dig me in! / Outta this mess, baby / Outta my head." Tucker's singing about how rock's monstrous noise rips off her skin, leaving her unprotected and gloriously unbound. As guitarist Carrie Brownstein turbocharges a riff rescued from Iggy Pop and David Bowie's "China Girl" and drummer Janet Weiss applies dominatrix discipline to her kick drum, Tucker alternately guides the music's onslaught and gives in to it. She lets the songs' electric momentum strip her down to her emotional core—a pure and antisocial humanity. From start to finish, *Dig Me Out* aims for this place of undiluted emotion, where girlishness yields to the rage and joy of women who feel no need to charm.

Nurtured in the pink petri dish of Olympia, Washington, where women's lib never went out of fashion and punk meant the gentle triumph of nerdy kids, Sleater-Kinney seemed at first like a glorious anomaly: politically radical artists whose rhetoric fired them up instead of weighing them down. Tucker's voice was one of those wonders of the world that turned listeners into pilgrims; Brownstein drove her own path with raggedy-ass, blade-sharp guitar, and the songs gleamed with quick eloquence. Yet for all the harsh allure of their 1995 debut and last year's *Call the Doctor*, Sleater-Kinney's music remained, for the most part, more no than yes, a reaction against sexism instead of an attempt to imagine life beyond it.

On *Dig Me Out*, a rockin' little collection of love songs and catchy dance numbers, Sleater-Kinney take the next step. Like the most radical feminist art, the album cuts into the meat of women's everyday experience, aiming for depths untouched by the buttons-and-bows (or nose-and-belly-button-ring) conventions that identify what's "feminine." This is not an easy task in the pop world, where most female artists trade in these conventions, occasionally sassing back, but ultimately staying within familiar boundaries. Many women assume they're liberated because they can choose which fantasy to modify. But self-determination doesn't mean shit when you didn't create the self you're determining. And one thing rock'n'roll's beat can offer is a momentary sandblast that frees raw consciousness. When Tucker sings, "I'll touch the sky and say what I want," she knows that the music is what opens her mouth.

It takes chops to achieve such a visceral liberation, and Sleater-Kinney now own them fully. Weiss, who joined the group last year, is both relentless and highly musical, and Brownstein has grown dexterous on guitar; her twisted melodicism, which always got its energy from wiry riffs instead of crunchy chords, is a full partner to Tucker's vocal aerobatics. Sleater-Kinney now deliver the punch their words describe. "Words and Guitar" leaps and skitters with the just-released repression of early Talking Heads; "Dance Song '97" uses a Farfisa for a new wave, DayGlo mood. Even "Little Babies," a fairly standard feminist protest against the maternity trap, gets an added bite from a rock-reveling chorus ("All the little babies go one-two-three-four!"). Over chords that sound like the Clash taking a walk on the wild side, Tucker and Brownstein giddily admit their own need to suck the mother's milk of the backbeat.

It's a blast to get charged up by Sleater-Kinney's suffragette rock, but Tucker and Brownstein make their most surprisingly radical moves within love songs. Most address women, and this unqualified declaration of lesbian desire immediately lifts them past typical wedding-bell romance. Both fragmentary and painfully intimate, the songs avoid erotic platitudes, instead exploring sexual longing in plain language. Tucker and Brownstein are listening to themselves, and what they discover isn't simple. In the magnificent "One More Hour," the chorus counterposes Tucker's irrational heartbreak ("I needed it," she repeats, her pitch rising) against Brownstein's rote rationalizations and deadpan clichés. The argument ebbs and fades; it could be lovers feuding, or one friend consoling the other, or the bereft Tucker split against herself. In this moment what emerges is the clarity of partial vision, the understanding that who you are is a process, not reducible to parts. *Dig Me Out* captures the noise of a soul-filled body shaking itself awake, and that's an experience that bridges any gender divide. In it, guys as well as girls will hear the rattle of their brains and the flash of their libidos. The catharsis Sleater-Kinney seek is more than just fun; it's a battle in earnest for the human right to know and possess yourself. Feminism was supposed to be about that fight, too, but it's still sputtering under the weight of its own complacency. Sleater-Kinney push us back into the fray. If they wanna be our Simone de Beauvoir, *Dig Me Out* proves they're up to it

---

ANN POWERS is the chief pop critic of *The Los Angeles Times*. She is the author of *Weird Like Us: My Bohemian America* and, with the artist, of *Tori Amos: Piece by Piece*.

THE **OUTSIDERS**

Middle-American
Gothic

Being odd man out at a Midwest goth festival

by JONATHAN AMES

APRIL 2006

Not to be too much of a kiss-ass brown-noser—God, those two phrases, especially when paired, reveal themselves to be rather vulgar—but I have really loved writing for SPIN. In life, I like to go on adventures and see what happens. If I can do this and combine it with journalism, then my work life and my life life happily cross paths. Essentially, I get paid for being an idiot and reporting on it! This, naturally, is in opposition to just being an idiot and not getting paid, which is what usually happens.

Anyway, a few years ago, SPIN sent me to a goth music festival in Illinois. At the time, I knew nothing of goth music or the people who like it. So this to me was an adventure, and I happily accepted the assignment. One of my early literary heroes was Hunter S. Thompson, and so I always like to thrust myself into the story I'm covering. This gives me an excuse to behave poorly, like my idol Thompson, and to make that part of the narrative.

One of the benefits of covering the goth festival, in addition to meeting some very sweet people, was that it prepped me for my subsequent SPIN assignment, a profile of Marilyn Manson, with whom I definitely behaved poorly. I will say that I was a gentleman at the goth festival and didn't get into trouble, but I'll let you find out for yourself in the following pages as to whether or not this is true.

■ ■ ■

'M **41** YEARS OLD and outwardly I may be one of the least goth people you could ever meet. For more than a decade, my style, fashion-wise, has been faux-preppy English professor, which means I wear sport coats and corduroy pants. To add a touch of flair, and to hide my bald head, I wear a tan cap backward, such that it looks like a beret. My musical taste, I should tell you, is similar to my clothing, which is to say it is decidedly nongoth. Twenty years ago, in college, I listened primarily to Cat Stevens, James Taylor, and Simon & Garfunkel; recently I've discovered Radiohead and find them to be quite good. So, clearly, I'm some kind of musical retard.

Thus, SPIN, being rather mischievous, thought I'd be the perfect person to cover Gothicfest 2005, which was the first of its kind, just as there was a first Super Bowl or world war. It was an all-day gathering of 20 goth bands in Villa Park, Illinois, a distant suburb of Chicago. The following is a diary of my adventures amid these dark minstrels and their loyal brood.

Saturday, September 17, 2005
The Odeum Sports & Expo Center

12:25 P.M. I'm wearing my checked sport coat, white shirt, tan cap, and jeans (to help me fit in a little), but I already seem to be attracting stares. There are roughly 100 people mingling about, and the Halloweenish costumes are causing a knee-jerk terror response in me. There's also pounding, scary music being played by a DJ.

I may have subconsciously chosen a white shirt to be defiant—everyone else is, of course, in black—and I just fantasized about being beaten to death as an intruder, getting kicked repeatedly while lying on the ground. A few of the fellows here look like neo-Nazi skinheads, which, I think, provoked this beating-to-death fantasy; also, I'm a little depressed and that always brings on suicidal thoughts.

Two chubby, expressionless boys stand to my right. They were once cute children, but now I imagine that they spend hours in dark bedrooms looking at violent porn. Or perhaps they have tender reveries about being sweet to the girls that they adore from a distance. I'd like to think about them in this generous light—that they are actually gentle young men—but it's hard not to stereotype them as potential serial killers. It's their eerie, still blankness that makes me think they're capable of murder—and the fact that I'm in the Midwest. The Midwest seems to cultivate serial killing. Must be the boxed-in geography.

One wears glasses and has multipierced ears and a scruffy pubescent beard. His hair is dyed red and spiked up. His dirty, loose jeans flow to the floor over his shoes.

His friend has a more mature beard but is fatter, shorter, and his nose is swollen with oil and clogged pores. His eyes are slits. He wears a winter hat, a dirty T-shirt, and filthy jeans. He really could be a medieval Visigoth; I can imagine him swinging an ax with vigor. I do like that these two are standing next to each other, that they are friends and are here together. It makes me think of my childhood best friend, whom I hadn't seen for years, and then learned two years ago that he had died. I miss him. In fact, I dreamed about him last night. Every few months I dream that we're friends again.

12:45 P.M. The Odeum Sports & Expo Center resembles an airplane hangar, with bleachers on one side. There are no windows, and though it's midday, it feels like night, which is fitting. There's a concession area at one end and a very large stage at the other. There are also about two dozen booths, selling various goth goods: CDs, black capes, plastic skulls, human skeletons, knives, and Vampire Wine. It's just wine, but when you drink it, I guess you pretend that it's blood. It reminds me of how, when I was a kid, you could get chocolate cigars and cigarettes and pretend you were an adult.

The first band, Dead Girls Corp., has just started playing. The singer keeps reminding the audience that they have driven all the way from California. He wants us to appreciate this sacrifice, which is understandable, but mentioning it repeatedly is a little tiresome. "Feeling empty because there's something to say," he sings. Shouldn't it be, "because there's nothing to say"? Then again, he might be right. All we really can express is pain. This diary and everything else I've ever written is actually a code for one word: help!

A fellow to my right is wearing a T-shirt that promotes the film *American Psycho*. Another young man's shirt says: BIOHAZ-ARD LEVEL 4. It occurs to me that I'm inwardly apocalyptic and these people are outwardly apocalyptic. I may dress like a somewhat libidinous college professor, but in my heart of hearts, I'm in a state of dark despair about the world. But are these people embracing the apocalypse, while I'm nervously awaiting it? I may not look the part, but in my own way, I belong here.

1:15 P.M. I'm in a side room reserved for bands, talking to the ceremonial host and hostess of Gothicfest, Mark and Michelle.

Mark, 19, is wispy, with large, vulnerable eyes and dark hair draped across his forehead. He wears a black shirt, a velvet scarf, and saddle shoes. His black jeans are decorated with the lyrics from a song he wrote, "Crimson Tears of Tragedy."

Michelle, 35, is short, pale, and voluptuous. She's got on a black satin ball gown made in Germany from a 16th-century design, bejeweled gloves, platform boots, and an elaborate dread-locked hairpiece.

"What do you get out of the goth scene?" I ask.

"The beauty of it," says Michelle. "The elegance. The history. There's so much conformity. We're nonconformists. We don't judge and we don't want to be judged. We're just artists expressing ourselves. I'm into traditional goth: Bauhaus and Joy Division. I hold true to the people who started the movement. My look is more classic, elegant, but some days I can go cyber."

"I fall more into the glam-goth scene," says Mark. "My idols were, like, David Bowie."

"What do your families think about you being goths?" I inquire.

"My mother loved the scene," says Michelle. "Like Peter Murphy. My father is totally sympathetic. Even when I was younger, into punk, he said, 'I will never have a square daughter.'"

"I live with my grandparents," Mark says. "My grandfather loves me for what I do—that I express myself. But my grandmother

Undead like me: The author is flanked by the hosts of Gothicfest 2005. © *Jim Newberry*

throws temper tantrums, calls me a fag because I wear makeup and I'm very feminine. I have an abusive relationship with my father. Constant beatings. I saw him in July, and he beat the shit out of me."

"Did you fight back?" I ask.

"I don't fight back," Mark says. "As much as I don't like him, I love him because he's my father. So I just take it. He wants me to be more of a man, not so fem. He wants me to be tougher, cold, heartless, an alpha male."

Later, Mark tells us how his uncle, a goth who had drug problems but was a true father to him, committed suicide by slashing himself. Mark found him as he was bleeding to death. Mark starts crying and Michelle and I try to comfort him.

"I'm sorry I'm crying," he says.

"It's all right," I say.

2:20 P.M. A band called Drake is playing.

The lead singer wears a long robe. He chants into the microphone in an ominous, froggy voice: "Dost thou leave me with such a myth / Falling into the abyss." I admire his rhyme scheme, but it would be much better if he had a lisp—"the abyth."

I eyeball the young man next to me, who is thin, brown-haired, and not very goth, except for his arms, which are encased in black fishnet stockings.

"Excuse me, could I interview you?" I ask.

"Sure," he says. "They call me Rain."

"Who's they?"

"The people at my college. I used to have purple hair and they weren't used to that there, so they called me Purple Rain, and it got shortened to Rain. My real name is Tim, but every Tim I know is a Melvin—an idiot—so I kept Rain."

"Are you still in college?"

"No, I'm 30."

"What's your take on Gothicfest?" I ask.

"Well, I'm here for the headliner, Hanzel und Gretyl. I'm actually more into industrial. Most of the bands here today are industrial. Goth is dying. The scene is, like, 20 years old. It should die. It's all regurgitating what was done in Germany ten, 12 years ago. Goth now is more about the clothing than the music. You can buy goth stuff at Hot Topic in the malls. Goth is dead in my world because it's packaged. It's not counterculture; it's pop culture. . . . Have you read Chomsky?"

"Not really," I say, embarrassed, and then add weakly, "I have a sense, though, of what Chomsky is about."

"A lot of the political message of industrial is voicing what Chomsky says—that we live in a benevolent fascist state."

"I really need to read Chomsky," I say. "Immediately."

"You should see this documentary about him, *Manufacturing Consent.*"

"Thanks for the tip," I say, and I sheepishly take my leave. I wasn't expecting to meet a Noam Chomsky fan at Gothicfest.

3:10 P.M. A band with female members, Ghost Orgy, is onstage. They have a lovely, femme fatale–ish violinist and a busty lead singer in high black boots. There are about 400 people here now, sporting a number of interesting T-shirt slogans: EAT A BAG OF SHIT; FUCK YOU, YOU FUCKING FUCK; and AN EXPERIMENT IN SICKNESS. A girl walks past me with a backpack shaped like a coffin.

The singer suddenly lifts up her skirt, revealing black panties. At that moment it hits me: I need to interview this young lady.

3:40 P.M. I'm sitting with Ghost Orgy's Dina Concina, who is in her mid-20s and even more beautiful up close. I compliment her on her performance, discreetly omitting the lifting-of-the-skirt part. She says she started her music career as a rock'n'roll singer but that she's been into goth for the last three years.

"I realized how much hate I have inside," she says, explaining her transition. "And I get to channel it onstage."

"What do you hate?" I ask.

"Our corporate jobs, shit like that. People. Our lives."

"Why do you hate your life?"

"Because I work a corporate job. Well, I just quit. But I was an engineer scientist for Kraft Foods."

"What's an engineer scientist do?"

"I created the recipes for cookies and crackers. I launched the new Cheese Nips. They're fucking good. You should try them."

"What do your parents think about you being in a goth band?"

"They don't even know the name of my band. They would kill me. They're old-school Filipino parents. But they're awesome. They know I'm in a band, but they don't know that I'm singing about death and demons and blood."

"They don't subscribe to SPIN, do they?"

She smiles, and then tells me that her neck is very stiff—she wrenched it onstage.

"I could give you a neck rub," I say, and I can't believe these words have come out of my mouth. It's like I have Tourette's. There's nothing more pathetic than a man who offers a beautiful young woman a massage.

"That would be great," she says. First a Chomsky fan and now a young woman who will let me touch her! This Gothicfest is remarkable.

I stand behind her and knead her neck. I feel like a dirty old man, and then I remember, I am a dirty old man.

4:10 P.M. I'm in the bleachers with Steve Watson and his 12-year-old daughter, Bethany, who are finishing up some hot dogs. Steve, 53, is friendly and articulate. He's wearing khaki pants and a golf shirt. Bethany is frail and cute, with black lipstick, a retainer on her teeth, and a tiara on her dark hair. "Bethany is into all kinds of music," Steve says. "Punk. Metal. And, quite frankly, I enjoy it as well. Living where we live, we're not exposed to all this." He waves his hand in front of him.

"You're a very open-minded parent," I say.

"I try to be. The community where we live is very affluent, and the people there are very intolerant. Not only are they intolerant of other people racially and financially, but if you don't fit in to the WASP lifestyle, you're shunned. Luckily for me, I have sufficient income so that I can say, 'Fuck you.'"

"Why do you live there?"

"Economic advantages. Schools are very good. Crime is zero. But it's not a utopia. Everybody is forced into conformity, and it puts the kids under a lot of stress. Bethany had some friends who wanted to come today, but their parents wouldn't let them. I tell you, we're treated more openly and accepting at these concerts than in our own community."

Bethany tells me she had a band but that they split up. Their name was Toxic Popsicle. "Not your average prom queen," Steve tells me. "But I'm cool with it."

7:15 P.M. I pass the booth selling skulls. They are very realistic-looking and can be used as piggy banks and candleholders. The short, smiling proprietress says, "Everybody likes a little head."

"What did you say?" I ask. The music is very loud.

"Everybody likes a little head."

"What?"

"Everybody likes a little head."

A male cohort tries to explain her sense of humor: "We usually work biker shows."

I move to the next stall, which is selling gigantic swords. I ask the woman standing behind a glass case of knives, "You can sell this stuff to someone right now?"

"No," she says. "At the end of the concert, they can get it, and then they're escorted out by security."

"That's good to know."

12:00 A.M. I'm exhausted. I've been listening to goth music for almost 12 hours. The last band is on, but I can't take much more. There are about 600 people here now—Gothicfest isn't a mad success, but it's not a failure, either. It's been a good day for the goths.

A pretty girl gyrating next to me shouts over the music, "Dance with me!"

"I'm too old," I say.

"No, you're not," she says.

"How old are you?" I ask. She looks about 19, 20.

"Fifteen," she says.

"Have a good time," I say and quickly head for the exit.

On my way out, I pass a fellow with spikes poking out of the top of his shaved head. It's like there are miniature traffic cones dividing his cranium in half.

"Are those spikes screwed into your skull?" I ask incredulously.

He puts his hand in his pocket, takes out a small bottle of glue, and says, "I'm not dumb, you know."

I nod and leave. Outside, there's a large, jaundiced moon in the black sky. I hope it's still there when the goths come out. I feel like a parent whose children prefer to stay inside and watch TV. The father pleads, "It's a beautiful day. Why don't you go play outside?" In this case, I feel like pleading, "It's a completely spooky night. Forget the loud music, come outside and have a blood sacrifice or something! There's a full moon!"

But I don't say anything to anyone. I bid a silent farewell to the expo center, and with the moon watching over me, I get the hell out of there.

JONATHAN AMES is the author of eight books, including *The Extra Man* and *Wake Up, Sir!* He is also the creator of the HBO series *Bored to Death*.

SCHOOL'S
OUT

Remembering
New York City's real
rock'n'roll high school

by **TOM SINCLAIR**

SEPTEMBER 2005

Growing up in New York City in the early '70s, I used to hear tales about Quintano's School for Young Professionals. The place seemed almost an urban legend, a school where the coolest, freakiest, baddest kids went to pass their high school years, getting high and screwing around. I was only dimly aware of its roots as an institution for young actors and musicians. Years later, when I became a rock critic, I learned that Aerosmith's Steven Tyler, Johnny Thunders and Syl Sylvain from the New York Dolls, and D Generation's Jesse Malin were among the alumni. It was when Malin told me about the male prostitution ring that allegedly operated out of the school in the '80s that I knew the Quintano's story had to be told. Five years later, I'm still running into Quintano's grads with stories as over-the-top as anything in the following pages.

■ ■ ■

JESSE MALIN NEEDED TO FIND a new school. It was 1982, and the then-14-year-old future frontman of glam punks D Generation (and, later, solo artist) had just been suspended from Junior High 194 in Queens, New York, for, well, let's let him explain: "These girls in Sassoon and Jordache jeans were making fun of me, and I didn't know what to do, so I went over to their desk in Spanish class, and I just took my penis out and banged it on the desk, and they *flipped*."

So did the school's principal, and young Malin soon found himself with some unexpected free time to ponder his educational prospects. School, as such, held little interest for him. A working-class kid obsessed with punk, he had recently formed his first band, Heart Attack, and was spending more and more time in Manhattan clubs. Too young to drop out, Malin felt he needed an environment that would allow him a larger degree of freedom than the typical public school.

Enter Andy Apathy (né Bryan), bass player for the punk band Reagan Youth. Apathy told him about a private school in Manhattan that was seemingly designed for kids like them. It was called Quintano's School for Young Professionals and ostensibly catered to teens in the performing arts. It was small—about 100 students—and had exceedingly lax academic and attendance requirements. "If you don't want to go, you just call in," Apathy told him. "You go there, but you don't *really* have to go." It sounded good to Malin, who turned to his grandmother for the tuition (about $1,600 a year), knowing she had a bit more ready cash than his working, single mom. He chuckles recalling how he told his grandmother it was a school for musicians, "like Juilliard."

While it's true that many musicians—among them Aerosmith's Steven Tyler, three-fifths of the original New York Dolls (Johnny Thunders, Sylvain Sylvain, and Billy Murcia), doo-wop legend Frankie Lymon, Tony Sales (who has played bass with David Bowie, Iggy Pop, and Todd Rundgren), Stevie Nicks and Linda Ronstadt guitarist Waddy Wachtel, and members of the Shangri-Las and the Jackson 5—passed through Quintano's doors, the school was about as similar to New York's prestigious Juilliard School as Smirnoff Ice is to Dom Perignon.

Though little known to the general public, Quintano's boasts a colorful, strange, and often unsavory history. Started in 1951 by Leonard S. Quintano—known as "Dr. Q," though he was neither an M.D. nor Ph.D.—it was a place most people heard about through word of mouth. It was where you sent your talented kid if he or she was, or wanted to be, in show biz; it was also where you sent your wayward brat if he or she had been thrown out of another school. A roll call of its famous Hollywood and Broadway alumni includes Patty Duke, Sal Mineo, Tuesday Weld, Gregory and Maurice Hines, Bernadette Peters, and Valerie Harper.

Malin's first visit to the school, then located on West 61st Street near Columbus Circle, left a distinct impression. "It was in a decrepit office building, on the floor right below *High Times* magazine," he says, laughing. "The place was barren, nothing on the walls, certainly nothing educational. There were about three small classrooms that looked like miniature *Welcome Back, Kotter* sets. The bathrooms smelled like pot."

Although future Academy Award nominee Diane Lane attended at the time, she was hardly typical of the student body. "There were a few actors and actresses, kids doing commercials, and a couple of us punk-rock musicians," Malin says. "But mostly they were rich kids whose parents gave them the [tuition], kinda hang-arounders who just wanted to fuck off. . . .

Student revolt: Heart Attack, featuring Quintano's Jesse Malin (right), in 1981.
Laura Levine

[When I first went in] all these kids were in the hallway, smoking and drinking forties!" They even, Malin discovered, brought their beers into class with no repercussions. *What a place*, he thought. *Loose!*

Yet chugging Olde E in social studies was nothing compared with the teen male-prostitution ring, allegedly organized by a school employee, which Malin and several other former students contend operated out of Quintano's. "There would be town cars double-parked downstairs," Malin remembers. "I'd be sitting in school, and guys in suits and mustaches would come in during the day and point to certain kids, and they would leave." Gradually, it became clear just what was going on. "One day Andy Apathy comes over and goes, 'Jesse, you wanna make some money?' And I was like, 'Well, I could use another guitar.' And Andy says, 'Well, uh, you go down to Atlantic City in these cars, and while their husbands are gambling, these women will spend a lot of money to be with you, will suck on your balls for hours. And, once in a while, you gotta be with a man.' "

"They'd pick out the pretty people and put the full spell on them," says Steve Poss, a student at the time, of the recruiting process. "That's when it got a little creepy."

Neither Poss nor Malin ever participated (Apathy died of an OD a few years ago), and within months the ring had been dismantled and the person allegedly responsible for its operation was fired—although the exact chain of events remains a mystery. Malin and Poss believe that the matter was handled internally and the police never became involved. (An NYPD spokesperson says that the department cannot give out information in cases where no arrests had been made.)

Latin pop singer Brenda K. Starr, who graduated from Quintano's in 1986, says she knew nothing about the alleged rent-boy ring and tended to steer clear of the school's wilder side. "There were kids there that were, like, smoking pot right in front of the school. I was, like, 'You guys are crazy.' But they were rock'n'rollers, what do you expect?" Whatever the truth, all agree with Brian Lima—a former soap-opera actor and Quintano's student who says he was approached to be an escort—that Dr. Q "had no clue about what was going on."

Says Malin of the scandal: "Even though I thought myself very adult, I was still kinda like, '*Wow.*'"

That was also his reaction when, years later, he found out his diploma was worthless and the school hadn't been accredited at the time of his graduation. "Now in my scrapbook I have this funny diploma and this connection with all these show-biz people that went there," Malin says. "And I wonder: How real or legit was Quintano's?"

TOM HOGAN, SUPERVISOR of the New York State Education Department Office for Non-Public School Services, remembers regularly fielding calls from distressed former Quintano's students, beginning in the mid-'80s. Like Malin, they had discovered their diplomas were of no value.

According to Hogan, a 1978 regulation stipulated that non-public schools must be registered with the Board of Regents in order to issue diplomas. "If you look at the requirements for registration, a school has to have certain facilities, which he apparently didn't have," says Hogan. "Perhaps because of failing health or whatever, Dr. Quintano's decision was not to bother with it at all." Hogan recalls a story told to him by an ex-student. After Dr. Q died in 1991, the supervisor says, "this person tracked down his widow somewhere in New Jersey. She told him that the school's records had been taken to the dump."

Just when did the school's long slide into chaos begin? By most accounts, things started to get weird in the mid-'60s. In a letter dated June 28, 1965, apparently in response to an application for a Regents charter, Anthony E. Terino, of New York's Division for School Registration and Supervision, called attention to some glaring deficiencies. "There is no science laboratory, no library, and no gymnasium," he writes of the school, which was then located at 156 West 56th Street, across from the back entrance to Carnegie Hall. "Mr. Quintano . . . is not really interested in expanding his facilities or making extensive changes to meet state requirements." In another letter the following November, Terino informed Dr. Q of the findings by a group of "specialists" who reviewed the school's final exams in English, social studies, science, and mathematics: "In most cases, their reactions are unfavorable, and I would strongly urge that you take the necessary action to improve your program."

By this time, perhaps for financial reasons, Quintano's had started accepting non-show-biz strays. Drug counselor Carrin Hare, who graduated in 1973, puts it bluntly: "You had the students that were there because they had real careers, and you had the fuck-ups." Some were a little of both. Moogy Klingman (who has played keyboards with Jimi Hendrix, Eric Clapton, and Bob Dylan) arrived at Quintano's around 1966. "I was thrown out of a high school in Great Neck [Long Island]," he says. "I started to become a rock musician and play in bands when I was about 16, and I heard about Quintano's. Tuition was incredibly inexpensive—$700 a year or something. You went and just kind of hung around. They would just graduate you, move you along. Most of the kids were pretty drugged-out, taking LSD and smoking pot. It was a completely out-of-control place filled with the wildest glitter-rock kids who were gonna be high school dropouts anyway."

"I hope there aren't any schools like that today," cracks Tony Sales, who went to Quintano's circa 1968. "I didn't consider it a school, really—it was more like a getaway, a place where I'd go hang out for a little bit and then decide where I was gonna go fuck off for the day." At the time, Sales was playing in a band, Tony and the Tigers, with his younger brother, Hunt. When the Tigers went on tour, Tony was dutifully given homework for the road. "Of course, everything stayed in my suitcase. They gave you the work, but they didn't say anything about *doing* it."

For future New York Dolls guitarist Sylvain Sylvain, winding up at Quintano's in 1967 (a year before his buddy Johnny Thunders) was a lifesaver. "If you wore bell bottoms and had long hair at Newtown High School in Queens in 1966, you were a 'faggot' and got your ass kicked," he says. "And if you were dyslexic like me, you were just [considered] stupid." Syl had heard about Quintano's from student Michael Brown (keyboardist for the Left Banke, who had a hit with "Walk Away Renee"). He enrolled along with Dolls drummer Billy Murcia and found that neither freakiness nor dyslexia were impediments to acceptance.

Steven Tallarico—better known today as Aerosmith singer Steven Tyler—was living at home in Yonkers, New York, and playing in bands like Thee Strangeurs and the Chain Reaction in the mid-'60s, when he was thrown out of Roosevelt High following a pot bust ("They put a narc in my ceramics class"). He soon landed at Quintano's, where he found like-minded souls who appreciated a high school where the emphasis was on *high*. "Everyone was walking around blitzed, tripping," says Tyler. "[In the mornings] I would get out of the subway and walk to Central Park, and in the snow, rain, whatever, a bunch of us would wind up sitting on the rocks with street people and smoking a fat [joint], and then going to school."

Tyler readily admits, "I didn't reap the scholastic rewards, because I didn't go to a lot of classes." He does, however, have vivid memories of Dr. Quintano. "Dr. Q was bald, skinny as could be, a bit of a Willy Wonka type. I remember coming in late and stoned, and he would sit and talk with me on the stoop outside the school, pep talks. He would tell me about the game of life and how it's played. He was a very witty, sharp guy. He's the one who told me about the type A personality. His theory was that, when you're loud and verbose, full of energy and alive, a lot of times society deems you an outcast, and type A personalities always got in trouble. He told me to hold my ground and embrace who I was. God, I remember it so well."

NO ONE WHO KNEW Dr. Leonard Quintano—who died in 1991 at the age of 91—would call him a type A kind of guy. Frank Mosier, 76, who taught at the school from 1960 to 1975, remembers Dr. Q as "a very private man, an odd little gentleman." He was, in fact, bona fide nobility. Born in New York City in 1900, he was the son of Italian count and classical violinist Giacomo Quintano, who came to the U.S. at the invitation of President McKinley to play at the White House. The younger Quintano, who was a public high school teacher early in his career, inherited many of his dad's old-world attitudes.

6 Extreme Metal Bands That Could Be Mistaken for Flavors of Herbal Tea

Kettle's on: Celtic Frost in 1984.

1. Celtic Frost

2. Autumn Leaves

3. Moonspell

4. Memory Garden

5. Jacob's Dream

6. Heavenwood

"He was in the wrong century," says Mosier, who today helps his wife run an arts foundation in California. "He was very Victorian in sensibility. He was this rather formal, almost delicate gentleman, married to this lady who had quite a bit of money and loved her dogs. He started Quintano's because he knew a young woman who needed a diploma and who was a performer—I don't even know what she was, singer, dancer, or what. He started it to give her a place to go to school, and he found there was a real demand for it."

"I think it was exposure to musicians in the classical world that got him interested in opening a school," says Leonard Quintano's nephew, screenwriter Gene Quintano (*Police Academy 3* and *4*). "He was a great character, all the kids really seemed to love him.

He used to say he was a sucker because he'd buy kids lunches if they didn't have money. He once said to me, 'If I don't pay for any more lunches this year, I should break even.'"

But it was apparently never about money for Dr. Q, who always kept his tuition lower than most private schools. His nephew believes that he opened up the school to other teens in the '60s because "he enjoyed all these kids. He was married for 60-some years, but they were never able to have children. I think a lot of it came from that."

"Gentle, gentle, gentle," is how actress Patty Duke, who attended Quintano's in the early '60s, describes him. "It was as if he grew there like a mushroom. As far as we were concerned, he had no prior life and no life outside the school." Yet for a man so married to his work, Dr. Q was in denial about the changing nature of his student body. In later years, after he was rendered nearly blind by glaucoma, his condition was the too-perfect metaphor for his unwillingness to see the drug problem that took hold of the school in the mid-'60s.

Mosier says that the various cliques "didn't socialize across group lines and almost pretended those other people weren't there. The faculty, of course, pretty much only identified with the better students and tried to forget about the losers: except for the assistant principal, which was me, who had to deal with them occasionally.

"I knew half a dozen drug dealers—they were my students," he continues. "I recall one day I called in seven sets of parents and/or guardians. I informed six of them that their children were heroin addicts and the seventh that their daughter was an alcoholic and a call girl—we had a few call girls among the students."

Eddie Kunze, a New York City–based photo retoucher, estimates that when he graduated in 1972, "a good third of the school was playing around with heroin." He recalls "kids hanging out in front of the school like it was a bar. We knew the place was under surveillance. The police weren't total morons—I mean, there were kids nodding on the steps."

Still, some former students maintain that it was possible to learn something beyond getting drunk, rolling joints, and snorting smack. That was especially true in the '50s and early '60s, when misbehavior was far more innocent. "The worst thing we ever did," says Patty Duke (mother of actor Sean Astin), "was go out of the building and goad Gregory and Maurice Hines into dancing, doing a half-hour riff on the sidewalk."

Yet even after things had changed—and the unofficial sobriquet "Quintano's School for Young Fuck-ups" had been coined—a percentage of kids willfully persisted in going to classes and doing homework. "There were people who were very diligent and into attending school," says former student Scott Farrington, citing his own accomplishments. "I was the sophomore class president, the junior vice president, and the student body president."

"The whole place was like an ideal democracy," says Mosier. "Or more properly, democratic anarchy without any real top-down supervision, including from me. It shook out like triage on the battlefield: The ones I could teach I spent a lot of time and energy on. The ones who were in the park scoring chemicals all day, or who simply never came, I refused to worry about."

Patti D'Arbanville, who attended Quintano's for two years in the '60s before launching her acting career with a role in *Andy Warhol's Flesh* (1968), chuckles remembering the laissez-faire attitude. "I maybe went to a couple of classes when it was raining really hard," she says. "We'd come in every once in a while and joke around with the teachers. They'd pretend they were having heart attacks: 'Miss D'Arbanville, my God, I never expected to see you here!' Nobody gave you a hard time."

AFTER NEARLY 40 YEARS of not giving students a hard time, Quintano's sputtered to a close at the end of the '80s. The office building that housed the school's final incarnation at 322 West 45th Street has changed hands numerous times in the past 20 years, and no one quite remembers what year Quintano's shut its doors— although Gene Quintano speculates it was around 1988. "My uncle never officially announced it was closing," he says. (A QUINTANO'S SCHOOL sign still hangs outside the building's second floor.)

Even to those who knew him, Leonard Quintano remains something of a cipher, a mild-mannered man who clung obstinately to the institution long after he had reached retirement age and his health was failing. More than one former student has likened the elderly Dr. Q to Mr. Magoo. "I was talking to Diane Lane," says Gene Quintano, "who said she used to see him coming into the school the last couple of years. He would bang into a parking meter and tip his hat and say, 'Oh, excuse me,' and then go on."

Sometime in the '80s, Mosier made tentative moves to buy the school. "I knew Dr. Quintano was getting older, and I was sounding him out about my maybe coming back and taking it over," he says. "In his own quiet but very effective way, he let me know I couldn't make a living at it. He said, 'If it wasn't for my wife's generosity and the fact that she shares my vision, I couldn't do this.'"

The ramshackle building across from Carnegie Hall, where the school was located in its early days, has been replaced by a modern office tower. "Whenever I go back to New York," says Patty Duke, "I always manage to walk down the block. In my mind, Quintano's is still there, and when I see it's gone, it triggers a real melancholy in me."

Steven Tyler is forever bumping into people who went there. "Especially in L.A.," he says. "I did this movie with John Travolta and Uma Thurman called *Be Cool*, and sure enough, I was talking to Danny DeVito and Quintano's came up. We were doing a scene at the Viper Room, and there was a guy sitting at the bar who had gone to Quintano's. I was like, 'Really! What year?' ''72.' 'Oh, I graduated in '68.'" Tyler pauses, laughing. "Or '66. Or '67. I don't remember. I have to ask my mother." *(Additional reporting by Jeanne Palomino)*

TOM SINCLAIR spent nearly a decade as a writer in the music department of *Entertainment Weekly.* These days he works as a substance abuse counselor and dabbles in rock criticism.

The Art
of the
HUSTLE

Pounding the pavement with rock's hungriest band

by **CHARLES AARON**

JUNE 2007

Sometimes, while writing about Atlanta modern-rock strivers Uncrowned, I wondered if I was portraying them fairly. Were they really an uncanny embodiment of the music industry's ickiest impulses? Desperately flailing careerism, manically incoherent networking, shot-pounding brocephus bluster, dangerously jolly self-deception, and musical homogenization of the most proficiently alienating sort. After all, they were pretty enjoyable company, and every band looks a bit craven while pushing their product at the annual South by Southwest music-industry chattel call.

Then drummer Scott Sellers called me for a follow-up interview while he was playing a round of golf. It was like so much about Uncrowned—an awkward reenactment of how rock stars supposedly act (circa 1998?), with social-networking double-talk substituting for actual record sales and, you know, fans. I just wanted to tell the guy to stop it, especially when he duffed his tee shot into a sand trap and then put the phone down in the rough so he could blast out into the fairway.

But why bother? In the music biz of today, with revenues dropping and consumer interest scattered elsewhere, being able to simulate the rock-star dream of fleeting fame and free drinks is all that's left for a majority of young musicians. Live fast, get out while you're still relatively young, and leave a good-looking brand. Last I checked, Uncrowned

were still "in the middle of writing more songs for the new CD, every-
one be patient, it will be worth the wait." Hope Sellers still hasn't quit
his day job.

■　■　■

I F YOU WERE to imagine the soundtrack for the death of the
record industry, you couldn't do better than an acoustic version of "Iko Iko" played by a graying white man in a Hawaiian
shirt and khaki cargo shorts standing in the bar-lounge of the
Four Seasons Hotel in Austin, Texas, on Friday night of this
year's South by Southwest music festival. Back in the go-go '90s,
this was schmooze central, where every wannabe player clocked
SXSW time.

Now, with sales tanking, labels consolidating, and staffs liq-
uidating, it's a comparative dead zone. Retired couples box-step
by the fireplace while a handful of industry grunts soldier on,
draining the last $13 martini out of their soon-to-dry-up expense
accounts.

"I'd rather drag my penis through ten miles of gravel than be
here," says Stephen Bazzell, lead singer of the unsigned Atlanta
modern-rock band Uncrowned. He slumps down in a plush
chair, scowling from beneath a baseball cap pulled tight over a
red do-rag. Bazzell and his bandmates are killing time while their
manager, Bret Bassi, is on a sofa across the way chatting with a
(seemingly sloshed) publishing exec from Universal Records and
a certain songwriter-for-hire.

"It's some guy who helped develop a band I fucking hate,"
spits Bazzell. He won't elaborate, but later I discover it's the mastermind behind the Oklahoma band Hinder, the most commer-
cially successful new rock act of the past year. Hinder's shtick
as a sleazier Nickelback is pretty crass, but they did record the
most undeniable power ballad of 2006, "Lips of an Angel" (also
a country hit for Jack Ingram), cowritten by the man on the sofa,
Brian Howes. Uncrowned, who are in the midst of recording
songs they hope will lead to a major-label deal, have already
met with a couple of cowriters—most notably Lee Miles, who

worked on one of last year's surprise rock breakthroughs, the debut album by emo-ish Florida pretty boys the Red Jumpsuit Apparatus, and who recently toiled on the latest for neo-grunge lifers Puddle of Mudd.

But as the members of Uncrowned gain more faith in their own abilities, they feel increasingly uneasy about the cowriting gambit, a driving force behind more of today's rock hits than anyone cares to admit. They're trying to forge their own sound, but they also want to succeed, or least make a living as a band, especially since Bazzell and headstrong guitarist Jack Andrad have been writing music together since 2001 and touring the Southeast with different lineups since 2003.

"Dues have been paid for a while," says Axel Lowe, the drive-time DJ at Atlanta alternative-rock station 99X, who has known the band for years. "They're tenacious and likable and talented, and I think they're getting really close. It's just a matter of getting that one hit song."

But is it?

In many ways, Uncrowned exemplify the volatile, vulnerable state of today's music business, a world rife with confusion, delusion, great promise, and great risk. With CDs being eclipsed by downloading (which brings in far less revenue), major record companies are more desperate than ever to score megapopular acts. A band that sells, say, 300,000 albums is negligibly profitable, at best. The large-scale services a major offers—distribution, marketing, promotion—are more suited to pushing Justin Timberlake from two million to five million copies sold. Few new rock bands approach that level, and it'll be obvious when they do: They will be the guys with the sculpted stubble and volumized hair, starring in a glossy video set in a church filled with flickering candelabra, directed by some guy named Nigel Dick. Prepare to grimace just so on the heartrending chorus (that you didn't write).

And what does a "hit" mean anymore? Radio rotates only a handful of songs to an ever-declining audience, and MTV airs just a smattering of videos. Fans are more likely to encounter new artists via TV commercials or soundtracks, video games, file-sharing, Internet radio, MySpace, YouTube, etc. People are listening to much more music, and it's not uncommon for a random track to get passed around or downloaded by millions in a weekend's time. But it's rare for a single song to capture the mass imagination long enough for it to translate into a real career for the artist. So why would a young, loud, aggressive rock band like Uncrowned, or their management, bank on that one demographically transcendent fluke?

"Their problem is, they're functioning in the old system of waiting to be swept off their feet by a label or some giganto marketing push that's going to propel them to stardom," says a record executive who has met with the band and asked not to be named. "The new paradigm calls for you to take care of your own niche first."

The new paradigm. Maximizing outside revenue streams. Monetizing digital content. CDs as loss leaders. More and more you hear these buzz phrases thrown around by the type of people who, back in the '90s, would've been arguing abstractly about whether Kurt Cobain was a hypocrite or a savior. It's finally a DIY world (bereft of political context, of course). Musicians across all

Schmooze moves: Uncrowned turn on the charm at SXSW in 2007. *Misty Keasler*

genres are necessarily, obsessively business-minded; it's not just gimme-the-loot rappers anymore. Since the Internet can reach millions of consumers directly, even standard indie labels soon may be passé—managers and booking agents wield the influence. The money isn't in record sales (down 20 percent this year), but in diversifying your brand beyond hoodie/T-shirt merch—just recently, press releases have hyped Beck's Sketchel shoulder bag, an All-American Rejects–designed Pepsi can, a skate-shoe partnership between Etnies and Chester Bennington's tattoo studio, and an Urban Outfitters indie-rock tour featuring the Ponys, Voxtrot, and Tapes 'N Tapes. Artists who have yet to release a record are pursuing publishing and sponsorship deals. One of the most talked-about indie bands of the past few years—Clap Your Hands Say Yeah—is perhaps more notable for its no-label business model than its music.

But the problem with a DIY approach is that you have to *do it yourself.* And that means a generation of artists who spend countless hours attempting to manage their own affairs and hustle every angle. But what if you're not Pete Wentz or Jay-Z or Arcade Fire? What if you can't trade on a punk or hip-hop or indie tradition? What if your numerous marketing ideas haven't quite panned out? What if you've got a killer MySpace page and consistently draw 300 people in clubs three states away and sell several thousand copies of your self-released record, but can barely pay the rent? What if you were a passing industry fancy a couple years back, but now that you're a far better band, interest has waned? What if you're so anxious to jump-start your career that you let your manager come hat in hand to *the freaking guy from Hinder*?

What if you're Uncrowned?

"HEY MAN, OUR dicks are like divining rods." It's Thursday night at SXSW, and Uncrowned—singer Bazzell, 25; guitarist Andrad, 24; bassist Stuart Clark, 25; and drummer Scott Sellers, 26—are surveying Austin's Sixth Street. The downtown area, closed off by police barricades, is a product tie-in petri dish, where the five-day festival's 11,000 registrants, 1,400 bands, and thousands more hangers-on try to cultivate a cultural buzz. But for Uncrowned, whose Friday show isn't an official SXSW event, it's a plum chance to scam—in a professional capacity, of course.

"If you're in a band and you walk up to a girl, it's an *event*, when normally it might qualify as stalking," says Andrad, laughing. With his perma-shades, carefully mussed thicket of hair, three ornate tattoos (all Dalí paintings), chunky silver jewelry, and confident, louche stride, he's the group's unquestioned leader. A diplomat's son born in New Jersey and raised in Italy, France, England, Spain, and Israel, he speaks five languages fluently. Tonight, his strategy is to take Polaroids with potential fans and write the band's show info on the back. Then the Polaroid can be used as a free ticket.

After the band promise their manager that they won't stop until the camera is empty, we're off. For the next two hours, it's a blur of clingy sundresses, numbingly tight low-rise jeans, blinding tans, pierced belly buttons, strappy heels, French manicures, and sheepish hugs. The guys' charm is easy and unflagging. The campaign peaks with a couple of athletic blondes in microminis and black stiletto boots.

"Equestrian instructors," confides Sellers, the husky, wisecracking drummer with a rooster-ish rocker 'do. "They invited us to go horseback riding out by the river and through the hills. They said they'd make it worth our while."

Do you think they'll come to the show? I ask.

"I can only pray," he answers, folding his hands.

Then, the group is suddenly confronted by one of the festival's most familiar sights—a street teamer hawking free Trojans. A late-20s brunette wearing a tennis shirt and slacks, she hands out samples and enthusiastically asks, "Are you a band?" The guys nod, give a perfunctory run-through of the Polaroid routine, and are quickly back on the move.

I think she really wanted to come to the show, I say to Andrad. Didn't you think she was cute?

"I don't do cute. I do hot," he announces, grinning.

Don't you wanna get any guys to come?

"I was always told that in order to be a rock star, you needed two things: The girls wanna have sex with you, and the guys wanna be you. If we get the girls, the guys will come."

Is that what you really think, or are you just bullshitting?

"That's your job to figure out," he replies, still grinning.

It's a fool's game to judge anyone by what goes on at SXSW. The hypercompetitive, overstuffed atmosphere can turn a meek Takka Takka–streaming blogger into a SoCo-swilling blowhard with an agenda. And away from the festival free-for-all, Uncrowned revert to being earnest, humble, committed musicians who just want their songs to be heard. The band's self-released debut CD, 2005's *Simple Sick Device*, is a skillfully arranged maelstrom of melodic post-grunge with electronic tinges and huge choruses. It's also an obvious triangulation of Smashing Pumpkins, Pearl Jam, and Nine Inch Nails, which Andrad admits ("It's like our little redheaded stepchild"). But a newer track, "Devil in My Hand" (recorded gratis by the owner of a cush Atlanta studio), which melds grinding guitars and falsetto vocals, and has a boyish cri de coeur refrain—"Say it with conviction / Say it like you lived it"—is as affecting as anything currently on modern-rock radio.

What gives Uncrowned a genuine artistic and emotional core is the intense, unlikely friendship between Andrad and Bazzell. The former grew up in relative luxury overseas, worshipping his father the Air Force military attaché (Jack was even recruited by the State Department at one point); the latter was born while his father the con artist was in prison, and spent his teen years in youth homes and with foster families. At age eight, he was singing "My Prerogative" on street corners for spare change, and at ten, he was helping his dad bilk a church mission and later rob the minister's house. Bazzell and his parents spent many nights sleeping in their Ford Fairlane. And at 11, he remembers watching federal agents chase his dad into the woods behind a Wendy's.

"That was a big year for me," he says with a trace of sarcasm. "We got caught in a hotel in Suwanee, Georgia. The feds knocked on the door, and me and my mom hid under the bed. Beforehand, my father had said we should bring the car across the street, and he'd meet us and we'd be out of there. I don't know how he got away, but here he comes, and he runs right by us, says, 'I love you,' and went down a hill, and that's the last I ever saw of him. Then these dudes with suits and .40-calibers stuck one in my face." Bazzell wouldn't see his mom for three years.

He was immediately on his own, but that's when things turned around. "I was finally taken in by this family—it's hard to find a home for an 11-, 12-year-old kid, everybody wants a two-year-old—and that's when the musical world came into focus for me. [Smashing Pumpkins'] *Siamese Dream* came out, and then Korn's first album—all these angry, energetic albums—and I had all this stuff that was pent up in me for so long. Those albums were really my epiphany."

Wanting to be more involved in music, Bazzell joined his school chorus, worked at strengthening his voice, and eventually was offered a scholarship to the University of Georgia—for opera. He lacked a few credits, so he attended a junior college in Gainesville. But the dream of Puccini arias soon ended.

"My grandfather, who was the only person I ever felt was a real father figure to me, was dying of cancer," he continues. "I just felt alone and started binge drinking and let myself go. I would be in there trying to sing 'Ave Maria' drunk. I started a punk band, my first band. I had dyed-orange hair and I'd pass out onstage. It was like this Nick Cave droning creepiness that would go into a drug-induced, Iggy Pop chaos thing. I just embraced that disdain for life, and the music was so passionate. Iggy Pop is a god, man. You find that and it's like, That's rock'n'roll! You wanna wrap your skin around it. But it just became too intense for me. I spiraled out over the edge."

And that's when the partners met. "Irony of ironies, Jack was at our last show. I walked up to him and told him that his band sucked, but he was good. And for some reason, he saw something in me."

Andrad was adrift at the time, as well. He'd been studying music at Miami Dade College North, but dropped out when his father died in 1999, and then moved to Atlanta. A cosmopolitan shredder who loved Judas Priest and Slipknot, he believed he'd found his singer, but the orphan ex-punk wavered.

"It was awkward in the beginning," says Bazzell. "He'd ask me for my vocal ideas, and I'd be out in left field; and I'd ask what his ideas were, and I couldn't comprehend what he was saying—so we made awkward music. But then a friendship grew, a true musical brotherhood. Jack could've ditched me many times, but he believed in what I could do. Basically, he saved my life."

Bassist Clark joined early on, but it took seven drummers and a few years before Sellers auditioned in 2004. And it has taken another two and a half years for the band to fully connect. "We're actually starting to make music from all of our influences," says Bazzell. "I feel like Jack and I are just finding our artistic voice. Before, we were getting to a place where we were gonna make art, but we weren't doing it. Now it's starting to feel like we are."

His words, which usually have a wounded, wary edge, sharpen. "I don't deserve anything for what I've been through—life doesn't work that way. But I do believe this band deserves to be heard. With my original experiences put with this music and these guys and this chemistry . . ." He pauses. "I just feel lucky to be alive. I wanna live 500 years."

IT'S PROBABLY NOT THE best idea to discuss your future over Jell-O shots and scrambled eggs. But that's SXSW. The Texas sun scorches the Iron Cactus patio, and everyone is squinting as Uncrowned and manager Bassi meet with Jason Spiewak, a founding partner of Rock Ridge Music, an "independent" label affiliated with Warner Music Group.

After some industry chatter—digital and mobile marketing, etc.—Spiewak leans forward, almost smirking. "So I'm curious about your little label-shopping expedition," he says, referring to the band's fairly public pursuit of a record deal. "What exactly are you looking for?"

"We're looking for an A&R who can really be a part of our family and grow with us," Andrad says, but Spiewak cuts him off.

"You know there's a chance that guy will be gone by the time your record comes out. Selling promise isn't good enough. It's about what you can bring to the table now."

Andrad's cool demeanor begins to dissolve. "Well, what we bring to the table is that we're a hardworking band with kickass songs and great stories," he says, a bit defensively. "We've done things that other unsigned bands haven't—we've got instrument endorsements from a half-dozen companies, we have a guitar in the Hard Rock Cafe's memorabilia collection, we've had songs on television shows. We've even done house remixes and Spanish remixes of our songs."

"Is that based on a fan base, or are you just hoping?"

"The Latin rock market is huge," Andrad replies.

"Listen," says Spiewak, "labels want to know basic facts: What sales history do you have? In what touring markets do you have a strong following? Do you have a substantial online presence? And we have to get back to the music. Music powers the format, not the other way around."

"All I know," Andrad says firmly, "is that we've put our lives into this band, and we're going to accomplish great things, and we've already accomplished great things, and if somebody wants to be involved with that, fine."

Finally, Bassi, who had gotten up to take a call while most of the ball-breaking transpired, suggests that we ask for the check. Nobody objects.

It's meetings like this that remind you why virtually every band that has any success, no matter how underground, has a cold-eyed manager. Even the savviest musician can buckle under the burden of writing songs, touring, and handling business. For years, Andrad was de facto manager, and if not for his dauntless ingenuity, Uncrowned would've crumbled.

But after playing a number of label showcases and not signing a deal, the band had a bitter split with their drummer at the time, and things took a turn. First, they entered and won the 2004 Shot at the Cabo Wabo battle of the bands, sponsored by the Hard Rock Cafe and Sammy Hagar's Cabo Wabo Tequila. The grand prize was an invitation to play Hagar's Mexican Meltdown birthday bash in Cabo San Lucas.

"I thought the battle of the bands was a bad idea, but they didn't ask for my opinion on that one," says David Prasse, an Atlanta attorney who works with Mastodon and the Whigs, and has supported the band pro bono since before it was even named Uncrowned (after a Charles Bukowski poem about an unsung boxer who defeats champions in nontitle fights). "It's too much like sports. I know, in a sense, music is competitive, but battle of the bands? It's art. It's not arm wrestling."

Still, the rock-star treatment was seductive: Hagar's driver chauffeured them from the airport to the lavish, all-expenses-paid Hotel Hacienda Beach Resort, where the staff greeted them with margaritas—"From Sammy!" As Andrad wrote in a blog post, they were "like four kids at Christmas." After the show, they were lured into a beer-chugging contest by the dark prince of multiplatinum rock cheesery, Nickelback's Chad Kroeger. To make a gross story short, Kroeger and Andrad faced off and slammed between 11 and 13 Coronas each, before nature said no. A queasy Andrad was led over to a trash can by Kroeger, who stuck two fingers down the guitarist's throat. Without blinking, Kroeger walked over to a sink, washed off his arm, and barked, "Bartender, two more." Next night was a party for TV's *Blind Date*, where the guys so captivated the producers that they were later flown out to Los Angeles to tape an episode. Three of the four band members participated (Bazzell had a girlfriend at the time), and at the end of the show, the band performed a set in a Hollywood club.

During this time, Bassi, who had heard Uncrowned's song "You Deny" on the online radio station GarageBand.com, e-mailed the group. A drummer for more than a decade who also has an MBA, Bassi, 29, had just started working with the Chicago firm KMA Management, which reps a number of young rock bands but is best known for breaking nü-metal ragers Disturbed. Laconically cool but persistent, he admired Uncrowned's skepticism. "They drilled me with question after question," he says. "They wanted a layout of what it would be like working together. They asked me about my time commitment, since I was working with other bands."

Bassi's first goal was to have the band refocus musically, suggesting that Bazzell take voice lessons and Sellers drum lessons. He wanted Andrad to concentrate more on songwriting. "We used to jump around onstage like monkeys on acid," says Sellers, "but Bret said cut that shit out and strip it down."

In a way, their SXSW show was the culmination of a two-year rehab. And when I speak with Jason Spiewak a week later, he relents: "I wish I'd seen them before we talked, because the live show is kickass. They have the one thing that you can't rehearse, and that's believability. I believe that they're up there and it's real."

But the fact remains that Uncrowned want to be stars in a way that is increasingly endangered. It practically takes a priestly blessing for a youngish rock band to cross over to a mainstream audience—i.e., be recognized by people who don't follow music—and remain artistically credible. Rather, the objective is to cut operating costs, serve your core audience, and forgo the foie gras.

Bassi demurs. "Our company approaches bands that we believe have the ability to be, and want to be, wildly popular on a nationwide scale," he says. "And that usually leads us down the path of a major label, because they have the marketing money and distribution channels. It's riskier than a DIY approach, where you sell your music online and keep everything in-house, but the rewards are potentially greater. In developing a band like Uncrowned, we try to do everything now that an indie label would be doing, so we can show a major they're taking the reins of a horse that's already moving."

He's backed up by an unlikely source. "I'd rather be on no label or a major label," says Nick Stern, manager of Clap Your Hands Say Yeah. "Indies usually can't sell a ton of records—and you only get a percentage of those sales, anyway. They can't pay you an advance and they can't give you tour support, so how are you going to make any money? How are you able to quit your day job, which is the goal for all these kids? At least a major label can cut you a check up front."

But Uncrowned have grander dreams. They want to put on the eyeliner and watch the lights come up on 30,000 people and eat Kobe filet and be respected artists. And after talking to Bassi a couple of weeks after SXSW, I find out what that kind of ambition ultimately means.

"This is a tough one," Bassi says slowly, "because David Prasse has been with the band from the inception. But we're transitioning into working with Jeffrey Light, the attorney for Christina Aguilera and Red Hot Chili Peppers. It's one of those things. The band is all about building a family, and David was, or is, a part of that family. But with the kind of contacts Jeffrey Light has, he can go straight to the top."

It's rare when you're working on a story that you get a legitimate chill, but I did when I got off the phone with Bassi. Prasse, who cut his teeth booking shows in Athens during the early-'80s underground-rock renaissance, is one of the smartest, most genuine, plugged-in people I've ever met in the industry. And there had been several times I'd wondered why he still had anything to do with Uncrowned.

"One thing that's different about those guys from the indie school," Prasse says carefully, "is that they're not precious about what they're doing. They wanna reach a lot of people. With some musicians, what they're doing is from the heart, and they don't care if anybody pays attention. Whether R.E.M. was like that or not, they convinced us they were, and it endeared us to them." He hesitates for a second. "With Uncrowned, I just don't know."

CHARLES AARON is the music editor of SPIN, and to quote esteemed white rapper El-Producto, is "stealth like a robot hidden in the fat asshole of Cartman." A native of North Carolina, Aaron lives in Brooklyn with wife Tristin, son Oscar, and bulldog Precious.

RUN-D.M.C.

Crown Royal

Arista

MARCH 2001

by **SASHA FRERE-JONES**

Sayeth the Elders of Arista/Bertelsmann unto the bards Run and D.M.C., "If ye elders of hippe-hoppe seek to feed our Modeste Village, Inc., ye must cast thine net very wide, so the wee and aged both may find your bate enticing." Sayeth Reverend Run, "Have thee read mine scripture *'It's Like That'*?" Sayeth the Promo Department: "Your Book is destined for the Table of Remainders. Get some *TRL* names on this bitch."

So, Run did venture into the Woodes and returned with Deal Papyri promising Pointes on Nette Sales to Fred Durst, Kid Rock, Ja Rule, Method Man, Everlast, Jagged Edge, Sugar Ray, Nas, Mobb Deep, and Stephan Jenkins. Run then Paused to reflect and said, "Sire, there is now no room for my ally of Rocke, the one called Darryl!" But the prince of A&R entered the Tunnel of Hollande and his Celle did lose Signalle.

And verily Run did enter the studio with a score of rappe-rocke yeomen. Some three years after (!) was produced a volume of songs, but the neighboring king of Wal-Mart did not therein detect a Single and so did send Run back for more Hookes. The young Jermaine Dupri of Atlanta was asked to create a Bounce Tracke, upon which he did allege that Run-D.M.C. "resurrected Aerosmith," a band for whose career path our heroes would trade their gold Adidas. Not yet despairing of Whyte People, the Everlasting performer was enlisted to cover a Steve Miller song, and the Master of Three Blind Eyes donated a Kravitz-like Thrashe tune called "Rock Show." Throughout the Album, the bard Run was heard to plead his case most Pathetically, even celebrating the treasure chests of his Brother, Sir Russell, who seems beside the Pointe.

A bugle blow came from across the ocean, and it was made known that the Doge of Bertelsmann had put Thee Album on a Release Schedule. And *Crown Royal* did become Producte, but loyal believers expecting the old boombap-type shite did draw long faces upon hearing the Grabbe Bagge of Popular Styles. Young citizens who had not before heard thee Artistes did giggle mirthfully because the flow of the barker sounded quite Odde. The principals of the Olde Schoole were issued an edict requesting that they stop rocking and thereafter retire.

SASHA FRERE-JONES is a musician and writer from Brooklyn. He plays in Ui and Calvinist, and is a staff writer for *The New Yorker*.

SIDE 4

THE RIGHT
PROFILE

Let Us Now
PRAISE
Women
UNCAGED

Extolling the virtues of Joanna Newsom and Karen O

by DAVE EGGERS

JUNE 2004

Benefiting from the generosity of Sia Michel, the editor in chief at the time, for a while I wrote a column for SPIN *called "And Now, a Less Informed Opinion." My hope for it, going in, was to write about music in a personal way, and to be careful never to imply that I had any expertise about music whatsoever. I'm a very uneducated listener to a wide range of music, and at the time of the column, there was—just as there is now, too—a seemingly unending parade of new and bewilderingly good music coming out; the column was just a place to talk about it, celebrate it, try to break it down. Looking at this particular column now is strange for a bunch of reasons. One, because this appeared pretty early in the career of Joanna Newsom, who of course is very well known now, though when I wrote this there seemed to be the possibility that an artist as offbeat as she is might not reach a wide audience. Two, I had forgotten that I was listening to Newsom's first album a lot on the way to and from visiting a friend of mine doing a year or so in a Connecticut prison; the music was very melancholy, and I felt that way and worse on those train rides. The good news is that that friend, Piper Kerman, is*

out of prison now and has published a book about the experience. So it
seems that these two people I care about are doing well, and it feels like
a nice bookend to this piece.

■   ■   ■

THAT WAS A CLOSE CALL. I was without it for two days and
I really thought I was in trouble. I was holding back a
powerful longing, cruel and searching, and I worried I'd
do something desperate. I'm writing from a hotel in Danbury,
Connecticut—long story—and for the first time in almost 54
hours I have been able to listen, on my laptop with its horrific
sound quality, to Joanna Newsom's album, whose title I don't
even know. Her music has changed my life and will, I'm sure,
make me a better person. How could I be without that kind of
power for 54 hours? Was I insane?

I have some kind of advance copy of the album, burned onto
one of those beautiful vinyl-looking Verbatim CDs, so I don't
know what label is putting it out, or even when. But I do know
that the music of Joanna Newsom is, day by day, listen by
listen—and we're up to about 81 times by now—making me
braver, making me feel that with it I could ride a horse. Into battle. A big horse into a big battle. This music makes my heart feel
stout, and enables me, with my eyes, to breathe fire.

IN MARCH I SAW Yeah Yeah Yeahs play the Fillmore in San
Francisco. I'd never seen them live, and I was astounded to
find that Karen O has no rock'n'roll maneuvers whatsoever.
She's got no studied poses, and the kind of action she's into
onstage—running around, spinning, bouncing like a very
happy nine-year-old—doesn't fit the trio's comparatively heavy-
tomorrow sound. She's clearly too full of joy to be leading a
band considered so downtown and dangerous. I was watching
the show from a side balcony, so far away that I could only see
enough to wonder aloud to anyone who could hear: "Is that
singer fucking smiling?" My friends squinted but couldn't tell

for sure. "Does that lady," I wondered, now to myself, because you have to project really well to be heard while wondering aloud at a concert, "does that Karen lady dare get up onstage and sing some low-down futuristic music and then smile, all carefree and unburdened by our expectations?" It was completely unprecedented.

Later, when I had the chance to see her up close, I noticed that not only did she smile a lot in general, but that night, she'd been wearing a fake smile drawn on her face. Crudely. With what looked like crayon. (It was lipstick.) She was, therefore, fake-happy and actually-happy, and of course either kind of happy confounds our Yeah Yeah Yeahs expectations. But by giving us nothing that we expected, and much more, she confirmed what we all suspected: that Karen O is the most original and unhinged onstage performer in music. Who could ever challenge her for that title?

THERE ARE ABOUT 40,000 albums released every year. So it would seem almost impossible for any music-making person or group to create anything even vaguely original. But nearly every week there's something brought into the world that sounds unlike anything before it, something that makes you smack yourself in the head and think, Of course! Last year we were given the Polyphonic Spree—about a hundred people who wear robes and sound like a Catholic school choir singing 5th Dimension songs—and every time someone breaks through the fog it seems both impossible and inevitable. If you're stuck in a logjam of tired ideas, then seeing the gaps—they're blue and wet—isn't that difficult, is it?

In high school I had some friends who were starting a band. I wanted so badly to be a part of it, but I had less talent than would seem mortally possible. Instead, I nudged my way into the role of manager. Producer. Consultant. They didn't know I sought these roles. To them, I was only irritating hanger-on.

I tried to have some influence. But when the band's initial lineup was decided upon and the heroes were established—the

Matters of the harp: Joanna Newsom in London in 2004. *Hayley Madden/Redferns*

Velvet Underground, Joy Division, the Smiths—I was shocked to discover that these people, my friends in whom I had limitless faith, planned to use the standard guitar/bass/drums configuration. It seemed like the most horrible sort of cop-out. Starting from scratch, with all earthly possibilities available, it was just wrong not to reinvent the idea of a band, from the instruments on up. Why a bass? Why a guitar? Why drums? Why not bang on raccoon skulls? Why not have 30 drummers and a singer who stutters? Why not have 30 children singing at once, with eunuchs slapping their own asses for percussion? There were so many things that had never been done! To use the most obvious building blocks was the ultimate act of laziness, my adolescent brain thought, and I told them this. They looked at me, blinking with displeasure, and banished me from all practices, meetings, and casual discussions on the way to laser tag.

Did this stop me? Well, yes. I gave up all music-related aspirations and soon found other hobbies, like inventing new games to play, alone, with a 16-inch softball. And where are they now, these tradition-bound friends of mine? Have you heard of a little band called the Walkmen? I love those guys. But I doubt my friends have heard of them, because most of them are now lawyers.

The point of all that was that we all feel great relief when any band departs from the expected, even the smallest amount.

THE MORNING AFTER the YYYs show, the sun was fighting off blues and grays, and I walked into my living room, squinting and barefoot. My wife was playing something unfamiliar, and after six or seven words I knew I had a new obsession, and that Karen O had competition.

"Who is this?" I asked.

"Joanna Newsom."

"Is she nuts?" I wondered, because the voice sounded nuts. It was unsettling, wobbly, and wavering, and stood nearly alone, with only the sparest accompaniment. "Is that a damned harp?" I asked. The singer was playing a goddamned actual harp. In a song called "Sadie," which would soon become my 92-plays-a-day habit, she sang of mercy and thirst and bones and blessings, her voice fierce but reed thin. The sound was country-tinged, backwoodsy, yet uncommitted to any traditions. But the voice was all: Joanna Newsom makes Daniel Johnston's voice seem perfectly sane, makes Bob Dylan sound as smooth as Teddy Pendergrass.

LET'S TALK ABOUT Bob Dylan for a second, and about music fending off evil. Not many songs can fend off evil. But the right song with the right voice can be a weapon; anyone who's listened to music through headphones while riding the subway or plowing angrily through a rush-hour sidewalk knows how it can and should separate you from them, allows you to say to the teeming masses that you are this and they are that.

Another Side of Bob Dylan did this for me a few years ago, in Los Angeles. I don't remember why I was in a cloudy mood that week, but I was, so in the middle of a bleached afternoon, when it seemed no one in California felt anything like angst, I stepped into Tower Records and bought *Another Side of Bob Dylan*. Walking and driving around, I flooded my head with Bob's fury, and "It Ain't Me Babe" and "My Back Pages" were my armor, my sword, my mount, my chain mail—I'm running thin on my medieval terminology—my sunrise, and a heavy blanket with which I could muffle the chatter of everyone I didn't want to hear.

The power of the music doesn't come from the words necessarily, and it doesn't come from huge sounds or big rock chords. With Dylan, and with Joanna Newsom, it comes from an unbeautiful voice—or a nontraditionally beautiful voice—singing . . . well, it's not really singing, is it? It's yelling. On the scale of ten to one, ten being *American Idol*–type all-craft/no-soul crooning, and one being the plain screaming of a lunatic, Dylan is about a two. Newsom is maybe a two and a half. There's just enough singing to prevent the music from sounding genuinely disturbing. To sing loudly, plaintively, and unhidden, without the benefit of distortion or backup, adds to the courageousness of whatever is being sung. Music like this can make you feel vulnerable, because it's vulnerable itself; it's bare and unflinching, which gives you the strength to be the same. Even if you feel strong when you start an album like Newsom's, you soon succumb, and then you need support, which it then provides. It breaks you, then builds you up again.

IT'S NOW THE NEXT day, and I'm still in Connecticut, on a train to Hartford. I just visited a friend doing time in a women's prison, and I'm in a car facing backward, and I'm watching the landscape, still wrecked by winter, pass the wrong way. The whole state is beige today, rust-colored and gray, and Newsom is making me sad and strong and then sad again and then strong. I have no idea what she looks like, and I'm wishing I never find out. I hope she's not pretty. Aren't we all tired of the most distinctive female voices, like Lisa Germano's or Hope Sandoval's, being attached to beautiful faces, implying that quirkiness is acceptable only if the face emitting the sounds is pleasant to look at, or worse, that only attractive people have the courage to sing? Wouldn't it be nice if a woman could become popular with a face that could melt cheese? If Joanna Newsom knows what's good for her, she should be covered in boils.

I picture her looking like Emily Dickinson. Newsom lives, I imagine, like a feral woman-child. Her dwelling is somewhere rural, and by a lake. But on a hill. On a hill, by a lake. The house is old, crackety, painted red like a schoolhouse. Maybe it is a schoolhouse! A former schoolhouse. And she's a former one-room-school teacher who's gone a little batty. She's painfully thin, and wears cracked glasses. She can't get them fixed, and why? Because she spends all day singing like a crazy person, that's why! The townspeople, after years of worrying about her, have come to terms with the loony former teacher who sings about unicorns, owls, and clipper ships, all alone in her red crackety schoolhouse. With a harp.

THERE HAS BEEN, as far as I can tell, one article written about Joanna Newsom, and I've made sure not to read it. The one thing I've gleaned is that, though they've never met, Joanna is a distant cousin of Gavin Newsom, the mayor of San Francisco. As a Bay Area resident, I will admit that during his candidacy, I was not Gavin's greatest supporter. Gavin, who looks like Gordon Gekko, was clearly a smart guy, and I didn't have any doubt that he could run the city competently. But he had a distinctly pro-big-business aura about him, and most of his supporters were from the wealthiest parts of town. The city braced for uninspired years from a centrist technocrat.

Instead, after only a few months in office, Gavin decided he would make one of the boldest gestures in history toward equal—completely equal—rights for gays and lesbians. No one was asking him to challenge state law regarding gay marriage. In fact, in 2000 California passed a referendum clarifying that marriage could only exist between a man and a woman. But apparently Gavin woke up one day and decided to basically shoot his political future in the foot. The majority of Californians disagree with him on gay marriage, thus ruling out the possibility of Gavin ever winning a Senate seat or a governorship. With his youth (he's 36), good looks, quick brain, and moderate views, he was a fast-rising star in the Democratic party. Now, chances are, the highest office he'll ever hold will be the mayor of the 13th-largest city in the country. His defiance of state law, of Schwarzenegger and Bush, was an act of courage and was committed simply because it was right.

So my question: Is there some genetic strain that runs through the Newsom family that makes them courageous, and even a little crazy? And is there any doubt that the two traits must always coexist? You never find courage without a touch of madness, and to live with madness in any quantity you must be strong as an ox. I wonder what Gavin was listening to when he woke up and decided to move history a bit forward. Does he own his distant cousin's record? I doubt it. So what was the music that broke him down and made him strong again? Whatever it was, we need more of it.

DAVE EGGERS is the founder of McSweeney's and has written six books, including *Zeitoun* and *What Is the What*.

LADY
Sings the
BLUES

Avoiding rehab with
Amy Winehouse

by **STEVE KANDELL**

JULY 2007

Fast as things happen in our culture today, Amy Winehouse's rise seemed particularly whiplash-inducing. We wrung our hands in early April 2007: Were we really going to do a cover story on someone we'd just introduced in our current issue and risk elevating a flavor-of-the-month in the wrong month? It was already clear "Rehab" was no fabulist lark, that she was every bit the libertine she prided herself to be in song, and that seemed like such a godsend at the time: a bona fide rock star. We—the magazine, pop music, the culture in general—needed her.

Looking back on my two weeks of chasing Amy, both at the Coachella music festival and through New York, what strikes me is how what seemed troublesome at the time feels so quaint compared to what followed, missing tooth and ravaged arms and all. Sure, there were whispers about her indulgences (her publicist insisted Amy was no different from any girl her age who liked to have a couple apple martinis—a triumph of either wishful thinking or nuanced euphemism). There were certainly concerns that her rekindled romance with Blake Fielder-Civil, he with the still-wet AMY tattoo behind his ear, was becoming a distraction of career-threatening if not yet life-threatening proportions. Her manager—the guy who replaced the guy who tried to send her to rehab—was clearly operating under a strict laissez-faire directive, damn the consequences. Certainly, the *rickety MTV taping that had execs staring at the floor uneasily would be considered a triumphant comeback if done today. In a culture where fame-chasing is the norm, it's hard to think of another recent artist who's been so content to let her moment pass.*

But what stands out the most is that, as exciting as it was for us to be doing the first extensive feature on Amy Winehouse, three years later, there's barely been another.

■ ■ ■

T'S 2 A.M. AND I'M WAITING for Amy Winehouse in the lobby of the Soho Grand, wearing a slice of tomato on my head. She bet me $100 that I couldn't walk to the bar across the street without it falling off, but just as we were leaving, she made an unannounced detour to her room. That was a half hour ago, and to be honest, I'm starting to feel like an ass.

Finally, the elevator opens and Winehouse steps out—a leaning tower of raven-black hair, supported, barely, by a wisp of a body—and sighs when she sees me. I follow her onto Grand Street, my head tilted high like a runway model. Seeds dripping into my eyes, I am the picture of poise and dignity, mere steps away from earning my bounty. Then she slaps me on the back of the head, sending the tomato slice to the sidewalk.

"Oops." Winehouse smiles impishly and bats her Cleopatra eyes like she knows it's enough to keep her out of trouble.

So far, it has been. But since her brassy retro-soul album *Back to Black* and its unapologetic ode to overindulgence "Rehab" came out of nowhere this spring to go gold and counting, Winehouse has garnered a CV that any rooster-haired, skinny-jeans-clad rocker might covet: problem-drinking, scandalous romances, coke-nostril gotcha shots in U.K. tabloids, wince-inducing weight loss, *Us Weekly* photo ops with Paris and Perez, and a refreshingly unpolished don't-give-a-fuck attitude toward all of the above. Three years ago she was an innocuous, girl-next-doorish, virtually tat-free, full-figured neo-jazz crooner with middling sales and no American distribution—now she's Sid Vicious. Music's most authentic punk is a 23-year-old white Jewish girl from the London suburbs who sings like a lost Supreme.

Winehouse walks into the bar, Toad Hall, hand in hand with her fiancé of two weeks, Blake Fielder-Civil, 23. He's the one with the week-old AMY tattoo behind his right ear and the Amy-as-mermaid on his right forearm that he got just four days ago. In a porkpie hat and Fred Perry polo shirt with the short sleeves rolled up, he knows a thing about impish smiles himself. (Two weeks from now, they will marry in Miami, and they were still married at press time.) Blake and Amy have matching crisscross scars and scratches up and down their left arms, presumably from a misbehaving house cat. The hickey on her neck looks fresh, and she's missing at least one important tooth (reportedly thanks to a drunken spill in London last March). Her sparkling engagement ring barely obscures a tattoo of the letter A, for her last boyfriend, Alex. When

Amy Winehouse is not onstage performing, she is making out with Blake Fielder-Civil, Nancy to her Sid.

The jukebox is broken, so Winehouse commands the bar's iPod—with the exception of Nas and Mos Def and *The Miseducation of Lauryn Hill*, she doesn't want to have much to do with anything post-1960s funk and doo-wop. "I don't listen to a lot of new stuff," she says, thick accent tripped up by the hint of a stutter. "I just like the old stuff. It's all quite dramatic and atmospheric. You'd have an entire story in a song. I never listen to, like, white music—I couldn't sing you a Zeppelin or Floyd song."

Fielder-Civil marches to the pool table in the back and writes his name on the board. One of the guys currently playing is bald, in his 20s, and seemingly hammered. "Hey, you know who you look like?" he asks Fielder-Civil. "You ever see *Can't Hardly Wait*? You look like that guy from *Can't Hardly Wait*."

Tat's entertainment: Amy Winehouse.
Andrew Haagen/Corbis

Fielder-Civil shrugs and takes a seat. He's charming and smooth, eager to talk about Don DeLillo, less so about his pending assault charge back home. And he's helpful enough to suggest that wearing a tomato on one's head might not be the best way to earn someone's respect.

"Ethan Embry! That's his name. Ethan Embry. He was in *Can't Hardly Wait*. Anyone ever tell you that you look like Ethan Embry?"

"No. No one. Anyone ever tell you that you look like Moby?"

Everyone laughs, albeit a bit uncomfortably. The bald guy continues to yammer to his friends about Ethan Embry. Fielder-Civil whispers into my ear cheerily, "Tell the guy who looks like he has leukemia I'm going to slit his throat."

I don't.

Though they've been involved on and off for two and a half years—much of that while dating other people—Winehouse and Fielder-Civil have only been back together for a month, and they are in the grips of some intense puppy love. Most of the songs on *Back to Black* are about their tortured romance and the self-abuse it inspired, but they are visibly enjoying its current, decidedly non-tortured status. To be around them is to stare at the ground uncomfortably while they grope and wipe saliva on each other—or alternatively, as increasingly seems to be the case, to gawk and take pictures. They couldn't give a fuck either way. The name BLAKE on the chalkboard has been amended; it now reads, AMY ♥ BLAKEY BIG BOLLOCKS.

Considering that Winehouse's previous album, 2003's *Frank*, was never released in the U.S. and that she was virtually unknown here before March, she must be taken aback by the alarming speed at which things have taken off, but she doesn't act like it. Three days ago she played her biggest American show to date, at a packed-beyond-capacity Coachella tent just before sundown. And though every rock act in the universe would be appearing at some point during the weekend, her arrival—delayed though it may have been—created the most palpable buzz.

She makes diva music, but Winehouse couldn't have looked less like one as she stepped onstage, wearing a white wife-beater and denim shorts that may well have been made for a nine-year-old. She strutted barefoot, and every time she took a sip of her drink, the crowd whooped appreciatively. Windswept, slept-on, and quite possibly ashed-into beehive notwithstanding, she looked no different from any other kid out getting wasted in the sun.

As celebrity well-wishers go, she seems to have a type: Before she took the stage, she was ambushed by Danny DeVito, who somehow managed to say he was "a huge fan" without anyone giggling. And immediately after her set, as she was rushing into the van that would bring her back to her trailer, there was this encounter:

"Amy, I'm Ron Jeremy. I just want to say I love you. You were great."

"Oh, wow, thank you! This is my fiancé, Blake."

"You're a lucky man, Blake. Amy, if you ever get tired of this guy, you should give me a call!"

Winehouse cocked her head a little and climbed into the van. "Fuck off."

OF AMY WINEHOUSE'S many tattoos, the cleverest is the pocket over her left breast (right below the word BLAKE'S). But the most noticeable might be DADDY'S GIRL on her left arm. Her father, a taxi driver named Mitch, is coming to see her in Toronto next week, and she can't wait. "We're good friends," she says, playing with a bowl of tortellini and escarole soup at an outdoor café in Manhattan's Chelsea neighborhood in early May, hours before her show at the Highline Ballroom. "He doesn't know what he's talking about and neither do I."

Winehouse grew up in Southgate, a suburb north of London (also home to posh rehab facility the Priory), until age nine, when Mitch and her pharmacist mom, Janis, split up. She was sent off to—and summarily kicked out of—a series of schools. She then won a scholarship to the prestigious Sylvia Young Theatre School in London, only to be kicked out of that, as well. "I was just disruptive, I suppose," she says, without elaboration. "I loved school and I loved learning, but things piled up, I guess."

Formal training or not, Winehouse was a quick study when it came to performing. At ten, she was the Sour to her best friend Juliette's Sweet in the Salt-N-Pepa–inspired tween-rap outfit, er, Sweet 'N' Sour. By 15, she was singing in jazz clubs, having been weaned on Dinah Washington, Tony Bennett, and Sarah Vaughan by Mitch and her older brother, Alex. Simon Fuller's 19 Management—the folks who brought us Spice Girls and *American Idol*—snapped her up, and a producer's demo featuring Winehouse on vocals turned into an obsession for Island Records A&R man Darcus Beese. "I snuck into the 19 offices to find out who was handling her, because they were keeping her a secret," he recalls. "I never heard a woman who lyrically put the shit together like she did, and I had to have her, so we did the deal. She's Etta James, she's Aretha Franklin, she's Mahalia Jackson, she's Courtney Love."

Frank was released in the U.K. in October 2003, and though it may sound much more like contemporary R&B than *Back to Black*, the album still had enough brazen chutzpah in songs like "In My Bed" and "Fuck Me Pumps" to sell around 300,000 copies. Nearly two years later, however, there was no sign of a follow-up; Winehouse was partying more and writing less, caught up in the turmoil with Fielder-Civil and starting a new relationship.

"It wasn't because she couldn't write songs," Beese says of this fallow period. "She just didn't have the subject matter to write about. She had to live it before she could write it."

There was a stark physical transformation as well—she gained a dozen or so tats, lost a couple of dress sizes—but Winehouse insists her metamorphosis was strictly a matter of taste. "I stopped listening to jazz and hip-hop, and started listening only to '60s music. That's pretty much it," she says adamantly. Mitch Winehouse has publicly stated that he personally prefers his daughter's previous appearance but trusts her to take care of herself.

The oft-told story has it that 19 didn't think her lifestyle change was quite that simple and wanted to pack her off for alcohol treatment, an invitation she famously declined. She then switched to a more tolerant management team, but it wasn't until Winehouse met 31-year-old London-born, New York–based DJ

7 Things You Should Know About Good Girls

In sink:
Cheap Trick, 1984.

1. They go to heaven, but bad girls go everywhere. (Cheap Trick)

2. There's one in particular who ain't searchin', she knows the score, and it ain't love she's lookin' for. (Kiss)

3. They're taken every time. (Joe)

4. They don't stay for breakfast, won't blow your evening, and have to keep it clean. (John Cougar Mellencamp)

5. They've all disappeared. (Ian Hunter)

6. One went bad 'cause bitches even gaffle boss ballers for cash. (Spice 1)

7. They don't, but he does. (The Knack)

and producer Mark Ronson that she found the throwback sonics perfectly suited to her stark new confessionals.

"She thought I was going to be some older Jewish guy or something," Ronson recalls. "I don't know if she thought I'd be like Rick Rubin or maybe Leonard Cohen. We listened to everything, like Earl and the Cadillacs and the Angels, and just started talking the way music geeks do when they get together." The next day Ronson came up with the foundation of what would become the record's title track, a midtempo weeper about getting wasted because the man she loves won't leave his girlfriend. (Another apparent obstacle to the relationship: "You love blow / And I love puff.")

"I write songs because I'm fucked in the head and need to get something good out of something bad," Winehouse says. "There were things I couldn't say to [Blake], but I never thought, 'This would be a great song. Who's going to hear this?' I thought, 'Fuck, I'm going to die if I don't write down the way I feel. I'm going to fucking do myself in.' It's nothing spectacular."

Ronson couldn't disagree more—he thinks it's her raw honesty that makes her spectacular and that that's why people are responding to the album. "How are you going to tell me Ashanti is more useful than Amy Winehouse?" he says. "Kids have been force-fed this homogenized teeny-bopper R&B, but Amy's stuff is so much more relatable to a 21-year-old going through a breakup or whatever. People forget that those '60s girls, like the Shangri-Las, were really subversive at the time: things like 'My boyfriend left me and I want to kill myself' or 'He hit me and it felt like a kiss.' It was rebellious music then, and that's what Amy's doing now. That's why I think it should sound aggressive."

That aggression is provided largely by New York–based R&B backing band the Dap-Kings, who are on the road with Winehouse now and appear on the six tracks Ronson produced. (Salaam Remi, who helmed *Frank*, handles four songs.) The result is familiar yet shocking—old-timey horns and rhythms backing straight-talk sentiments like "I should just be my own best friend / And not fuck myself in the head with stupid men." Universal Republic signed Winehouse in the U.S., and *Back to Black* debuted at No. 7—the highest opening position for a British female solo act ever . . . until a fellow Brit, blue-eyed soulstress Joss Stone, trumped her one week later. The album has barely dipped since.

Prince is dying to cover her, Lily Allen picks fights with her. Long before Britney Spears got her hands on electric clippers, the jig was up for the last crop of prepackaged pop tarts—look, there's Hilary Duff's latest, well south of *Back to Black* on the *Billboard* charts. We don't want the freshly scrubbed myth right now, we want rough-around-the edges reality, and edges don't get rougher than Amy Winehouse's. She is a demographic perfect storm: The rock crowd loves the attitude and the look. ("A lot of practice, a lot of back-combing and hair spray," Winehouse says of her voluminous 'do.) The hip-hop audience responds to the hosannas from the likes of Ghostface Killah, who raps a verse on "You Know I'm No Good." Boomers are drawn to the familiar musical tropes.

For all this, Winehouse largely has "Rehab" to thank. It has already reached a near–"Hey Ya!" level of ubiquity, yet the song has only recently been officially released as a single, complete with a new verse courtesy of superfan Jay-Z. Six months from now, after your aunt has already picked up a copy of *Back to Black* as an impulse buy while ordering a caramel Frappuccino, half the cool kids who packed into the tent at Coachella to see Winehouse will turn up their noses at the mention of her name and swear they were across the field watching Silversun Pickups at the time. (If you don't feel like waiting that long, the T-shirts at her merch table read I HATE AMY WINEHOUSE.)

And the guy who caused all the inspirational misery and heartache is again in the middle of it all. "We were always close, but we got to the point where it was hurting other people for us to keep seeing each other . . ." Winehouse's voice trails off a little, then perks back up. "It just made sense for us to be together. I'm still singing about it every night on my knees, crying onstage. But when I'm with him, I feel like nothing bad can happen. I can't explain it."

She doesn't need to—the attraction's hard to miss. Primping and preening and making friends with a giant rooster at her SPIN photo shoot, she avoids getting burnt-out during the long session by taking many bathroom breaks, then later checks her nose in a shard of broken mirror. Fielder-Civil, who's worked as a production assistant on music videos and commercials, documents the afternoon with a video camera, and Winehouse's face visibly brightens every time he enters her line of vision—everyone and everything else cease to exist, including the photographer. Between setups, Fielder-Civil lands this exclusive interview:

BLAKE: What's been the highlight of the day so far?
AMY: Five minutes from now.
BLAKE: What happens then?
AMY: I'm going to bring you into the toilet and fucking eat your ass.

Romeo and Juliet it's not, but that doesn't mean it isn't deeply romantic in its own scatological way. Just as her heartbreak feels sloppy and real on every groove of *Back to Black*, so does her happiness now. Listen to the lyrics in "Wake Up Alone"—"His face in my dreams, seizing my guts / He floods me with dread"—and, as she stands against a wall, flashes popping as she gently carves I LOVE BLAKE onto her bare stomach with that shard of mirror, don't be worried for Amy Winehouse. Be happy. She's earned this.

"I SWEAR TO FUCK, I'm not usually this shit." Amy Winehouse and the Dap-Kings are on the *TRL* set in the MTV studios, now decorated to resemble a swanky nightclub. She's flubbed the opening of "Tears Dry on Their Own" twice. This is the taping of the first episode of a new show, *45th at Night*. Flickering lightbulbs on cocktail tables appear to the camera's eye to be classy candlelight, and the studio audience isn't shrieking at Damien Fahey, but rather sitting silently and awkwardly. The beer they're drinking is real, for that extra night-on-the-town touch. In the greenroom, a cabal of label muckety-mucks pick silently at their cheese cubes, watching pop's great white hope regain her composure.

"Where's Blake sitting?" Winehouse's manager grumbles under his breath.

Nearly every song requires at least two takes, which may not entirely be what the network had in mind when it proposed this intimate, spontaneous performance series, but Winehouse is more interested in getting it done right than getting it done quickly. One of her heroes, Mos Def, arrives (late) to freestyle a verse on "Mr. Magic," a *Frank* outtake that is, Winehouse tells the audience, "about weed," and requires four takes. "You guys get to go home if you want," she tells the audience, "but I'll be here till Thursday if I have to." This winds up not being necessary. After two hours, the taping finally wraps, and Winehouse works the industry-heavy receiving line like a gracious pro.

"That was fucking horrible," she recalls a few days later, sitting on the sidewalk outside a housing project on West 16th

Street. It's a flawless day, cloud-free and 78 degrees. She tilts her face to the sun. "When I'm nervous, I stutter, and I had to keep stopping and starting. I wanted to die."

This is in stark contrast to the experience of riding with Winehouse to the stage at Coachella, when she was casually bullshitting in a van with her BFF Kelly Osbourne and Fielder-Civil, admiring a Polaroid he'd just taken of himself with his cock out. ("It's me with my cock out!" he explained.) Less than a minute later, she was accosted by DeVito, and less than a minute after that, playing the biggest show of her career. None of this fazed her in the slightest.

A fat man with a camera approaches. "Hey, Amy, you know what would be so funny?" he says. "If I take a picture of you in front of that beer truck. That would be so funny." He cackles so horrendously that I'm quickly introduced to my own inner Sean Penn, but Winehouse is unfailingly polite, allowing this inter-loper to snap a quick photo of her, but right here's much better rather than next to the truck, thanks so much. This is the byprod-uct of the particular brand of celebrity she has cultivated, will-ingly or not, and it's the reason her audience hoots and cheers every time she takes a chug of her Jack and Coke onstage. Maybe she isn't Etta James, Aretha Franklin, and Mahalia Jackson. Maybe she's Dean Martin.

"It doesn't bother me," she says after the would-be paparazzo waddles away. "I mean, I write about it. I'm not going to turn around and kick the camera out of his hands. But I haven't been getting up and drinking and playing pool all day and sleeping it off, and getting up at one in the morning and going out again. I've been working. If anything, people saying stuff like that to me makes me miss going out and fucking having at it, you know what I mean?"

Winehouse claims the best advice she ever got was "Shut up," but she became a British tabloid editor's dream by con-sistently failing to heed that counsel, detailing her bouts with manic depression, bulimia, and boozing with a candor rarely heard from chart-topping superstars-in-waiting. She's largely complying with it now, though understandably perplexed as to why having a gold record means having to justify herself to strangers bearing tape recorders. Ask Winehouse why she thinks her classic-sounding songs and nakedly unmanaged (or unmanageable) persona are striking such a chord at this particular time, and she doesn't grasp that she should even be part of the conversation. Explain to her that one reason for her new-found mass appeal may be that her messiness feels so human and that audiences are starving for a little humanity in their pop stars, and she says she wouldn't know, she's not a pop star; she's a musician. Inquire as to whether she's proud of helping to introduce Motown and classic soul to a new generation of curious music fans, or what she thinks of the fact that the most productive source of new singing talent is a contest on TV, and she just stares through you, weary. Wonder aloud if she finds it hypocritical or unfair that the media go after her for partying, and those staring eyes glaze over entirely. Her reticence can't be due to shyness—this much we've already gleaned—but maybe to a genuine bewilderment over her rapid ascent that renders her unable to properly contextualize it just yet. Or, even more likely, she genuinely doesn't give a shit.

"I don't care," she finally says with a sigh. "I don't care about any of this, and I don't have much of an opinion of myself. I don't think people care about me, and I'm not in this to be a fucking role model. I made an album I'm very proud of, and that's about it. I don't think I'm such an amazing person who needs to be written about. And if I did, I'd be a fucking right cunt, wouldn't I? Just ask me a silly question, like, What's my favorite flavor of Tootsie Pop?"

Okay, Amy. What's your favorite flavor of Tootsie Pop?

"Cherry," she says, flashing a grin that's perhaps seen one Tootsie Pop too many. "See? It's easy! I'm just a very silly girl."

But she seems more exhausted than silly. "Maybe I'm a bit resentful because all I do is work now. If I'm not working, I'll be up for three weeks at a time, just like the old me; but I guess I'm just bored at the minute." She softens a bit. "I suppose that sounds ungrateful. I'm a lucky girl."

If staying awake for three weeks straight is her idea of stress-relieving R&R, and if making it to a 3 P.M. soundcheck and a 9 P.M. sold-out show feels like drudgery, maybe she could use a supervised time-out. And if being packed off to the Priory or Promises isn't the answer for someone who might be losing the plot, what is? Winehouse's shoulders slump. This again.

"Personally, I've had friends who have really benefited from rehab. I'm gonna go find Blake." She stands up. "We're done here, right?"

It's a rhetorical question.

STEVE KANDELL has been the deputy editor of SPIN since January 2007. He was previously at *Blender* and *Maxim* and also writes for *Details* and *New York*, which is also the name of the city he lives in with his wife and presumably impressed infant son.

The **Rebirth** of
COOL

Introducing the Strokes

by **MARC SPITZ**

JANUARY 2003

*They were edgy and rattled about what was happening to them. The
fantasy came true. Real fame after handing out flyers and playing empty
bars. Their first big tour with the roadies and the techs and the caterer
and the security because it's necessary. I was edgy and rattled because
of what was happening to me. The fantasy came true for people who
do what I do: I was embedded with a real-deal band at the pop and fizz
of their moment after years of writing about Sugar Ray and Third Eye
Blind. We were all of us doing our best to look and keep very, very cool
despite the nerves. Strokes on the bus. Me in the rental car behind the
bus. The D.C. sniper at large as we drove through D.C. Osama bin Laden,
too. The whole world changing. I read this piece now and I can see
how hard I was trying to get it right. It almost suffers from that sense of
"This is important." As if we all knew it wasn't meant to last, and someone had to collect the info.*

■ ■ ■

S IT OKAY to let the girls in?" Smoggy asks.

The Strokes' amiable, ruddy-faced security man, dressed
in crisp English sporting gear, ducks into the dressing
room of Portland, Maine's once-grand State Theatre to see if
singer Julian Casablancas is ready to meet some jailbait.

It's been 15 minutes since the band burned through the opening night of their fall 2002 Wyckyd Sceptre tour. As usual, there was no encore. Just a confident march backstage, a brief analysis, and another strange after-party.

"I don't care," replies Casablancas, shrugging, a bottle of red wine in his hand. "I have a girlfriend." Indeed, he is faithful to New York–based painter Colleen Barry, even if he doesn't much resemble a responsible gent—or a rock star. In fact, you'd probably give him a money game if he wandered into a pool hall dressed the way he is now—yellow polyester shirt, appalling blue-and-white-striped tie, tailored suit pants with the right cuff ripped open, tattered red Chuck Taylor Converse All Stars. Then you'd wonder if he was a hustler when your bank disappeared.

For all the angst and confusion in his lyrics, Casablancas is brimming with confidence tonight. He's a billiards buff, and opponents go down one by one while he strikes Tom Cruise-in–*The Color of Money* poses. "You are about to get fucked in the ass, my friend," he tells me before gracefully sinking another game-ending eight ball. The guy owns his own cue, and one gets the feeling he doesn't lose much. Not these days.

"Nick Cave is not party music!" proclaims guitarist Albert Hammond Jr. as he enters, an inside-out Journey tour jersey clinging to his skinny torso. All kinky hair and sleepy eyes, he immediately frets over the sequence of his home-burned CD mix. "Change it," he begs. Nikolai Fraiture, the largest but least imposing Stroke, ambles in and takes his regular post, an empty corner. As the room fills with Marlboro smoke, rangy guitarist Nick Valensi (taking snapshots) and drummer Fabrizio Moretti (grinning, fresh off a stage dive) wander over.

Smoggy finally opens the door, and a dozen 16-year-old girls surge forward clutching paper for autographs. Their hometown may smell of New England chimney smoke, but these girls have their Lower Manhattan ensembles down—thrift-store tees, leather jackets, tight vintage cords. They're too young to drink or shag or do anything, really, except gawk at the politely indifferent, chain-smoking, pool-shooting, beer-drinking, new princes of rock'n'roll. And they are thrilled.

Reclining in the black T-shirt, stick-tapered trousers, and high-top Adidases that he will wear for the next five nights, Valensi starts to protest SPIN's choice for Band of the Year. "The White Stripes are Band of the Year," he insists, lamenting that he missed Jack and Meg White's free afternoon show in New York City's Union Square today. You sense that he's not just being humble. He really believes the White Stripes deserve the honor.

But he's wrong.

PACKING TWO GUITARS, a bass, drums, five pairs of Converse All Stars, and miles of streetwise New York style, the Strokes are 2002's Band of the Year. Like the White Stripes, they are a great rock group that seems to get better with every show. But during the past 18 months, on the strength of a debut, *Is This It*, which has sold around 750,000 copies in the U.S. (and more than 1.4 million worldwide), it was the Strokes who led the movement to recast the way rock looks, sounds, and sells.

"They're the ones who made that positive change," says comedian David Cross (the Strokes' tour is named in honor of the ultra-stoked gay metal band Cross cocreated with Bob Odenkirk on their HBO sketch comedy program, *Mr. Show with Bob and David*). "They paved the way for bands like the White Stripes. They were just way better than nü metal. It got to a point where those douchebag assholes lacked anything to say, so they just got more piercings and played louder."

Says Casablancas simply: "From the beginning, our goal was to make something that was less popular but that would be appreciated later."

"Our music didn't fit in between Puddle of Mudd and Staind," says Valensi. "Record-company people, radio people, journalists, they all told us, 'The recording quality isn't good enough to have any mass appeal,'" Fraiture remembers.

But their music did get on the radio. And on MTV. And like Nirvana a decade ago, the Strokes sneaked into the mainstream, this time on a wave of Internet buzz and U.K. media frenzy heard across the Atlantic. "Last Nite," a smart, tough, punkish single

In the New York groove: The Strokes in 2001. *Andy Cotterill/Camera Press/Retna*

oozing urban ennui, seemingly willed itself onto modern-rock playlists. Its follow-up, "Hard to Explain," became a cult classic when bootlegger the Freelance Hellraiser mashed it up with the vocal from RCA labelmate Christina Aguilera's "Genie in a Bottle." Heretofore obscure acts like the Hives, the Vines, and Black Rebel Motorcycle Club became headliners, beloved by girls who had recently screamed for 'N Sync and by newly horny boys who realized they weren't gonna get laid at a Papa Roach show.

"We'd been stuck in a musical rut for a while," says Perry Watts-Russell, senior vice president of A&R at Warner Bros., "and this is the new movement—bands that are reminiscent of things that came before, but doing it in a different way. I've signed a band called the Sun, and I would say that was influenced by the fact that the Strokes and Vines have gone on to success."

At once modish and skanked-out, the Strokes unwittingly forged a new aesthetic out of nothing more than the unwashed clothes they picked up off their bedroom floors and threw on before a night at the local bar. "You're talking about jeans and a fucking T-shirt," Cross says. "I live in the East Village. People in the East Village dress like that." But what of the L.L. Bean-ers in Maine who now look like they're hanging out on Avenue B or the kids in England who are blowing a week's wages to look like they've just been foraging on Bedford Avenue in Williamsburg, Brooklyn?

"Our style happens to be one of not giving a shit," says Moretti, wearing the same worn Coca-Cola T-shirt and collarless denim jacket he'll keep on all week. Though Hammond insists that he's been dressing the same "since I was 18," everyone from Courtney Love to Avril Lavigne has adopted his new-wave skinny ties and badges (Love, ever quick to pick up on a zeitgeist shift, quickly wrote the song "But Julian, I'm a Little Older Than You" as a Strokes endorsement). And in the year following September 11, downtown New York City became a (rock) center of the world for an entirely different reason: The Strokes live there.

Hammond wore a Yeah Yeah Yeahs badge during a January *Saturday Night Live* performance, and a major-label bidding war ensued for the Brooklyn trio. Other New York bands like Liars, the Rapture, Interpol, and Strokes tour openers the Realistics started getting taken to lunch. "The guys can't acknowledge it," says Strokes manager Ryan Gentles, 25, a former booker for Lower East Side rock club Mercury Lounge. "But when I see CBGB T-shirts being sold at, like, Wal-Mart in Omaha, I know that's because of us."

In England, where the band's three-song *The Modern Age* EP (a demo released in January 2001) hit the charts, the Strokes could probably kick the Queen in the shins with their dirty Chucks and remain beloved. But Americans seized on the theory that the son of a notorious playboy (Julian's father, Model Management founder John Casablancas, has been divorced from Julian's mother for years) who was educated at Manhattan's private Dwight School and briefly at posh Swiss boarding school Le Rosey, couldn't possibly write a decent rock song.

"I never lived with my dad," Casablancas stresses. "Everything we got, we've worked for." It's clear from his tone of voice that he's uttered this disclaimer an awful lot.

"If you think you can't go to a good school and make good art, then you'd have to forget Mick Jagger, Keith Richards, John Lennon, Pete Townshend, and Joe Strummer," says Cross, who opened the Strokes' New Year's Eve 2001 show at Harlem's Apollo Theater. The fact that Hammond's dad, Albert Hammond Sr., is a singer/songwriter whose credits include the Julio Iglesias and Willie Nelson kitschfest "To All the Girls I've Loved Before" wasn't exactly cred-building. But it hardly warranted the rumors that the bandmembers' parents hired songwriters for *Is This It* and called in favors to get them a deal with RCA.

"It's like the new-kid-in-class thing," says Casablancas. "The girls like him, but you immediately want to hate him. You're like, 'Who is that guy?'"

That "the girls" included celebrity rock-boy predators Drew Barrymore (who dated Moretti earlier this year) and Winona Ryder didn't help. In truth, there was privilege—four of the five Strokes grew up on Manhattan's tony Upper East Side—but stardom was not handed to the band as a graduation present.

Only a few family and friends witnessed the Strokes' first show at the Houston Street hole-in-the-wall the Spiral in September 1999. They rehearsed at a shared space in Hell's Kitchen, then showed up at local clubs like Don Hill's with fistfuls of gig flyers. Fraiture worked in a video store. Hammond worked in a record store. Casablancas tended bar. Even as their crowds tripled in New York, leading to a weekly residency at Mercury Lounge, they were unknown everywhere else.

"They went to Stamford, Connecticut, and played in front of five jocks and an old man," Gentles says. All the griping about the band's pedigree, along with the fact that they've been schoolmates or bandmates for nearly a decade (Casablancas and Fraiture's friendship is pushing 20 years), may account for the Strokes' aloof exterior. That insular quality has fueled more than a few "Strokes haters." But now, when the five virtual brothers exchange inside jokes and near-telepathic glances, hug and kiss one another (and tweak one another's nipples), it seems more necessary defense than secret handshake.

The past year and a half has been characterized by exciting, nerve-wracking firsts—first TV appearance, first huge outdoor show (England's Reading Festival, where they headlined over Weezer and Jane's Addiction to a crowd of 60,000), first taste of seriously surreal fame. "My best friend in L.A. gets calls from people he hardly knows asking for tickets," Hammond says. And as easy as the band's camaraderie is, more often than not, you can sense major group jitters.

"You never lose your nerves, you just disguise them better," says Hammond (who insists that he and his bandmates are "really shy"). "It still feels like we're walking into a bar full of strangers every night."

SOUND CHECK AT Boston's Fleet Center is over, and it's time to get hazed. The Strokes are on a Harvard campus bus, speeding through midday traffic. This being a vehicle filled with rock stars, beers go round, smokes are lit up, and John Lennon's "How Do You Sleep?" is cranked on the stereo. "Is Natalie Portman gonna be there?" Valensi asks. The band's formally attired collegiate escorts huddle together, force smiles, and apologize for Queen Amidala's absence, but the Strokes remain psyched—they're being made honorary members of Harvard's 127-year-old humor magazine, *The Harvard Lampoon*. They'll soon join the esteemed likes of Bill Cosby, Peter "Columbo" Falk, and last year's inductee, Elijah "Frodo" Wood. Bow Street is glutted with students as the bus pulls up in front of *The Lampoon*'s office in "the Castle," a low-lit, Flemish structure furnished by onetime staffer William Randolph Hearst. The Strokes are ceremoniously led into the circular library.

"You're all so dressed up," Moretti exclaims. Firm handshakes and awkward, high-strung introductions from the clean-cut *Lampoon* brainiacs cause the band's security team to actually tense up. The disheveled but courteous Strokes head for the free booze, then to a common corner of the well-appointed study to sit on real thrones (!) and stave off the sensation that they've crashed a party in their honor. Well-lubricated, the band is finally led back out to the street.

Here, in the shadow of high academe, the Strokes will challenge "the Hives" for the dubious title Best Rock Group of the Millennium. The band is to choose its "form of competition," and a previously briefed Moretti grabs a bullhorn and shouts defiantly, "Go-carts!" A crowd of students cheers, and on cue, two go-carts whiz around the corner in front of the bemused, slightly freaked-out rockers. One is driven by a *Lampoon*-er done up in Hives drag—black shirt, white tie, etc. Moretti pulls on an old yellow football helmet and gets behind the wheel; Hammond climbs into the passenger seat. At the bullhorn signal, the two carts tear off, speeding through the Cambridge streets. When Hammond and Moretti finally return to the Castle with "the Hives" trailing, it's clear the fix was in. The Strokes are presented with their trophy—a plastic, baby carnival giraffe, stolen from an unlocked study hall.

"Thank you, my friends," Casablancas says through the bullhorn. "Now, do your homework."

Such are the new distractions, very different from the old distractions. According to Fraiture, the band's new unofficial motto is: Get your shit done, then have fun. Wyckyd Sceptre is their first big-venue tour as headliners, and it's got all the rock-god trappings: a traveling caterer adept at whipping up an array of sushi or a large Italian feast; a security/road-management team; drum and guitar techs; and a semi loaded with sound equipment, instruments, and lighting. Everything's timed to the minute, run very professionally. "Every night now, in my hotel room, I get a piece of paper slipped under my door telling me the whole deal," says Valensi. "It gets much easier when you've got a whole crew taking care of your shit. Making sure your fucking luggage doesn't get lost."

This year, everybody wanted the Strokes. And so they played for everyone and nearly cracked up in the process. "There's only so much time you can be on the road before you lose your mind," says Hammond. "We were pushed everywhere. Different time zones, different languages. Jet lag. Finally, we were like, 'If you don't give us time back in New York, we're not gonna be a band anymore.'" The pressure culminated in Paris, where Casablancas scuffled with a record-company exec after objecting to the band's heavy European promo schedule. Later, he performed with a serious knee injury, singing from a stool.

"It seems like if you don't play the game, you get screwed," he says. "Like, if you don't play ball with radio stations and MTV, no one hears your music. Sometimes I think we should get some MTV director to do a video the way he wants to. I mean, I liked Nirvana growing up, but the way they did stuff, like videos, the way they toured, maybe that was their mistake, you know?" He stares deep into the cherry of his lit cigarette, as if searching for some misplaced clarity or much-needed energy.

Casablancas has been composing songs since he was 14. "I wrote really cheesy stuff," he says of his early rock years. "It's not like I picked up a guitar and was prolific, you know? It takes time. I started with figuring out how to play Nirvana songs on one string."

After years of studying and relentlessly pushing himself, Casablancas is becoming one of his generation's best songwriters. But he can't write on the road. He hasn't packed a notebook or a tape recorder. Nearly every song on *Is This It*, as well as the five new songs the band play on tour, was written in his apartment in New York City. The process is simply too lengthy and complex. "It's weeks of misery till the song is done," he says. "It's getting down to the deep, deep details. Like, what a bass can do with a certain part, and if that's okay, what the rhythm should be and then getting a guitar part to go with it. And, of course, you've gotta have a chorus that's kind of pretty." Frequently, he brings a fully arranged song to the band.

On tour, though, he barely has time to figure out the lyrics. "Some of these new songs we're playing, I'm just making shit up," he confesses. Many of the new songs, like "Meet Me in the Bathroom," address familiar second-album subjects, like how touring and fame are trying his mind. On "You Talk Way Too Much," Casablancas nearly screams, "Gimme some time! I just need a little time!"

"The responsibility has definitely changed," he says. "It's gone from, like, 'You don't have to worry about rent and stuff' to 'Now my job is to worry about the music.'" And everyone else's job is to worry about Julian, a heavy drinker since his teens who admits, "Nothing I do productive, I do sober." "That guy," Gentles says, "he's got a lotta fuckin' pressure on him. A lotta pressure."

Gentles, who could be mistaken for a sixth Stroke with his skinny ties and pegged Levi's, has the unenviable job of fielding every offer and relaying it to the band. "Anytime I pick up the phone, Julian's always ready to talk, but I know if I say anything he's going to dwell on it for 24 hours," says Gentles. "It's like 'Okay, Jules, I really want you to do this, but I don't want you to fucking die if you do this.'"

There are things the Strokes won't do on principle alone. While they altered *Is This It*'s cover (an ironic black-and-white shot of a leather-gloved hand touching a woman's bottom in profile) and replaced "New York City Cops" with "When It Started" on the American version of the album after September 11, they declined a lucrative offer from the Gap. And they said no when MTV invited them to join the Hives and the Vines for the now-infamous "garage-rock battle of the bands" at this year's Video Music Awards. Instead, they invited Mos Def and the Realistics to play a party at Chelsea's Milk Studios.

But then there are the offers you can't refuse. Tomorrow they will travel to Landover, Maryland, to open for the Rolling Stones on two dates of the Stones' Forty Licks tour. Casablancas' newfound willingness to play the game is evidenced when he casually reveals that he doesn't really like "the world's greatest rock'n'roll band."

"I respect them," he says. "I was just never a fan, you know?"

THE ROLLING STONES have granted an audience to their support band at a quarter past the hour, but there are complications. "[I know] it's 7:15," Casablancas moans, "but I gotta shit." Worse, Hammond and Valensi appear to be totally Cheech and Chonged.

Red-eyed, they shift in a corner of the cement bunker beneath the 80,000-seat FedEx Field, home to the Washington Redskins and, tonight, three generations of Stones fans.

"I don't wanna go in there," Valensi says, worried. "Don't spoil this for me," Moretti pleads. Gentles finally rounds up the entire band and ushers them in to meet the Stones. Ten minutes later, they emerge, all wearing sheepish smiles. No matter what the Strokes think of the classic-rock geezers, they've obviously been starstruck by Keith Richards' no-bullshit cool (Mick Jagger was somewhat distant). They even autographed a set list for Ron Wood's daughter, Leah.

The stadium is less than a quarter full when the Strokes walk out. A roadie informs them that it's okay to smoke onstage, provided they deposit their butts in the designated ashtrays. "Even Keith does that," he says cheerfully. All one can see from behind the stage is an expanse of blue and red lights emanating from novelty pens issued at the gate. When Moretti hits the jail-door drumbeats announcing "New York City Cops," the thwack travels so far across the canyonlike field that it echoes. Minus the video screens, backup singers, horn section, and pyrotechnics that the Stones wheel out, the Strokes are dwarfed. Only "Last Nite" is faintly recognized. Then it's over.

"The show sucked," Valensi says, laughing. "Rolling Stones fans don't know who the Strokes are. I felt like we were little kids at a grown-up party. People were looking at us like, 'Aw, look at these little kids, doing their rock'n'roll. Bring on the real.'"

The following night at the smaller Hartford Civic Center goes much better. Preshow, the band hunker down in another locker room, this one littered with porno mags left over from a hockey practice. Casablancas has finally changed his clothes. He wears a maroon school blazer and a tie with a pink shirt. Record-label reps stand around, oblivious to the crew thumbing through glossy *Barely Legals*.

The arena is nearly full when the Strokes go on, and the cheers are the kind you'd expect for a headliner. Girls scream and shake their hips in the stands. Even the bearded acid casualties tap their sandaled toes. Buzzing afterward, the band gather to watch the Stones show in its entirety. Even the Stones are better tonight, and Jagger seems to know the Strokes are watching. He shimmies down the walkway toward them more than a dozen times, hip-shaking, whooping, and sweating.

Moretti, Hammond, and Fraiture beam like schoolkids. Casablancas keeps his head down, unimpressed, again very much in his own head. He cradles a bottle of red wine in one hand and once again stares deeply into his cigarette. For a minute, I think I see him exhale blue smoke, then cup it in his hands, and splash it back toward his cheeks like senses-reviving cold water.

THERE HAVE BEEN six teenage girls sitting outside Philadelphia's Electric Factory since ten in the morning, doing their homework and waiting for the doors to open so they can get as close to the stage as possible for tonight's Strokes concert.

Post-Stones, the Strokes are excited to be back on their own. Hammond and Moretti are fresh from a quick shopping spree on South Street. Danny, the security guy, drops off a pair of size 11 Converse All Star "flames" for Valensi (the box is scrawled with a fan's phone number). Moretti and Fraiture play foosball in the backstage rec room and blast Tom Petty's "You Don't Know How It Feels." Strokes pal Ryan Adams tinkles on a candy-striped piano in the corner.

"Let's get to the point!" bellows Casablancas, like a full-fledged Heartbreaker. "Let's roll another joint. You don't know how it feels—to be meee!"

The space is lined with posters from bands who've played the Factory over the years. Some went on to become significant stars (Radiohead), and some are now mere footnotes (Squirrel Nut Zippers). How it feels to be Casablancas right now is edgy and hopeful. The follow-up to *Is This It* will be recorded next year in New York City with the debut's producer, Gordon Raphael (onetime keyboardist for the Psychedelic Furs). The five songs already written are "Meet Me in the Bathroom," "The Way It Is," "I Can't Win," "You Talk Way Too Much," and "Ze Newie." Although "You Talk Way Too Much" is markedly aggressive and

"Meet Me in the Bathroom" has a bass line funkier than anything on *Is This It*, they're both unmistakably Strokes-ish and fit seamlessly into the live set.

"So many times, when you hit on something, you want to expand on it so quickly," Casablancas says. "And I don't want to be like, 'We had success, let's get weirder' and call it art and be arrogant about it. If anything, I'd like to make it sound a little more modern, because I don't want people to hear the second record and think, 'Oh, it sounds like '60s garage punk.'" He lights another cigarette.

"We might find that no one gives a shit about the second record," says Moretti.

Whether the follow-up is the Strokes' own *The Bends* (Radiohead's artistic breakthrough) or their . . . *But the Little Girls Understand* (the Knack's career-stopping follow-up to 1979's smash *Get the Knack*), one thing's for sure: People will certainly "give a shit." So much so that it will probably be the most anticipated rock album since, well, Nirvana's *In Utero* in 1993.

And no one knows that better than Casablancas, who has a lot of intense smoking, drinking, and worrying ahead of him.

"I'm the one anticipating it the most," he says, laughing.

MARC SPITZ wrote one more cover story on the Strokes after the thrill was gone. He is the author of five books, including *We Got the Neutron Bomb* (with Brendan Mullen), *How Soon Is Never*, and *Bowie: A Biography*.

15

BRUCE'S
Transparent
DOGSHIT

Dissecting
the Boss

by **RICHARD MELTZER**

NOVEMBER 1985

*Deconstructing Springsteen. A lousy gig but someone has got to do it.
Done!*

■ ■ ■

BRUCE, UH, SPRINGSTEEN? The youth-demographic Wayne
Newton/Bette Midler? In *this* mag as opposed, y'know,
to that other one? Is he even an issue anymore? (Don't tell
me he's on the cover—I'll find out soon enough.)

I have never liked the youth-demographic Newton/Midler. I
have nearly always loathed him. I've rarely been able to even
look at the boring little prick without muttering expressions
like "master of ersatz," "the absolute voice of the status quo," or
"the emperor's new jeans and workshirt." Pompous as kneejerk
responses go, maybe, but here's this guy, see, the absolute
nonirony of whose most prevalent guise ("earnestness") has

always struck me, on sheer scale alone, as more than a trifle pompous incarnate. But fuck *me* (right?)—whuddo I know?

Basically, I've just never gotten the point. Well, I have gotten the point of his appeal to consumers of the rampantly consumable. That much is obvious: boogie on *down*, not only without guilt but *with* social conscience—all bases, or let's just say both bases, covered—three hours for the price of one.

It makes total sense, for inst, what my lady friend Irene sees in this shit. She's a show fan, see, Broadway and whatnot, a somewhat late (but eager) arrival to the rock-roll shores. She finally takes to rock and what she takes to is Bruce—and I ain't listening. Eventually she gets her way, sits me down perchance to educate me (lout that I am), plays me some Bruce and, lout that I am, I jump up (she forgot to tie me down), wave my arms (*to the beat* so she knows, at least, I am no crackpot), conduct the room to a round of "O! . . . klahoma! Where the wind comes sweepin' down the plain!" and dang me if she does not *chuckle* (as opposed, y'know, to sending me home) (lout I forever will be) because (a) she is no fool and (b) I have got the sturm und drang of it not far from purt near *correct*. And I know—and she knows that I know—that Bruce is naught but her long-awaited Conrad Birdie, or whatever their names are from *West Side Story*, made flesh. Or at least made ongoing product.

Which is fucksure cool but, um, note the connection. Just note it.

Or, for further inst, take my pal Scott Kempner. Scott's basic rhythm-of-life shtick has always been the Rock 'N' Roll Fan Club Meets Here. Before Bruce was his boss boy, it was Peter Townshend. But ever since that week in '75 when its Face made the covers of *Time, Newsweek*, and all three trades, the Bruce Gestalt has, for Scott, role-played one consistently grand *advertisement* for the Power and Glory of Rock Rock Rock 'N' Roll, as if by the mere fortuity of its scale 'n' bombast (not to mention its benignity) we are assured that—this time around—they cannot and will not dare bust "our music." Somehow, in this picture a seminal (and terminal) wedding of creative lifeblood to marketplace/culture death is overlooked (or ignored). But, heck, that's cool too—there's people, I'm told, who actually regard rock videos as *gifts* (as *primary* objects of experience!). And, hey, couldn't the, y'know, fact of Reagan be regarded as glorious evidence of the persistence of electional demo- . . . what's the word? . . . demogracy?? i.e., *you want a ring implanted in your cultural nose, well someone (by golly) will implant it.*

But, mea culpa, I digress. The *specific* side of the Kempner plug-in to Bruce—sorry, Scott, but use you I must for nefarious purpose—is . . . well, I'm not sure about now, but in '75 I asked him flat-out "Whuh?" and he says, "If the Fonz had a band, it would be Springsteen." Yes! The Fonz!! This, of course, was before we knew, or *could* know, that the incredible lovable li'l

**Bored in the U.S.A.:
Bruce Springsteen.**
SGranitz/WireImage

leather schmuck, the most palatably inaccurate (yet life-affirming) peer group archeTVtype since Maynard G. Krebs, was but an accident on the road to grown-actor oblivion for one Henry Winkler. Can't knock actors as pump-primers for purported *real thingers* in principle, no sir, but when you've got your Ersatz Quotient up there in a *supreme* falsification-of-reality range . . . hey (weepy-eyed stick-in-the-mud humanist that I am), I'm knocking. But not mocking. It is *sad* what folks sometimes fall for. And *remain* fallen for ten fucking years down the chute . . . fuggit.

Or for final inst, 'cause I'm itching to get to what genuinely *pisses me off*—back at the dawn of the '80s I had this punk show on a Pacifica station that the Revolutionary Communist Party was bugging me to play their band Prairie Fire on. Finally I go see 'em and they're, well, they're not Public Image (or the Fall) (or even the Clash). They're just your basic formally reactionary get-down boogie band with largely *im*plicit rad/topical "message" super-added. Structurally sound reiteraters of an already mega-told tale (American Music Revisits American Myth); one more entry in—and I don't *really* mean to insult them—the Springsteen Sweepstakes. Far from being insulted, their spokesperson hears the Bruce reference and . . . like wow. Gee, she tells me, if *only* they could harness that *familiar sound*, Bruce's or its ilk, which People and y'know Workers *already relate to*, and wow, like songs're so liberating and freeing and . . . and god am I one godless stick in the mud.

I hit her with (and she rejects) my whole entire rant re: the need to reject Prevailing Form (the "No Excuse for Bruce After Punk" routine). She winces at but stands up to my drivel re: Bruce as (a) Hubert Humphrey (if even that much) in contempo-softshoe drag; (b) nose-ring yanker of the palace guard; (c) learning-disabled child of the '60s to whom that decade never even *registered*. We're bouncing all this one-dimensional quasi-*political* claptrap and then we start talking lyrics, poetics. Bruce's, that is. We're no longer talking Prairie Fire. We bounce "bourgeois" about. I ask (pray tell) what the *non*bourgeois—shall we even maybe say *revolutionary?*—import might be of such Springsteenisms as *wind blows through my hair (and yours) in my '56 Chevy and my wonderful new sneakers embrace bright lights of etc*. And she says, "Bourgeois romantic or not, such lyrics *give hope* to so many." And so be it.

6 Misguided Attempts to Falsify Rock History

1. Fleetwood Mac, "Gypsy"

   Lyric: "So I'm back, to the Velvet Underground."

   Fact: Stevie Nicks was never a member of the Velvet Underground.

2. Elton John, "Philadelphia Freedom"

   Lyric: "I used to be a Rolling Stone."

   Fact: Elton was never a member of the Rolling Stones.

3. John Cougar Mellencamp, "Small Town"

   Lyric: "Another boring Romantic, that's me."

   Fact: The Coug was never a member of the Romantics.

4. Bruce Springsteen, "Tenth Avenue Freeze-Out"

   Lyric: "When the change was made uptown and the Big Man joined the Band."

   Fact: The Big Man never joined the Band. The only big man in the Band was Garth Hudson.

5. ZZ Top, "Jesus Just Left Chicago"

   Fact: Jesus was never a member of Chicago. Many people make this mistake because Jesus looked just like the trombone player.

6. N.W.A, "Gangsta Gangsta"

   Lyric: Girls say, "We wanna fuck you, Eazy!" Eazy says, "I wanna fuck U2!"

   Fact: Eazy-E didn't really want to fuck U2, except maybe the drummer.

A different stripe: Elton John in Holland in 1976.

And so be it all. I mean, yeah, I certainly can dig how among the teeming zillions various lames and non-lames alike have plugged into Bruce. It seems like the sum of the some-of-the-people you can fool all of the time has gotten a little unwieldy, but at heart I'm a pluralist. Not all mass delusions make me puke. I just cannot see, really I can't, a single sight, sound, or accident *within* the delusion that is anything but monochromatic blah.

Is there anything grimmer and grayer than the Myth of America? I am sick of the Myth of America. Granted, Bruce's America is at least fractionally different from *Rambo*'s—a *good* bad sitcom compared to a *bad* bad one—but since we're talking belief systems and the goddam marketplace, how many billion consumers do you think have bought both? Bruce and *Rambo*. Without missing a beat.

None of which would mean shit to a shithook—and, really, let's not be so *ad* mass *hominem*—if it weren't for what Bruce, or his shill Dave Marsh, did last October to avoid endangering any *possible* cross-constituency of consumers of the left and/ or right. A couple weeks left till the election—remember?—and Reagan starts quoting Bruce. But instead of saddling his sturm und drang, riding out and yelling, "Vote for Walter! Our president wants us dead!" (and winning Walt Delaware and possibly Hawaii in the process), the little cocksucker passes it on to his publicist Barbara Carr, who passes it to her wonderful husband David. I don't remember the exact words, I've looked and I just can't find it, but "rock critic Dave Marsh" did an *outstanding* hem-haw on page one of the respected newssheet I happened to catch. Something to the effect that if the President *would only look at such and such a Springsteen album cut*, he would clearly see that au contraire blah blah bluh. Don't say anything, don't stir anything, don't lose a single customer! *Fuck these people!!*

And fuck me for getting so steamed. I'm an old grouch alright, but after punk, after Reagan—after everything and anything— why does this transparent dogshit remain an *issue*, for crying out loud? Next we'll be asked to write about Garfield the Cat.

RICHARD MELTZER is the Father of Rock Writing As We, Uh, Know It. Period.

FOO FIGHTERS

Foo Fighters

Roswell/Capitol

SEPTEMBER 1995

by **TERRI SUTTON**

Think of *Foo Fighters* as the first post-suicide release by a former member of Nirvana. Ha ha—that's a joke. Try thinking of it another way, though—as the debut album from Mike Watt's opening band, or from Tom Petty's drummer—and you're still reading about it in the lead review because this is the first post-suicide release by a former member of Nirvana. And I'm here with you, spooked and queasy because my editor just joshed, "Make sure you get all the Kurt references," and I was already feeling too much like Geraldo scavenging an old plane wreck for a bloodstained sneaker.

So what do you want to know? Whether it rages or regrets? Who it blames? Hmmm. Let's put it this way: There's a gun on the booklet cover, and when you open the CD, it's aimed straight at you. Which may or may not be intentional, but, hey, I got my hands up anyway. Yessir, guilty as charged: I don't know fuck-all about Dave Grohl except that he drummed like a literate caveman for the most brutally lyrical band ever coughed out by alternative rock. Maybe after listening to this band featuring Mr. Grohl on all the instruments (he's since been joined by ex-Germs/Nirvana guitarist Pat Smear, and ex-Sunny Day Real Estate bassist Nate Mendel and drummer William Goldsmith), I'll have a wider appreciation of his interests and concerns. . . .

Many spins later, I still know fuck-all about Dave Grohl. But I think I really like him—precisely because he refuses to be read. He's taken this great, ghastly burden, this what's-he-got-to-say-about-Kurt-or-Courtney-and-how's-he-dealing-with-the-loss tabloid moment, and made it as difficult to see through as the proverbial final curtain.

To begin with the obvious, I'm assuming that Grohl's thin holler has been deliberately drowned in the guitars' wicked heave—especially since the submersion is not only a matter of volume but of clarity. Even when the riff tides ease up, his words are somehow smeared and flattened, as indistinct as the reflection off a greasy lake. This voice will never turn the world on with its wiles—bland and average, it says Everyman truer than the symbolically typical warblings of Jeff Tweedy and Stephen Malkmus. Still, when Grohl wants to be heard, he comes through like Jesus versus the moneychangers. As in: "I / Don't / Owe / You / Anything." Or "Get out / Get out / Get out." What words I can figure—with a lyric sheet, mind you—may as well be fists protecting a vulnerable face.

The album's first half, rife with quietly pretty verses and tank-like refrains, owes much to *Nevermind*, and it's tempting to hear it in the way *Nevermind* taught us to hear, i.e., violent noise equals violent emotion, confrontation, and rage. Except that between then and now, such bands as Candlebox and Collective Soul have used that sound to take note of a broken fingernail. I get the impression Grohl hides behind his rapacious hooks like he disappears between his words—this by now commonplace style is yet another impenetrable veil. *Foo Fighters* seesaws efficiently, even rambunctiously, but there's a distance, a sheen to it, that reminds me of Queen's tongue-in-cheek responses to p-rock on *News of the World*.

Which is why I'm increasingly partial to *Foo Fighters*' more whimsical later tracks. Not necessarily less noisy or opaque, these songs still manage to allow a little air into the room—an opening for the expression of something beyond defensiveness. Something close to weirdness, a sardonic, self-conscious anger, even (dare I say?) grief. "For All the Cows" swings snarky and insouciant as Grohl snorts, "I'm called a cow / I'm not about / To blow it now / For all the cows" between choruses like blisters. I first thought he was talking about drummers (sorry), but now I'm guessing it's cash cows, given the hellacious, invigorating anti-biz rant "Watershed" two tracks later. Then there's "Weenie Beenie," the splintering Big Black parody with its double-edged final chant: "One-shot nothing" (ouch).

That these three tracks are interspersed with three uneasy, carefully coded laments (requiems?) provokes a certain tension, one that might be phrased as a question: How can I keep my secrets from being mass-produced, marketed, and profited from until all the truth has been leached out of them—until they are bloodless, disgusting lies? Or, as Grohl sneers in "Watershed": Hey man, can't you tell it's still a problem?

For now, Grohl ducks and weaves, hoping that if he can't be caught, he won't be bought. So it's no surprise that the most direct tribute to an old bandmate here is an absence: On an album framed with guitars, there is but one guitar solo, which finally gets swallowed into a big aching hole of empty on the very last track. And just writing that, I feel like a snitch. Call me Geraldo.

TERRI SUTTON lives in Minneapolis.

VOICES CARRY

16

Don't
Look Back in
ANGER

Chatting with Oasis'
Noel Gallagher

by DOUG BROD

OCTOBER 2005

This is an expanded version of an interview that was conducted for a special 20th anniversary issue of SPIN. It was my first experience speaking with Noel Gallagher, whose band Oasis—fronted by his brother Liam—I'd adored since hearing their debut album in 1994. His reputation as one of the last of the eminently quotable rock stars proved to be well earned. I found him to be charming, arrogant, self-effacing, and very, very funny. And, as it turned out, not exactly prescient. Despite his protestations below, he split from the band in August 2009, admitting in a statement, "I simply could not go on working with Liam a day longer."

■ ■ ■

SPIN: Starting out, did you think the band would last this long?
NOEL GALLAGHER: To be honest, when we signed our six-album record deal, I was quite confident we had six albums' worth of material in us. It's weird: You hope you're in it for the long run, but you just have to think, "Oh, something's bound to go wrong."

Was there a point when you said, "Oh no, this is going under right now. I hope it recovers."?

I suppose when Bonehead [Paul Arthurs, former guitarist] and Guigsy [Paul McGuigan, former bassist] left in the same week while we were mixing *Standing on the Shoulder of Giants*. The first single hadn't even been released and I was like, "Well, fuckin' hell. Yesterday, there was a band, and today there's me and Liam." If we were in the middle of some time off, it might have been, "Well, what do we do?" But we were already committed to a load of gigs that were sold out, so we had to get it together to go and do it. Had we been at the end of a tour and people left, maybe we would have considered it differently. When Andy [Bell, bassist] and Gem [Archer, guitarist] joined and we went out on the road, the plan was just to complete the tour and then see what we all felt about it, but immediately it was like, "Fuckin' hell, man! This is gonna work."

The 13 or so years Oasis have been together, you've gone through the full life cycle of a rock band: You've had the quick success, an even bigger second album, drugs, rivalries, critical drubbing, lineup changes. It feels as if you should be a much older band.

Yeah, there's been that much history in the short space of time already. I like it like that. It kind of weirds me out when people put us in the same bracket as U2 and R.E.M. and the Rolling Stones. Bono and Michael Stipe are, like, ten years older than we are, and yet we've managed to catch up to them in 13 years. This particular year, putting out [*Don't Believe the Truth*], apart from one or two prejudiced reviews in England, universally people have said we're still making good records. To me, that validates what we do, and it means that we still got it.

Do you have any regrets about some of your records? I mean, you've said things like, "*Be Here Now* was done when I was all coked up, and that's why it sounds like shit."

Well . . . there are two things I regret in my life, and one is not taking more time out after [1995's *(What's the Story)*] *Morning*

Glory. After selling all those records, we should have gone away for a couple of years and got all those drugs and that [stuff] out of our system before we reconvened to make a record. Whereas, in fact, we went for one tour too many in the States, and we kind of imploded. We came back, and instead of going our separate ways and having a year out, we went straight into the studio [and recorded 1997's *Be Here Now*] to end the speculation of whether the band was gonna stay together. The other thing I regret is switching to Marlboro Lights from Benson & Hedges.

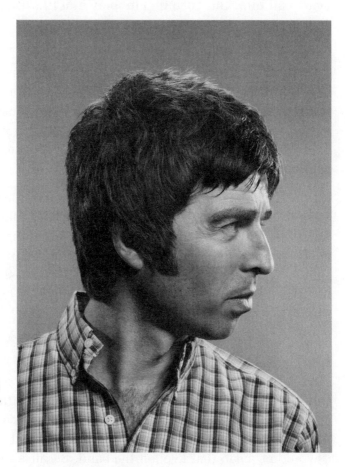

His big mouth: Noel Gallagher in 2008. *Alan Clarke*

Why is that?

You know, the lungs can't handle the full power anymore. I'm afraid I've gone a bit like a woman. Other than that, I think, I'm glad it's all part of the story.

How has your relationship with Liam changed over the years? Has the bond become stronger?

Not really. The way it's changed is I've kind of learned that instead of arguing stuff out with him and ending up in a fight, I work on his psychology. And he's completely freaked out by me now. He's actually frightened to death of me.

So what you're saying is, you can read him?

I can read him, and I can fuckin' play him like a slightly disused arcade game.

Give me an example.

I can make him make decisions that he thinks are his, but really they're mine. Without fightin'. It's an art I've learned. Our relationship's the same, but we're getting older. Instead of it all ending up in insults and fist fightin', it's now more veiled psychological warfare through the press, which I excel at, thank you very much.

I'd guess you feel that people do not necessarily have to like each other to be in a band together. You see the Pixies, Dinosaur Jr., and Smashing Pumpkins either reuniting or planning to, and obviously there's a lot of tension between some of the principals.

I think that the most tension comes from the cash runnin' out. It's like, "Fuckin' hell, I've got no more money left. Maybe we should get the band back together."

So you don't see that happening with you guys for a while, do you?

Well, we would never split up—for the simple reason that we would have to come back. We may take a hiatus, but there's no point in saying, "Today we've called a press conference to announce that Oasis have split up." If I wanted to go off and do other stuff, it wouldn't mean that I've left the band. Because then you'd just have to call another press conference to announce that you're going on a fucking comeback tour.

5 Pieces of Terrible Advice from AC/DC

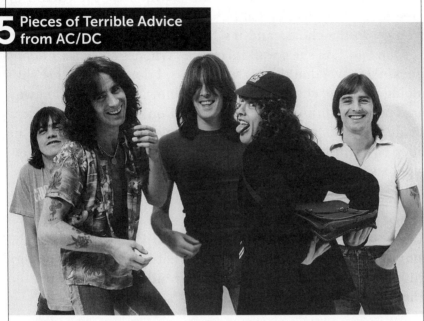

AC/DC in 1979.

1. If your high school principal is sexually harassing you, hire someone to assassinate him. ("Dirty Deeds Done Dirt Cheap")

2. If you are convicted of murder and receive a relatively light sentence—say, 16 years—you should immediately try to escape. ("Jailbreak")

3. When drinking alcohol, never consider the consequences. ("Have a Drink on Me")

4. When receiving oral sex, it is totally acceptable to compare your sexual partner to a domesticated animal. ("Given the Dog a Bone")

5. When discussing romantic courtship, always change the subject back to poker. ("The Jack")

I just saw the band at Madison Square Garden. It must make you feel good that the biggest audience reception now comes during "Don't Look Back in Anger," which you—and not Liam—sing.

Yeah. It's kind of taken over for "Wonderwall" as the anthem. It's like a hymn. To be quite honest, I sing that song every night, and there's that groundswell when it leads to the first chorus. But

I think: What the fuck are all these words about? "Stand up beside the fireplace." What the *fuck* is all that about? And then you get to the chorus and it's "So Sally can wait / She knows it's too late / As she's walkin' on by." Where's she goin'? *I don't fuckin' know.* I don't know who she is. I don't know what she's doing or where she's going, but you know, her soul's slid away, and now she turns around and says, "Don't look back in anger." *What?* [*Laughs*] And "Champagne Supernova." I still have no idea how one can slowly walk down the hall faster than a cannonball.

Maybe someone should do a study of the physics of Oasis songs.
Can you slowly be faster than a cannonball? Surely, it's fuckin' physically impossible. But that's what I struggle with every night. "Slip inside the eye of my mind." How does one do that? Hmm . . .

What are you proudest of contributing to the musical canon?
As a whole, *Definitely Maybe.* If there's one song: "Live Forever," because it's so universal. It's so about being young, and it came out of being the complete opposite of an artist I admire very much, Kurt Cobain; you know, "I hate myself. I wanna die." It came directly out of the mindset of "*Fuck* that, man! The world is a great place. It's just the people in it who are assholes. We wanna live forever."

What has been your biggest thrill over the years?
Meeting virtually everybody that I had posters of on my bedroom wall and actually knowing them on first-name terms, and them knowing me without me having to introduce myself. John Lydon, Morrissey, Pete Townshend, Neil Young, Ringo Starr, Paul McCartney, George Harrison, Mick Jagger, Bono. It's like, "These people actually know who I am." Get your head around that.

Have you become friends with any of them?
Yeah, Paul Weller is one of my best friends. Johnny Marr is one of my best friends. The rest are all kind of reclusive. In any case, who'd wanna be Mick Jagger's best friend?

In the mid-'90s, you had a vicious rivalry with Damon Albarn and Blur. If you ran into Albarn today, what would you say to him?

I don't know. I've got a lot of respect for him—as a musician. It's very difficult for me to explain this to people, because it all boils down to him moving his single [Blur's "Country House"] to coincide with ours ["Roll With It"]. I've come to realize that it was a clever move, 'cause ten years on we still talk about it. So he still has his name—and Blur's name—connected with ours. But what would I say to him? I don't know. It depends what he was wearing. If he was wearing something ridiculous, I'd tell him to sort his fuckin' wardrobe out. If he looked cool, I'd say, "Hey, fuckin' hell, man, you're looking well." But if he wasn't, I'd say, "You're looking like a fat idiot, why don't you go get on the treadmill?"

Now, I know you're not a big fan of hip-hop—

Is anybody?

Well, some of our readers are.

Oh, really?

But have you heard *The Grey Album* by Danger Mouse?

Yeah, it's shit. I was embarrassed for him.

You didn't think it worked?

No, it was just a pretty atrocious attempt to try and make the Beatles hip-hop. I bet Paul McCartney loved it. And if he could find any way of convincing Yoko Ono, it'd be in the fucking record shops now. Hip-hop is shit at the best of times—don't involve John Lennon in it. What's next? A hip-hop version of *Highway 61 Revisited*? I'll personally slap that cunt if he does that.

What do you think is the most spot-on thing someone's either said or written about you and the band?

Graham Coxon from Blur was interviewed in a guitar magazine and he'd seen me playing the guitar on a TV show the night before, and he said, "It looked like he just didn't give a fuck." I was reading it going, "That's kind of not an insult." Also, the usual "Oasis are a bunch of wankers." That's probably quite spot-on.

What's been the greatest cultural development of the last 20 years?

I would have to say the Internet, even though I don't really have a computer, I don't download, I don't have an iPod. But the way that people can communicate with each other—fans of bands all around the world—is pretty spectacular. It also means that there'll never be anything approaching the Holocaust again 'cause word gets out pretty quickly.

What do you think has been the worst?

I'm not saying this just for effect, but I think that the rise of so-called hip-hop culture is a bad thing. When I was a kid, hip-hop culture stood for something: It was socially pure and socially aware. It was really noble. This—what's masquerading itself as hip-hop-slash-R&B—is just fuckin' horrible. These guys will go on the telly going, "Hey, kids—stay in school, don't do drugs," and then they'll be shooting each other down at the shopping mall. It fuckin' bends my head. The disregard for women, stuff like that, I find quite sickening. And the clothes they wear, and it's all about "me, me, me" and "I wanna fuck you up." It's like, "Give it a rest, you bunch of idiots."

Who's your favorite artist of the past 20 years?

I would have to say U2. I'm not saying they've made the best records. They've made *some* of the best records, though. I think *Achtung Baby* and *All That You Can't Leave Behind* are two great pieces of work. When I first heard "Beautiful Day," I was like, "Fuckin' hell, you bastards, how do you write something like that after all those years?"

Have you ever thought about what you'd want on your tombstone?

It would probably be something very, very simple like HERE LIES A GENIUS. KEEP THE FUCKIN' NOISE DOWN.

DOUG BROD has been the editor in chief of SPIN since 2006. A former editor at *Entertainment Weekly,* he has also written for *The Village Voice* and *The Hollywood Reporter,* among other publications, and is quoted in the book *The 776 Nastiest Things Ever Said.* He lives in Brooklyn with his wife, daughter, and French bulldogs, Serge Gainesburger and Jane Barkin.

17

Street
HASSLE

Surviving Lou Reed

by **DAVID MARCHESE**

NOVEMBER 2008

If you're like me—and the fact you're reading this book suggests that at least on some level you are—then you're likely aware of Lou Reed's reputation as rock'n'roll's premier ornery interview. For more than 40 years, the guy has made a habit of leaving hapless journos squirming on the end of pointed barbs. Though it makes for some absolutely killer reading/rubbernecking, the Lou Reed interview experience is, I can assure you, decidedly less fun in person.

In fact, when asked if I was interested in interviewing Reed, the only reason I didn't beg off was that I felt I was too new on staff to say no. But looking back, despite the sheer discomfort of the experience—and being unable to endure Reed's music for a solid six months after—I'm glad I did it. I've gotten more responses to this story than from any other I'd done for the magazine—including correspondence from other writers who shared with me their own Reed horror stories. I'd been initiated into the Survivors of Lou Club. Our motto: We did it for you.

■ ■ ■

LOU REED DOES NOT ABIDE. Nor should he. Not when the lifelong New Yorker exploded rock's borders with the Velvet Underground and invited cross-dressers and speed freaks onto the charts with "Walk on the Wild Side." Sure, Reed's restless muse often leads to the likes of 1973's sepulchral concept album about suicidal lovers, *Berlin*, and 1975's feedback opus *Metal Machine Music*, but he doesn't care what you think anyway. "Do I feel vindicated?" he snaps over artichoke salad at a chic West Village café, as he discusses those albums' recent critical reevaluation. "For what? I always liked *Berlin*." Reed's 2006 live performances of that album are out now on DVD and CD.

Testy moments aside, Reed has aged well, being feted at this year's South by Southwest and, last April, finally marrying performance artist Laurie Anderson. Despite his iconic status, he, like mentor Andy Warhol, was never one for nostalgia and, as always, brooks no bullshit. The implication, as with so much of his work, is this: Take nothing for granted.

SPIN: You're so closely associated with New York. But you haven't written explicitly about the city since—
LOU REED: I wrote a song for Cartier that you can download from my website. Have you heard that?

Yeah. "Power of the Heart."
I did two songs for [2007's] *Nanking* documentary: "Gravity" and "Safety Zone." Have you heard those?

Not "Safety Zone."
Research, research, research. It means everything. [*Sighs*] You were saying? [*Beckons his manager*] How could this guy have heard "Gravity" but not "Safety Zone?" [*Manager responds, "I don't know. It's on the website. It's also on iTunes."*]

I didn't find it on your website.
[*To manager*] How come it's not on the site? [*Manager responds, "I'm sure they're on there somewhere. Some songs play without prompting. But there's a tab that says A GIFT FROM LOU, and that lets you listen."*]

Well, I couldn't find them.
Do you find the website hard to navigate?

I do. The menu keeps bouncing around.
That's exactly what I've been saying! It has to change. [*To manager*] This is a young guy! We should make it easy. I'm complaining about my own website. Plus, the font is too small. Call our website guy

now. Seriously. I want the truth—that's why I asked. The thing's impossible to navigate. [*To interviewer*] Have you seen *Super Monkey Ball*?

No.
It's for an iPhone. There are people who told me that they think the iPhone is an elitist thing. But they have cellphones. Anyway, you were saying?

Stark, raven, mad: Lou Reed in 2008. *Portrait by Mark Mahaney*

Has the fact that the city has been cleaned up made it a less interesting subject for you?

I would hope to write about more than just the city. Raymond Chandler managed to write about L.A. his whole career. Should I keep going writing about New York? Is that what I should be doing? Songwriting doesn't work that way.

How does it work?

I write whatever shows up. That's good enough for me. I'm part of the first generation that wants to still do original material and not tour around as an oldies act. You know, Chuck Berry is still out there playing. No one can play his music like he does. My stuff's the same way. [*His phone rings*] Sorry, I have to take this. [*A minute passes*] That was my 99-year-old aunt. You know how it is.

You put together the track list for 2003's *NYC Man* career-spanning anthology. As someone who doesn't listen to his own music much, did you hear anything in your old songs that surprised you?

I heard the same things wrong that were wrong the first time. The first generation of CDs sounded terrible. Any chance to remaster would make the music sound better than what was already out there. People at the record company do not give a shit. They don't care if the tapes are sitting on a warehouse floor somewhere. When they say music is disposable, they're not kidding.

Aside from sonic issues, did the songs mean anything different after hearing them again?

Sound quality was the reason I listened to those songs. That's it. They sound better now. They're not vinyl, but they can be killer. The *Berlin* DVD, I'll match that up against anything. The sound is murderous. *Murderous.*

Okay, let's talk about *Berlin*. It was pretty poorly received when it came out. Then, in 2006, you were approached to make the album into a concert film directed by Julian Schnabel. Did you get a sense that people's feelings about the album had changed over time?

You know, it's funny. It's making me think, like, if you were talking to Bill Burroughs, would you have said, "Now, Bill, they put together the new version of *Naked Lunch*. What do you think? Do you still feel the same way, Bill?" Can you imagine being put in a position where you're trying to justify *Naked Lunch*? How are we supposed to answer that? You gotta be kidding me. *Berlin*, you know, we tried. It's such a simple idea that it barely qualifies as an idea: Instead of all the songs having different characters, why not have the characters come back and deal with each other? How much simpler can it get?

Does it matter to you that the album has been given a second life?
I mean, I'm glad people get to hear it. People never really got to hear *Berlin* because of the critics. Then critics ask you if you feel vindicated by other critics. I didn't like critics then, and I don't like them now. There you go. I've always been outside the mainstream, and it stayed that way.

The year before *Berlin* came out, you released "Walk on the—
I followed up my one big hit with *Berlin*; *Berlin* has got this rap that it's depressing. Are you joking me? You can't handle it? You ever read *Hamlet*? Who are you talking to that's so stupid? Are you joking? You're kidding me.

When you were touring behind *Berlin* in the mid-'70s, you were doing some risqué stuff onstage. [Reed would feign injecting drugs during concerts.] You were singing about domestic abuse. And people clapped. Did you ever wonder if they were clapping for the wrong reasons?
I have no control over the audience. I have no idea what they think. My heart's pure. I can't do anything. I really can't do anything. I don't know what goes on in the crowd. I've had them show up and throw beer cans at me. I caused riots in most of the major cities. What can I do?

Singing about gay life on albums like [1972's] *Transformer* was definitely transgressive at the time. But now, playing with sexuality and gender is part of the mainstream. Do you feel like the center has come to you?
That's truly a critic's kind of question. I have absolutely no idea about anything.

Is that really true, though? Do you think your music has been something of a guide for people to learn about behavior they might not otherwise encounter?
[*Reed stares and remains silent*]

Is there a moral aspect to a song like "Heroin"?
I don't know what to think about something like that. I don't think anybody is anybody else's moral compass. Maybe listening to my music is not the best idea if you live a very constricted life. Or maybe it is. I'm writing about real things. Real people. Real characters. You have to believe what I write about is true or you wouldn't pay any attention at all. Sometimes it's me, or a composite of me and other people. Sometimes it's not me at all.

Does that confuse people?
You know, I wanted to be an actor. That was my real goal. But I wasn't any good at it, so I wrote my own material and acted through that. That's my idea of fun. I get to be all these things in the songs. But I present it to you like: This is how it is. Simple. But a guide to doing things that are wrong and right? I mean, Othello murders Desdemona. Is that a guide to what you can do? The guy in *Berlin* beats up his girlfriend. Is that a guide to what you can do? Is that what you walk away with? I don't think so. Maybe they should sticker my albums and say, "Stay away if you have no moral compass."

You've been doing a radio show for Sirius—
It's a very cool show, have you heard it?

No. I don't have satellite radio.
How can you ask me a question about a show you haven't heard?

Because your answer won't depend on my having heard it.
Did you know I did a version of "Jesus" with the Five Blind Boys of Alabama at the U.N.? Hard to believe, right? That the same person who wrote "White Light/White Heat" was singing at the U.N.

I don't find that particularly hard to believe.
It makes perfect sense to me too. I used to have a radio show when I was studying at Syracuse. It was called *Excursions on*

a Wobbly Rail. I played jazz and R&B. I have a much broader palette now. I'm more interested in Rabbi Josef Rosenblatt. Go look it up.

He's a cantor from the 1910s.
Anybody can Google anything nowadays. I heard about him from Ornette Coleman.

Let's talk about the earliest days. In the early '60s, you started out in what was essentially a bar band, right?
It *was* a bar band. A really bad bar band. My first regular gig was factory songwriting for [budget label] Pickwick Records. It was real cheap, hack stuff. Whatever was popular, I'd write an imitation. Ten racing songs. Ten surfing songs. Some of them weren't bad. Kids find this stuff now and then sell it online. Go figure.

Given that you cut your teeth writing to order and playing covers, was it difficult to develop your own songwriting style?
That happened when I was in college and starting to write the stuff that ended up on the first Velvet Underground record. That was me trying to write myself. I don't remember if it was the first song I wrote, but "Heroin" was the first one where I remember saying, "I'll leave that one alone." This is 1963, '64.

Syracuse is where you met [Velvet Underground guitarist] Sterling Morrison?
Yeah, Sterling was up there. Then we moved to New York. I met [VU multi-instrumentalist John] Cale in New York when Pickwick needed people with long hair to be a make-believe rock group and play a song I wrote called "The Ostrich." Cale was one of them.

Did you meet Andy Warhol soon after?
That was a little later. I first met Andy when he came down to hear the Velvet Underground when we were playing on West Third Street in New York at a place called the Café Bizarre.

How important was Warhol's support?
To have Andy Warhol say you're on the right track . . . it meant a lot to me that he liked the material. It was everything.

It's easy to think of New York as this great incubator of bands. But that wasn't the case for the Velvet Underground, was it?
Is this going to be all about the Velvet Underground now?

No. Did it hurt or help that you guys developed apart from a scene of bands?
The Velvet Underground was part of Andy's group, and Andy wasn't part of anything. I suppose you could say he was part of Pop Art, but he was really off on his own thing. I don't know what things would've been like if he hadn't been there to support us.

Did the confidence you got from Warhol help you decide to go solo?
I've never been superconfident about anything. The work is never as good as it could be.

How does an unconfident person put out _Metal Machine Music?_
I've thought a lot about that question. If something of mine ever got popular, maybe I could've stuck with that. But that was never the point. I had other goals.

Which were?
Hubert Selby. William Burroughs. Allen Ginsberg. Delmore Schwartz. To be able to achieve what they did, in such little space, using such simple words. I thought if you could do what those writers did and put it to drums and guitar, you'd have the greatest thing on earth. You'd have the whole pie. It's a simple thought. There's nothing complicated about me. I'm as straight as you can get.

Your popularity sort of waxed and waned in the '70s. Then, in the '80s, you did some film acting, you were on the Amnesty International tour with U2 and Sting, you did an ad for Honda that used "Walk on the Wild Side." Were you making a concerted effort to enter the mainstream, like David Bowie?
Those were projects that came up at the time. Warhol used to do all kinds of ads to fund projects. I thought I could do the same thing, but people got really upset, so I didn't do it anymore. Now people have their music in ads all the time and no one seems to

care. It's very strange. This has nothing to do with music, so I don't know why you're asking, but fine.

Tell me about having folks like Moby and My Morning Jacket play at your tribute concert at South by Southwest.

That was amazing. Dr. Dog played, too. And they were all songs I wrote. It was astonishing to see. I couldn't believe all those songs.

It's funny, you can tell which bands are into *White Light/White Heat* and which ones are into *The Velvet Underground*. What's interesting to you about the influence you've had?

My work goes from "Pale Blue Eyes" to "White Light/White Heat" and all stops in between. Generally speaking, you wouldn't figure that one person is going to write both those songs. But I haven't a clue about my influence. I mean, I really don't. Someone will say, "Have you heard that so-and-so sounds like you?" Why? Because they sing out of key?

How did collaborating with the Killers on the 2007 track "Tranquilize" come about?

They asked me. It was a good song. I liked the singer. I did it.

What other younger bands do you like?

I'm not gonna list bands for you. I mean, I could look at my iPod. Battles. Holy Fuck. Melt-Banana.

Tai chi training inspired your most recent album of new material [2007's *Hudson River Wind Meditations*]. Has studying martial arts affected your approach to music?

Everything affects the way I make music. I don't understand what you want to know. I could say "yes." Would that be better?

From what I understand, tai chi has a spiritual component as well as a physical one. Has that spiritual component found its way into your music?

It's a really profound study. I couldn't possibly sum it up for you. The problem is that I don't think you know what you're asking about. When you say *tai chi*, you're just saying a generic thing like *yoga*. If you want to ask a question, you should know what you're asking about, don't you think?

It's hard to find a story about you that doesn't mention your reputation as a difficult interview. Does that perception bother you?
You could judge for yourself, can't you? You want me to comment about other critics as though they matter. You save this question for last? I don't know why you brought it up, seeing as we got along fine. Unless I'm mistaken. What answer do you want?

I want to know how you feel about the way you might be perceived.
You're talking about critics and journalists. Listen, you're not talking about music. I don't want to get into this stupid subject with you. You brought it up. You shouldn't have. We had a good conversation, and now we're done. You feel better now? Did you find your angle? Do you think you did a good job?

The question wasn't a trick.
I didn't think you were trying to trick anybody. This is the kind of shit you wanted all along, and you saved it for last. What should I say?

I'm not looking for any particular answer.
You could've talked music, but this is what you wanted.

Haven't I been asking about music this whole time?
You're not interested in music. We're done talking.

DAVID MARCHESE ended up as a SPIN associate editor through a combination of wishful thinking and sheer dumb luck. Previously, he wrote for Salon.com, *The Village Voice*, and a bunch of blogs he sometimes wishes didn't exist.

18

Armageddon
in
EFFECT

Confronting Chuck D

by JOHN LELAND

SEPTEMBER 1988

In 1988 it was possible to take rappers' revolutionary aspirations literally and treat their threats against journalists—in this case, me—as part of the figurative oratorical surround. I wrote a mixed review of Public Enemy's first album in The Village Voice, *under the headline "Noise Annoys." In response, Chuck D told the British music paper the* NME *that he wanted to "fuck [me] up." Better, he wrote the song "Bring the Noise." As I saw it, we were two suburban loudmouths who liked hard music, hard language, and hard argument. I took his threat in that context, and still do. When the group's minister of information, Professor Griff, made anti-Semitic remarks, I invited Chuck to continue the battle of words. He brought a tape recorder. He was late. The conversation, I think, made him human and approachable: not the formidable voice from the group's recordings, but a guy who would mix it up and laugh (almost) at his own pretensions.*

Hip-hop was smaller then. You could banter with it and it would banter back. It seemed more important, capable of doing even the things it said, but history has not been kind to this view.

■　■　■

T WAS AN OLD-STYLE PROTEST HANDBILL, unsigned, dropped anonymously on every seat at the New Music Seminar's panel on racism. Across the top, handwritten in artless capital letters, it read, DON'T BELIEVE THE HATE. And for the remainder of the page, in cramped, single-spaced type, it presented its case:

> The World According To Public Enemy:
>   "Cats naturally miaow, dogs naturally bark, and whites naturally murder and cheat. . . . White people's hearts are so cold they can't wait to lie, cheat, and murder. This is white people's nature. . . . Whites are the biggest murderers on earth."
>   "There's no place for gays. When God destroyed Sodom and Gomorrah, it was for that sort of behavior." (*The Face*, July/Aug. 88)
>   "The White Race or the Caucasian Race came from the Caucus mountains. . . . It was not black people who made it with monkeys, animals and dogs, but it was white people. . . . White people are actually monkeys' uncles because that's who they made it with in the Caucasian hills."
>   "They say the white Jews built the pyramids. Shit. The Jews can't even build houses that stand up nowadays. How the hell did they build the pyramids?"
>   "If the Palestinians took up arms, went into Israel and killed all the Jews, it'd be alright." (*Melody Maker*, May 28, 1988)

It was July 18, the opening day of the Democratic National Convention, and the emotional circus that had been building around Public Enemy all summer just kicked up a notch. By the time the night was over, and Public Enemy lead rapper Chuck D had denounced writer and supporter Greg Tate as the *Village Voice*'s "porch nigger," New York was swinging. We'd never seen anything like this before.

It was also nine business days after the release of Public Enemy's second album, *It Takes a Nation of Millions to Hold Us Back*, and the record had already unofficially gone gold, sating the very different hungers of black and white audiences. It seemed to be booming out of every car at every traffic light in the city. The *Wall Street Journal* had recently discovered car stereos that approached the decibel level required to bore a hole in a piece of wood, and this was the perfect program material—dense beats, fragments of sound and meaning, vituperative word-association: "*Suckers, liars, get me a shovel / Some writers I know are damn devils / From them I say don't believe the hype / Yo Chuck, they must be on the pipe, right?*"

What might have been a simple, bodaciously funky message of black self-determination, delivered by two college friends from Long Island, had turned into a liberal apologist's nightmare, a martyrdom in the making. At the center of it all, Chuck D, a virtual red diaper baby with a degree in graphic design, compared himself to Marcus Garvey and Nat Turner, and let the contradictions swirl.

For the record, Chuck D didn't make the statements quoted in the handbill. They belong to Professor Griff, Public Enemy's Minister of Information, and leader of the S1Ws (Security of the First World), Public Enemy's plastic-Uzi-toting, paramilitary Muslim security force.

Like Chuck D's logo, a silhouette of a black youth inside a rifle sight, and like the S1Ws' plastic Uzis, Public Enemy merges the rhetoric of militancy with that of advertising in ways that sit

No. 1 with a bullet: Public Enemy's Flavor Flav and Chuck D give it their best shot in 1988. *Richard Reyes/Retna*

uneasily for both camps. The crew is both rational and hysterical at the same time. It offers hysteria as a rational response to the times.

Chuck D: "It's definitely Armageddon. The black man and woman is at war with himself or herself, and with the situation around them. Armageddon is the war to end all wars. That's when everything hopefully will be alright, the last frontier. Of course we're in it. I'm in it. Maybe you're not in it. You can afford not to be in it, because it doesn't confront you on a daily basis. Black people in America are at war."

SPIN: **Chuck, what's your reaction to the handbill distributed at the New Music Seminar?**
CHUCK D: They're making a whole lot of shit about nothing. A lot of paranoia going on. People think I got the ability to fucking turn a country around.

Do you back the statements that Griff made?
I back Griff. Whatever he says, he can prove.

You mean he can prove that white people mated with monkeys? That it wouldn't be such a bad idea if the Palestinians were to kill all the Jews in Israel?
Now, that was taken out of context. I was there. He said, by Western civilization's standards, it wouldn't be bad for the Palestinians to come into Palestine and kill all the Jews, because that's what's been done right throughout Western civilization: invasion, conquering, and killing. That wasn't mentioned.

It's no secret that white people lived in caves while blacks had civilizations. Marcus Garvey said the same shit Farrakhan's saying today. Black people know this. White people do not.

Now, people think we're building up some kind of anti-Semitic hate. Black people's feeling around the country, 98 percent of them say Jews are just white people, there ain't no difference. That's my feeling. I don't like to make an issue out of it.

Doesn't Griff speak for Public Enemy?
He speaks for himself. At the same time, Griff's my brother in Public Enemy. People are gonna see that Griff said this, and in the same interview, I said something else. It's up to them.

Do you consider yourselves prophets?

I guess so. We're bringing a message that's the same shit that all the other guys that I mentioned in the song have either been killed for or deported: Marcus Garvey, Nat Turner, all the way up to Farrakhan and Malcolm X.

What is a prophet?

One that comes with a message from God to try to free people. My people are enslaved within their own minds.

Rap serves as the communication that they don't get for themselves to make them feel good about themselves. Rap is black America's TV station. It gives a whole perspective of what exists and what black life is about. And black life doesn't get the total spectrum of information through anything else. They don't get it through print because kids won't pick up no magazines or no books, really, unless it got pictures of rap stars. They don't see themselves on TV. Number two, black radio stations have neglected giving out information.

On what?

On anything. They give out information that white America gives out. Black radio does not challenge information coming from the structure into the black community, does not interpret what's happening around the world in the benefit of us. It interprets it the same way that Channel 7 would. Where it should be, the black station interprets that information from Channel 7 and says, "This is what Channel 7 was talking about. Now, as far as we're concerned. . . ." We don't have that. The only thing that gives the straight-up facts on how the black youth feels is a rap record. It's the number one communicator, force and source, in America right now. Black kids are listening to rap records right now more than anything, and they're taking it word for word.

I look at myself as an interpreter and dispatcher.

To get a message across, you have to bring up certain elements that they praise, or once did praise, 'cause I've seen a change in the last year and a half.

What do you have to bring up that they praise?

Violence. Drugs. I'll give you a good case, I'm warming up, you know. It takes me a while to warm up into an interview.

Two years ago black kids used to think that saying nothing was alright; getting a gold rope, a fat dukey gold rope, was dope, was the dope shit; it's alright to sniff a little coke, get nice for the moment; get my fly ride and do anything to get it, even if it means stomping on the next man, 'cause I got to look out for number one. It's alright for a drug dealer to deal drugs, it's alright 'cause he's making money.

1988, it's a different thought. Because consciousness has been raised to the point where people are saying, "That gold rope don't mean shit now."

Are you taking credit for these changes?
Yes. When I say, "Farrakhan's a prophet and I think you ought to listen" [on "Bring the Noise"], kids don't challenge the fact that Farrakhan's a prophet or not. Few of them know what a prophet is. But they will try to find out who Farrakhan is and what a prophet is. It sounds good to them first, then at the same time they're going to say, "Well, it interests me, let me get into it." Their curiosity has been sparked. Once curiosity has been sparked, the learning process begins. You can't teach, or a kid can't learn, unless their curiosity is sparked.

Okay. ". . . That I think you oughta listen to." Kids will say, "Let me listen to the man." I think the man lays down a decent game plan that has been misinterpreted. He lays a solution and he inspires and challenges the black man to use his brain and understand what has happened before. Which brings up the point of, "Listen, that was then, this is now." Farrakhan says no. That phrase should never be used. Because you're dealing with the after-effect. When I offer that line, that's what goes off in kids' heads. Or, "Supporter of Chesimard." Twelve-year-old kid would not know about Joanne Chesimard [a.k.a. Assata Shakur, a member of the Black Panther Party and Black Liberation Army, who was convicted in the killing of a New Jersey state trooper; she escaped to Cuba]. But their curiosity is sparked.

When I came out with my first records, I had to be shocking in order to be heard. My job was just to tune the radicalness a little bit more. And to be shocking once again sparks the curiosity.

You make a lot of assumptions about black youth. You treat them as a singular idea, and as having one attitude, one mind, one situation.

Yeah. On the whole. Because on the whole, everybody's falling victim to the same obstacles. To be able to dissect and understand what's happening to them or what's happening to us, it takes years, or it takes constant teaching. And these things aren't being taught in schools. They throw a bunch of facts about history, they throw you math and science, which are needed, and a bunch of things that are not needed in life. And the kids are not trained to challenge the information. For example, the kid that says, "Listen, I just don't agree with you" to the teacher, the teacher can't deal with that most of the time, because they have to move the class on. They can't go back. So a lot of black kids can't challenge information.

And that's where rap is filling a void, where before the parent used to talk to the child and say, "Listen, you watch this program, son, this is what it's about, this is what he's saying here," and the kid is not getting his information just through what he's watching or what he's listening to or what he's reading. He's getting an interpretation from the parent who understands. Right now we're in a situation where the parents don't understand. Or if they do understand, they don't know how to break it down for their son or daughter, because they don't know how to communicate on a regular basis. Or in most cases, it's not a father around, it's a mother around, and she's young herself, she ain't got nothing in her head, or she ain't got time.

I happened to fall into a situation that allowed me to have a thorough education because if something came across and my mother said, "This is what it's about," my father would say, "I don't think so." Even if they got into an argument, this would be interesting to me. My mother was a social activist in the '60s. I guess whatever movement went down, she would support it: Angela Davis–type shit. My mother was very strong. She always gave me that sense of radicalism from day one. And this weekend happens to be my mother and father's birthday. I'm planning a big shindig. It's probably going to be the happiest day of my life, to throw a party for my father.

What was the Afro-American Experience?
Afro-American Experience was a supplementary educational program for the black youth of Nassau County, Suffolk County, and Queens, run by Panther leaders.

Which ones?
I can't tell you who exactly. I remember Brother Lee. It wasn't any big leaders. 'Cause the Panthers had headquarters in every black community back then. The Nation of Islam had temples in most of the communities. The Black Panther Party was viewed as a positive organization for the betterment of black people and their communities, to get what they wasn't getting. And they joined together with college students to create this program.

How old were you when you were in this program?
When I went I was 11. Don't print my age. I was 11 in 1971. Don't print my age.

Why not? What's the big deal?
The big deal is that in order to communicate to the youth you have to be recognized as a peer. Something has to be there that they can say, "This is me." So I'd rather not have my age printed. But at the same time I was 11 years old in 1971. My parents sent me, and I was reluctant at first, 'cause I felt I shouldn't have to go to no summer school. I did well.

The program consisted of eight hours, Monday to Friday, education. I think it had maybe 1,500 kids. Hank Shocklee [Public Enemy's producer] was there. We dealt with classrooms. I'm not saying disciplinary actions are right, but a couple times kids got out of line, and how a lot of the brothers would discipline the kid, everybody else would have to punish this person. Not by beating him up or spanking, but everybody would talk to him at once and tell him how fucked up he was for acting the way he did.

Were you ever punished?
No, no.

How did you like administering punishment?
I felt good, because I was convinced that it was for the betterment of all of us. Like a person broke a window on campus.
Somebody was going to get yelled at, usually the brothers. First
of all, they weren't wanted on the campus. The communities
forced the campus to allow this program to exist. So I felt
pretty good.

**You said in the *NME* that you went to the SPIN party looking for
me, that you wanted to fuck me up bad.**
I sure did. You appear to be a nice guy. Did you used to have long
hair? I just wanted to speak to you mainly that night. I heard you
was hiding out.

Everybody's entitled to their opinion, I guess. But it's bad that
you keep your opinion limited. Because the whole market of rap
is basically unable to judge information. I know that most of the
market doesn't read the magazine, but some do.

Black kids and the black market right now, they're unable
to challenge information. Or they're unable to weigh logic.
My challenge is to put A and B up and say, "Damn, don't you
see B is fucked up, and that A would be a lot better for you?"
They have to get this, 'cause they're not getting it in the school
systems.

**But do you really think they're getting it from you? The objec-
tions I raised were that a lot of your lyrics were sloganeering.**
Yeah, they're getting it from me. You got to understand, the black
market is schizophrenic. A lot of things are said with words or
body language or things meaning something else. It's like, if you
go up to somebody and he says, [*sputtering*] "nigga bugging,"
he's saying a lot of things besides nigga bugging. It's felt.

And I could understand it. Some white person with a middle-
class background or little contact with black people won't understand that shit at all.

There's a lot of people in Creedmor [psychiatric hospital]
that people can't understand. You have to find people that are
able to communicate to those that are unable to communicate to
the rest of the world. Rap is a true reflection of the streets. It's

what R&B once was: the slang that you invent through music or the slang that you can pick up on the streets and then present through music. Motown was once that. Marvin Gaye comes out with "I Heard It Through the Grapevine," based on his interpretation of what his mother told him. It became slang in the street. It was a teaching process. And it was a reflection at the same time. R&B doesn't do that anymore. Rap does it. It's able to open doors to the mind. Rap deals. It's abrasive. It doesn't hide shit. R&B hides shit. It's Barry Manilow, it's Frank Sinatra.

I hate to talk about communism as Western civilization knows it, or even communism as it's known today, 'cause it's not fair, it's not people dealing with people. There's still somebody at the top, manipulating people. But I think capitalism should be a mixture. I think people should be treated fair from day one. In this situation right here, in the United States of America—I don't even want to get mad at the fact that it's so unfair.

If you get mad, what do you get mad at? Where do you direct your anger?
I try to direct the anger on trying to do something constructive for my people that are at a disadvantage.

That's what you do with it. But who do you get mad at?
Right now, it's hard for me to say, because it goes by the moment. There's a lot of people I could get mad at, but I understand people, so there's no hatred. I just try to throw a monkey wrench in the motherfucker. It all goes back to people saying, "Chuck D, what kind of government system would you have here in America in 1988?" I say, "One that says black people shouldn't have to pay taxes." It's compensation. Matter of fact, it's overcompensation that we need to be behind the eight ball from 1609 to 1865 and thereafter, 120 more bullshit years. Slaves were brought to this continent in 1609; 1865, 256 years later, the so-called black man was free, quote-unquote "free." So that's 256 years of free labor to build this country. And then the animosity and hatred that went with the package afterwards. When I say black people shouldn't have to pay taxes, it's because we haven't been compensated. I think that's fair. Do you think it's fair?

No. No I don't.
Ha ha. That's one thing I think should happen. Black people shouldn't have to pay taxes.

That's a bullshit reform.
That's a bullshit reform. Also, we should be compensated $250 billion or whatever it takes to get each black family on its feet. Not saying that it will help a whole lot, because there's still no brains. The slum of black America is in the mind of black America. But it would help. I'm talking about that's a solution, a plan. That will never happen. So we're talking fantasy. People say, "Well . . ." What do you think I am, fucking Albert Gore? If I could give you A to Z, I might as well run. But I can do it. Give me some time.

People are always looking to catch me in fucking doubletalk and loopholes. They treat me like *I'm* Jesse Jackson. I'm not running. I'm just offering a little bit of a solution, or at least explaining why things are the way they are. Which are fucked up.

Are you paranoid?
No, I'm not paranoid. I know there's other things for me to do in this music. If it has to come through other means, I could give up doing records.

Your last single, "Bring the Noise," was basically about what other people are saying about you . . .
Oh yeah, that was about you. I was talking right about you. . . .

And now your new single, "Don't Believe the Hype," is also about what people are saying about you . . .
"Don't Believe the Hype" is about telling people, "Listen, just don't believe the things that are told to you." Go out and seek, challenge information. "The follower of Farrakhan / Don't tell me that you understand / Until you hear the man / I bring the book of the new-school rap game / Writers treat me like Coltrane, insane / Yes to them, but to me I'm a different kind / We're brothers of the same mind, unblind." We both know what's happening, but we're treated like we're bugging. That's why I say I'm treated like Coltrane. 'Cause when Coltrane took his stance in the

mid-'60s, a lot of writers came crashing down on him because of his radical stance. He started becoming more and more radical until the day he died, started speaking his mind. A lot of people thought he was losing it. Today they recognize the man as a genius. I'm not telling you I'm a Coltrane fan because I'm getting into Coltrane. You probably know more about him than I do.

You call yourselves Public Enemy, and build a strong identity on that, but then the minute you get a little piece of criticism, you fly off the handle.
Don't you think that makes it a little exciting?

It makes it exciting. It also makes it untrustworthy.
Listen. The only one I'm furious at over the past year is Greg Tate [who, in a review of *Nation of Millions*, suggested that the group's "misogyny is a result of PE suffering from LOP: lack of pussy"]. That motherfucker sold out. I'm pissed at him, man.

I think that's because you can't take criticism.
I can't take motherfuckers calling me a motherfucker.

Aw, big deal, Chuck.
I ain't got to feel bad. At the same time, was it an album review or a character review? I also deal on "Louder Than a Bomb" with the FBI tapping my phone.

Have they really, or are you just guessing?
I'm guessing. Because it's happened to most black leaders. It's no secret. The FBI does get involved with somebody even a slight bit outspoken. So it would be ludicrous and naive to believe that they won't do it today. So if they do it, so what? What I say comes through on records and in interviews. It's no secret at all what I say, 'cause I'm louder than a bomb. They can tap my phone. The FBI had King and X set up. "Party for Your Right to Fight" deals with COINTELPRO, FBI, CIA, assassinations, and destruction of the Black Panther Party, Martin Luther King, Malcolm X, the Nation of Islam.

You don't believe that X was killed by the Nation of Islam?
No. And if he was, it was a set-up, some snake that was paid.

Do you have any reason to believe this, or is it just something that's convenient for you?
It's something that's convenient for me. But also, if you look at it, it's a pattern. It's a real good guess.

You used to come out in the beginning of your concerts and say that the Klan was outside, ready to shut you down. But there was no danger of this.
No. But at the same time, I was letting people be aware that these forces exist.

And you feel justified in manipulating the facts in order to make that point?
Uh huh.

That's the mark of a politician, to manipulate the truth to get across an agenda.
To manipulate the truth? You tell me another way to tell the truth to black people if they don't want to hear the truth straight out. I'm open to answers.

You've complained constantly, in interviews and on records, that you can't get your records on black radio, because black radio perceives you as being "too black," too aggressive, too loud. So you make louder records, and you get them on black radio. Does that mean that you're wrong about black radio or wrong about the records?
My whole point is that black radio has a responsibility to the black community. It's responsibility, if the black community and the black youth wants to hear 50 percent rap records in that community, it's black radio's responsibility to play 50 percent rap records. Now, don't get on the demographic trip of trying to reach 25 and over of demographic black females, who aren't listening to radio at night anyway. My wife don't listen to radio. She's watching TV till she falls asleep.

But you listen to the radio. I listen to the radio. Anyone in a car listens to the radio.
No. Anyone that drives in a car listens to tape decks. See, we're dealing with different sciences here. That's what's accelerated

the rap album public: car tape decks. Ten years ago, you bought an album so you could take it home to your turntable to play. I know, because I was there—I went out and bought an album to play on the stereo system at home, that I couldn't play loud.

Over the last ten years, the advent of the car stereo, the tape player, and also the box, and the Walkman—now a kid says, "I can take my tape, and I boom that shit loud." Motherfuckers going out now and getting big systems, and it's music to play loud. It deals with loudness. It deals with noise. I can turn it all the way up, park myself in the car, and play the tape that I just bought. Which explains why people are buying every rap album.

This is not a music that you can go home and kick up your feet and listen to. This is music that requires activity; or if you're gonna cool out, you're gonna be in something that can be active in a minute, like a car.

Like I wrote "Bring the Noise" driving along the ocean where I live. Matter of fact, I wrote my first album in a car. I had a track in the tape deck, and I'm writing it on the Long Island Expressway, I'm writing it on the seat.

What's the function of noise in your music?
To agitate, make the jam noticeable. When I originally made it, I wanted some shit where, when a car passed my house, I know that's my song. It grew into a political thing, but I'm telling you the basis. Do you really find that much noise in our music now? It was something that we just put a label on, and found that people believed the label. Now it serves as a uniform. We wear it sometimes, and sometimes we don't. We try to set trends, so we don't stay on things too long. Now you hear it everywhere.

Nobody wants to judge us on our music. Everybody wants to judge us on our character. Journalists only cover me because right now it's exciting. It beats the hell out of covering Morrissey 30, 40, 50 times, talking about the state of rock'n'roll, which isn't exciting at all.

Why do you take the bait every time an interviewer offers it?
Taking the bait? I'm not actually taking the bait. Sometimes the bait is thrown at you and you can't get out of the way. It's easy to attack us.

It's no problem at all. It's a matter of throwing you guys a noose and letting you put your neck in it.

Uh huh. But at the same time, I don't look at it as putting my head in a fucking noose, because it's not really dying. The music they can't stop.

I'm just saying, being that I'm the only one that's making this shit kind of exciting for a little period of time, don't take this shit so seriously that you get hurt. 'Cause I got a job to do.

Alright, Chuck, I'm straight. We can wind this up.

C'mon, you can't be straight, man. Let's keep talking. . . .

JOHN LELAND was one of SPIN's original columnists. He is now a national correspondent at *The New York Times* and author of two nonfiction books, *Hip: The History* and *Why Kerouac Matters: The Lessons of* On the Road (*They're Not What You Think*).

19

Dearly
BELOVED

Presenting an oral history of Prince's *Purple Rain*

by BRIAN RAFTERY

JULY 2009

Nobody talks to Prince.

Well, that's not entirely true. I'm sure the guy talks to somebody, if for no other reason than to replenish his supply of platform heels and glyph thongs. But with rare exception, Prince avoids dealing with the press. As a fan, this reticence makes me love him even more: While his superstar contemporaries navel-gaze to the point of self-demystification, Prince remains rock's biggest tease, the source of countless late-night hypotheses and rants. If he were to answer all our questions, what would we have left to discuss? I mean, there's only so much to debate about the subtext of Shalamar.

Thankfully, Purple Rain *was birthed during what turned out to be the last relatively unguarded period of Prince's career, and he had plenty of co-conspirators willing to talk (though there were a few holdouts, most notably the Time's Morris Day, who was presumably off having a confab with a gilt-edged mirror). I found out later that Prince wasn't crazy about the story— but until I hear from him directly, I'll never quite know why. So, Prince, if you're reading this: Call me. I still have plenty of questions for you.*

■ ■ ■

DEARLY BELOVED, we are gathered here today to get through this thing called life. And 25 years ago, life seemingly revolved around an elfin horndog with a rococo fashion sense, an alpine voice, and a purple motorcycle twice his size. *Purple Rain* is remembered for its music—the soundtrack album produced four Top 40 hits and is a pop masterpiece—but the movie, released on July 27, 1984, remains the nerviest act of his quixotic career. As the Kid, a struggling Minneapolis rocker, he feuds with his alcoholic father, slaps his adoring girlfriend, and seethes with jealousy over his zoot-suited rival.

But *Purple Rain* wasn't some widescreen ego trip; the spectacle of a famously image-conscious artist introducing himself to the mainstream as fragile and occasionally cruel could have easily killed his ascendant career. Prince rarely talks, and when he does it's not about *Purple Rain*, but in new interviews with his former collaborators, he is always front and center: a headstrong leader who inspired both devotion and disgruntlement. *Purple Rain* may not be an autobiography, but it may be as close as we'll ever get to his true story.

Let's go crazy.

On April 10, 1983, Prince played the final show of his Triple Threat tour—a five-month jaunt that saw him traveling the U.S. with his protégés, the Time and the risqué girl-group Vanity 6. Though the tour began in theaters, Prince steadily upgraded to arenas, thanks to such hits as "1999," an upbeat, apocalyptic dance-off, and "Little Red Corvette," a first-person locker-room brag that's either about a two-seat sports car or a clitoris (or both). Those tracks would help his 1999 album eventually sell more than five million copies worldwide, while the accompanying videos introduced the world to Prince's backing band, a multiracial, sexually cryptic collective known as the Revolution.

LISA COLEMAN (keyboardist, the Revolution, 1980–87) From the very early days, we were controversial. We were black and white, we were girls and boys, and we were traveling together. We'd go to truck stops in Bible Belt country, and people would look at us like they wanted to kill us. But we were like brothers and sisters. We loved each other.

BOBBY Z. (drummer, the Revolution, 1978–87) We were kind of a carnival troupe.

DEZ DICKERSON (guitarist, the Revolution, 1979–83) One of the things that made the chemistry of that band unique is we shared a certain ethos and certain values. All of us wanted to be the best. None of us were party animals. We knew how to have fun, but it wasn't in a nihilistic, destructive way. Prince would pay for these elaborate parties, and we'd show up for 12 minutes and go back to the hotel.

WENDY MELVOIN (guitarist, the Revolution, 1983–87) Pre–*Purple Rain*, we were still seen as part of the underground, psycho-punk scene. I was proud of that.

DR. FINK (keyboardist, the Revolution, 1979–91) During that tour, we kept running into Bob Seger and the Silver Bullet Band. After one of the shows, Prince asked me what made Seger so popular. I said, "Well, he's playing mainstream pop-rock." Michael Jackson and Prince were breaking ground,

Paisley perk: Poster of Prince and the Revolution included free with *Purple Rain* album.
© *Tom Medvedich*

but there was still a lot of segregation on mainstream radio. I said, "Prince, if you were to write something along these lines, it would cross things over for you even further." I'm not trying to take credit for anything here, but possibly that influenced him.

COLEMAN The idea of doing a movie had been bubbling for years. Prince carried a notebook, and he'd always come up with little scenarios on a plane or on buses or, back then, in the occasional station wagon.

BOB CAVALLO (former manager) We managed Prince in '78, '79, something like that, until '89, the ten really good years, as far as I'm concerned. I call [partner Steve Fargnoli] and he's on the road with Prince: "Steve, there's about a year left on our deal, mention to Prince that we'd like to re-up." A day or so later I get a response: "He'll only sign with us if he gets a major motion picture. It has to be with a studio—not with some drug dealer or jeweler financing. And his name has to be above the title. Then he'd re-sign with us." He wasn't a giant star yet. I mean, that demand was a little over the top.

COLEMAN You know how he is—it wasn't about coming out with the next record. The next record had to be a whole environment.

MELVOIN It was exciting, but I was concerned it would be cheesy. I was just turning 19, and even at that age, I was this odd, geeky cinephile. I was one of those kids watching *The Tin Drum* and *Seven Samurai*. So I was really concerned with doing a rock movie and it not being as cool as *A Hard Day's Night*.

ALAN LEEDS (former tour manager) Two pop hits doesn't mean you're a movie star. And this was before MTV had any significance, particularly with black music. But I don't know how you describe his obsession. It was beyond confidence. It wasn't even arrogant. It was destiny, and either you're on board or you're going to miss out.

With no previous filmmaking experience, newly minted producer Cavallo began pitching Prince's idea around Hollywood, taking meetings with such potential investors as Richard Pryor and David Geffen.

CAVALLO Prince just kept pushing, and everybody turned us down. Nobody wanted to give me the money. We were gonna make a movie in the late fall, in Minneapolis, with unknown black people in front of the camera and me as a first-time producer. I went out to find a writer because no one would do it. Finally I found a TV writer who'd won Emmys.

WILLIAM BLINN (screenwriter) I was the executive producer of *Fame*, the television series. I went to Hollywood, where Prince was putting together final touches on a video. Met him at an Italian restaurant in Hollywood. What I remember more than anything was that he was the only person I had ever seen in my life who had pasta and orange drink. I didn't get it then, I don't get it now, but what the hell. He had definite ideas of what he wanted to do—a generalized story line, broad strokes. It wasn't his life, but it was about his life. Not that it was wall-to-wall docudrama, but he knew where he'd come from, and he wanted the movie to reflect that.

BOBBY Z. I think there always was a battle-of-the-bands story line—the Triple Threat tour was definitely the impetus. We had an epic food fight with the Time that could've easily been in the movie; it spurred the whole Time-versus-Revolution myth. It went from the show to the hotel and back to the bus to the airport and never stopped for about three days.

JELLYBEAN JOHNSON (drummer, the Time) We're onstage, and all of a sudden, [Time singer] Morris Day's big bodyguard grabs [Time guitarist] Jesse Johnson and snatches him offstage. And Prince takes his place, playing guitar. They take Jesse backstage, chain him to a coat rack or whatever, and proceed to pour syrup, or whatever food was in their dressing room, all over him. Now the band is wondering what the hell's goin' on: Prince is still playing guitar, and Jesse's gone, and then they got Jerome [Benton, dancer and backing vocalist] too. So when we got done with the last song, we decided, "We're gonna kick their ass." We took all our suits off and got into some dirty clothes, and we got eggs and everything, and we made them quite uncomfortable. We wouldn't do it while the show was going on, 'cause we figured we would've got fired, but the minute the show was over, it was on. We got all of them. We didn't discriminate.

BLINN Shortly after meeting Prince, I went to Minneapolis. We went to a couple of clubs, and I kinda picked up what I could on that scene. We were certainly an odd couple: I'm a fairly large human being, about six-three and 190 pounds. It was hard for me to just blend into the background. We found a way to work. He respected what I was doing, and I respected what he was doing. I did a couple of series with Wilford Brimley, whom I genuinely liked, and you could not pay me enough to ever work with him again. Prince was never a diva. He was there to do the work, and he worked his ass off.

With Blinn's first draft in hand, Cavallo set out to find a direc-
tor. He was eventually steered toward Albert Magnoli, a film
editor and recent USC grad with a jazz docudrama as his sole
directorial credit.

ALBERT MAGNOLI (director) I had problems with the script. It just didn't have any truth. If a film like this works, it works because it's speaking to the kids and it's coming from the heart.

CAVALLO We meet for breakfast, and [Magnoli] is jumping up and down and kneeling on the floor, telling me how he was gonna take the last scene of *The Godfather*—the famous montage of the christening while the guys are getting rid of all of Michael's enemies. He said, "That's how we'll open the film. Prince will be performing, but we'll introduce all the characters as we cut back and forth between Prince getting ready to go for the gig."

BLINN I think we had a better first draft—more mysterious and offbeat. The character of the father was a suicide, not an attempted suicide, and he was gone. The overall thrust of the picture was the Kid being torn between the dark allure of death—what it does to a kid when a parent commits suicide—and music and sexuality.

MAGNOLI I was told, "You're gonna sit in a hotel room for a couple hours, and then we're gonna meet Prince at midnight. We're gonna go have a meal, and then you'll talk about the script." They picked me up at 11, and I sat myself down in the lobby near the elevator. At midnight, the doors parted and Prince walked out. That put the last 30 pages of the screenplay in my mind—I was able to discern a tremendous amount of vulnerability in him, which the material I'd studied hadn't given me. Because when Prince is performing, he's extremely assured. But what I saw walking across the lobby was a very vulnerable kid.

CAVALLO You know how he's called the Kid in the movie? Well, that's all I ever called him: Kid.

MAGNOLI We got to the restaurant—it was just a Denny's or something like that—and sat in a booth. I ordered a grilled cheese sandwich; Prince ordered spaghetti and orange juice, which was one of his favorite meals. I launched into the same pitch I'd given Cavallo the day before: A kid from the other side of the tracks, someone that's not appreciated, he's in this wonderful musical world, and he's got parent problems.

PRINCE (to Tavis Smiley, 2009) My father was so hard on me. I was never good enough. It was almost like the Army when it came to music. . . . I wasn't allowed to play the piano when he was there because I wasn't as good as him. So when he left, I was determined to get as good as him, and I taught myself how to play music. And I just stuck with it, and I did it all the time. And sooner or later, people in the neighborhood heard about me and they started to talk.

MAGNOLI Prince and I then walked out the door and got in the car. He started to drive and didn't say a word. We were on a freeway for about five seconds, and then we got off, and I swear to God we were driving in a complete vacuum of blackness. There was about five minutes of complete silence, and then he said, "Do you know me? Have you read anything about me?" I said no. So he said, "Do you know my music?" And I said, "1999," "Little Red Corvette." And he said, "That's it? How is it that you can tell me my whole life in seven minutes?" When he dropped me off at the hotel, he says, "I have over a hundred songs produced. Maybe you can come by tomorrow and listen to them, because I think some of them might be good for the movie."

Magnoli signed on to direct the film and rewrite Blinn's screenplay. In August 1983, he relocated to Minneapolis, where he conducted interviews with Prince, the Revolution, and the Time, and immersed himself in the local music scene.

DAVID Z. (producer, Prince collaborator) Minneapolis was a very reclusive, isolated place for a long time. We were trying to get a hit record out there for 35 years, and nothing would happen. Nobody would come and see us, 'cause they all thought we had nothing going on in our backyard. And then two things happened: [Lipps Inc.'s] "Funkytown" and Prince.

COLEMAN "Funkytown" was more along the lines of what was considered the Minneapolis sound, because it was tight, funky, gizmo-synth kind of stuff. But it's funny, because "Funkytown" was about wanting to get out of Minneapolis and being miserable there.

PAUL PETERSON (keyboardist, the Time, 1983–85) I've lived there my entire life. The musicians that were around then all pretty much knew each other. We all sat in together at different clubs. There were the different cliques—Soul Asylum, the Replacements, and all those people. We didn't necessarily interact with those guys, but in the funk scene, we all hung out.

DICKERSON Prince was the game-changer. One of the reasons the area had always been cover-band-dominated was there wasn't a template of "Do this, put together a showcase, get A&R people." Nobody knew anything about that. So there was no label presence until Prince. Once that happened, people started coming in. So you have Hüsker Dü and Soul Asylum and the Suburbs and those bands benefiting from that.

To prepare for Purple Rain's *grueling production schedule— Magnoli had only eight weeks to shoot—Prince enrolled the cast members in dance and acting classes at Minnesota Dance Theatre.*

LEEDS You had one guy who couldn't do a push-up and someone like Prince who could do splits in his sleep.

COLEMAN I wish I had films of those things, because it was hilarious. We took a proper jazz/ballet class, and we were doing jazz hands. And imagine Jellybean, the drummer from the Time, doing pirouettes across the floor.

JOHNSON That was bizarre for me, being a kid from the streets.

FINK We'd sit in a circle and play mind-development and memory games. The dancing was required for a while. Then Prince didn't make it mandatory after several weeks, because some people were not into it. It was mainly to get in shape. The instructor was playing the old Jane Fonda workouts first thing in the day.

For the film's love interest, Prince cast Vanity, née Denise Matthews, as an aspiring singer torn between the affections of the Kid and Morris.

MAGNOLI When I met Vanity, I was at [nightclub] First Avenue, in the mezzanine area. Before anyone even said a word, I felt a quickening in the air. Within seconds, people started buzzing, "Vanity's here, Vanity's here." I saw her coming through, one of the most beautiful women you could ever lay your eyes on, packed into latex or whatever second skin, looking exquisite.

COLEMAN Vanity was supposed to be the lead, but she left right before the film. It almost tanked the film. I don't know what happened. Maybe it was a personal issue between her and Prince. They were dating.

MELVOIN My only speculation was that they had a big blow-out. That's what I heard. They had a huge blowout and she bolted.

MAGNOLI What happened was—and it's the Hollywood story— Martin Scorsese was casting for *The Last Temptation of Christ*, and they gave her an offer to play Mary Magdalene. She came to me and said, "Listen, I've got this offer, my agent wants me to take it, what should I do?" I felt bad for her because I knew she was in a terrible bind. In the end, she and her representative made the determination that they would do the Scorsese project, which then got delayed because of financing.

CHRISTINE HARRIS (secretary to Pure Heart Ministries and Denise Matthews) Being that Denise did not appear in *Purple Rain*, she would not have anything to add to your story. God bless.

JILL JONES (actress, singer) When she pulled out, a good friend of mine, Gina Gershon, auditioned for it. That would've been a totally different film.

MAGNOLI I saw hundreds of girls, and Apollonia was the last one. She came in with sweatpants and a sweatshirt on, no desire to glam up or impress. I called Prince and said, "You gotta come and see this girl."

APOLLONIA KOTERO (actress) I was in South America and Mexico— singing in nightclubs, doing commercials, TV series, films. I had to submit my tape with songs and the acting reel, meet the producers in L.A., and meet Prince in Minnesota. He was shy. And he smelled real good. Like purple. [*Laughs*] We sat there and stared at each other for the longest time.

COLEMAN Apollonia came and saved the day. But she was not a singer. She was an actress. So the poor thing was thrown into the studio: "Here, you have to sing this." She was like, "Oh my God, I don't know how to sing." And she did the best she could. I doubled her vocals on "Take Me With U" to make it sound a little better.

KOTERO I don't remember that. But I would imagine she's on [the song].

Much of the Purple Rain *soundtrack was recorded over the summer of 1983 at a warehouse in suburban Minneapolis and live onstage at First Avenue.*

MARK CARDENAS (keyboardist, the Time, 1983–84) On one side of the warehouse was Prince's huge stage; on the other side was the Time's little club set-up. It was a constant reminder of how big Prince was and how little the Time were.

MELVOIN [For the title song] Prince came in with the melody and the words and an idea of what the verses were like. I came up with the opening chords, and everybody started playing their parts.

BOBBY Z. My first reaction was, "Wow, this is almost a country song." It had a different feel than anything we'd been rehearsing for the rest of the album. I realize now it was probably, in his mind, the centerpiece of the story. But that's Prince—his ability to thread the needle, so to speak.

BLINN The first time you hear that song, you realize that this person who's built like a jockey and speaks barely above a whisper can just knock something out of the park.

One of the album's most enduring moments is the spoken-word introduction to "Computer Blue," featuring Coleman and Melvoin.

COLEMAN I have a Facebook page and I can't tell you how many people post, "Is the water warm enough?" on there. I don't know what it means. Prince handed us a piece of paper and said, "Will you guys go out there and say this?" I didn't think twice. Honestly, I hate to say that it doesn't mean anything. Is it tea? Is it a bathtub? Whatever you want to think. It was just us being cheeky.

MELVOIN We had no idea that it had some weird psychosexual connotations. Now it's like some odd tagline for us. I roll my eyes, because some people say it like I've never heard it before.

COLEMAN [Our relationship] was never meant to be a secret. We were just who we were. She was my girlfriend, and that lasted until just about six years ago. We were married for 20 years. I mean, not married, but together.

MELVOIN We were very quiet with the press. You could call it closeted, but we didn't want to put our relationship at risk. And everybody loved the mystery: "I bet they are. I bet they're not."

With a final budget of just over $7 million, Purple Rain *commenced shooting on November 1, 1983.*

MAGNOLI We had over 900 extras who came to the set every day excited. They gave the whole scene a tremendous amount of realism. And we didn't know it at the time, but those images had a tremendous amount of influence on the direction that MTV took.

COLEMAN When it came to shooting, Prince was very focused and specific about the way he wanted things to look. He got very involved. He made you feel safe and proud.

JONES He would just let you be who you were and try to help bring it out. When you're in his company, you're like, "Yeah, we can do this." That's a great quality, even with all the socio-pathic behavior that he can exhibit.

KOTERO One minute we're hanging out, playing basketball like two buddies, and then the big kiss scene. It was in the barn and I had to be topless. He was really a gentleman—he looked straight in my eyes. We have great chemistry. But the whole world has this idea we dated. At the time, I was seeing David Lee Roth.

MAGNOLI I didn't find it very difficult to direct them. Because they were already performers and because the story was organic to them, all they had to do was be themselves. But I feel that Prince, Morris Day, Jerome Benton, Apollonia—they were who they needed to be in those roles. There was no embellishment, there was no flourish. They stayed true to their characters.

LEEDS No one was going to win any awards for acting. No one had any illusions that they were. The majority of the music-buying public hadn't seen what a remarkable performer Prince was. Whatever success the movie was going to have depended entirely upon how well the performance scenes came off.

CAVALLO We were a few weeks behind, and we had four weeks set to shoot the music. So I said to Prince, "You know, Albert is gonna want to do 20 takes, he's gonna want different angles." And Prince, he almost changed color. "I'll give him one take for each song." I said, "No, that's extreme. What if we just did a couple of takes with a bunch of cameras?" We got a bunch of cameramen, and Prince, who's unbelievable, always hit his mark. If he did three takes, there was no change. Within a week, we had done the four weeks' work.

MELVOIN We were rehearsing the live material for six months. We didn't have to worry about that part.

STEVE MCLELLAN (former owner, First Avenue) The fact that the movie didn't show what was going on musically beyond the funk circle and was so narrow-focused—it had no sense of reality to me. Then, after the film came out, people came to the club just to see if Prince was there. I thought, "These people are kind of shallow, aren't they?"

What is perhaps the most frequently quoted scene in Purple Rain *takes place not in First Avenue, but on the banks of a chilly lake outside of Minneapolis, where the Kid cruelly tests Apollonia's loyalty by asking her to "purify [herself] in the waters of Lake Minnetonka," prompting her to strip down and jump into the drink.*

KOTERO Some crew guy comes over with a flask of Courvoisier and goes, "It's like magic Jesus juice! This is gonna help ya!" I was like, "You know what, I'm okay." I jumped in and, basically, there was a little sheet of ice, and that was the very first take. When I came out, I was supposed to have dialogue and I lost it—I was completely in a state of shock because it was colder than I ever imagined. Hypothermia was setting in.

Later in the film, after it's revealed that Apollonia has been spending time with Morris, a jealous Kid attacks her. The film's portrayal of women drew charges of misogyny from some critics.

KOTERO I discussed all of this when I was doing the tour to promote the film—the movie had to do with alcoholism and a dysfunctional family. There was an abusive relationship, and it paralleled the relationship he had with his parents.

Though the Time scored two hits as a result of Purple Rain— *"The Bird" and "Jungle Love," both widely believed to have been cowritten by Prince—the band was in shambles: Founding members Jimmy Jam and Terry Lewis had been fired by Prince during the 1999 tour after missing a gig, causing tension between Prince and Day.*

LEEDS Morris was not happy with what Prince had done: "It's my band, but I have no voice in this." Of course, the hypocrisy was it never really was his band.

COLEMAN All the different bands he has created have been sides of his personality: Vanity 6 would be the sexy girl, Morris Day would be the comedy guy, and then Prince was the rock star.

MELVOIN Morris was the guy who could make him laugh more than anyone on the planet. I never saw it as being a subordinate relationship, but I knew Morris was helping Prince out. Morris would wash his car sometimes for a couple bucks or something. I didn't see it as being as strained as it was portrayed in the film.

DICKERSON The Time was a collaborative effort, an arrangement between Prince and Morris, who had been friends for many years. But the Frankenstein aspect of it was that the Time became such a force as a live band that there was this onstage competition— they pushed us to the limit. Which was a good thing. We were out to blow one another off the stage every night.

JOHNSON You imagine something you created is beating your ass in all these towns down South? Prince was the one who had the money and was putting us all out there, but you're talking about hungry kids from the ghetto trying to get their groove. The only power we had was those 45 minutes onstage, because it's a dictatorship. He ran everything. He still does that to this day.

According to Johnson, tension between Prince and Day eventually led to an on-set scuffle.

MAGNOLI That's news to me.

JOHNSON I was there; I broke them up. Why did they fight? I have my theories, but I can't tell you. Morris is my brother and I have to work with him, and Prince, I still have to deal with his punk ass. What Rock and Roll Hall of Famer has time to be looking at what is said about him and watching every word and all that bullshit? He, unfortunately, is one of them.

In the spring of 1984, as Prince began prepping a new tour, Cavallo and Magnoli were trying to convince Warner Bros. that Purple Rain *wasn't just a rock star's vanity project.*

MAGNOLI They originally were gonna release it in 200 theaters. Prince had a hit album [with *1999*], but so what? He was an urban-based musician. They thought no one understood him besides the urban base.

CAVALLO We had our first screening somewhere in Culver City [California]. Kids were fighting over the passes; we had fan-club kids telling us they had their passes taken away from them by bullies. We knew it was pretty hot. But Warners gets the numbers back, and they're too good to be true.

MAGNOLI [The studio says,] "We need to go to Texas now and screen this in front of an all-white, redneck audience." A week later, we fly down to Texas and put it up in front of 300 white kids. Within three minutes, they're all up on their feet. Bob was able to get the studio to understand that they needed to get this into the heartland.

CAVALLO We got 900 theaters, which was enough for us to be a huge success.

MAGNOLI Rick Springfield had a movie [*Hard to Hold*] coming out at the same time. Warner Bros. says, "We're nervous." So I got to a screening, and this was my report: "Guys, we have nothing to worry about. It's got nothing to do with reality, nothing to do with the world of musicians. They tried to make him into a movie star. Not gonna work."

On June 9, a month and a half before Purple Rain*'s opening, Prince released "When Doves Cry," a stark downer that addressed the film's themes of personal and familial tumult. It became Prince's first No. 1 single.*

CAVALLO We wanted to precede the picture with a song that would appear in the movie like a video.

?UESTLOVE (drummer, the Roots) Before *Purple Rain*, brothers had a hard time embracing a bikini-clad, high-heel-boot-sporting, five-foot, Midwest, light-skinned guy with a falsetto. But the second after my block saw the "When Doves Cry" video, and he was getting on Apollonia, that changed a lot of opinions.

COLEMAN Prince had a lot of meetings with wardrobe people, and all the clothes were made for us. There was a little bit of consulting, but it was more like, "This is your look, and this is your look, and this is what we're going to do."

BOBBY Z. He was really good at style, and he knew that when you feel good in something, your character comes out. He could take people and find their strengths. I had a mustache and curly hair, and it's pretty easy to turn that into a suave character. Who doesn't want to be suave?

FINK I wore a gold satin tuxedo once; I looked like a freaking waiter. From there, I moved on to a black-and-white jail suit. In late '79, we got on tour with Rick James, and he had this big oversize jail suit, and the front of it was Velcroed together so he could tear it off and be half-naked. So Prince said to me, "I think you better change your image."

COLEMAN Prince actually got mad at me because I was such a jeans-and-T-shirt girl. He was like, "God, you look like a roadie. What if Mick Jagger sees you?" He was always imagining the absolute nth-degree scenario. I was like, "Dude, it's okay. I'm going to 7-Eleven."

FINK Prince said, "Did you have any other ideas when you thought of the jail suit?" And I said, "Well, you gave me this khaki paratrooper's jumpsuit. I could wear that again." He goes, "No, that's passé." I go, "A doctor's suit?" And then the light bulb went off above his head: "That's it." He had his wardrobe gal run out to a uniform shop in Chicago and get me authentic scrubs. And Prince goes, "I'm going to get an easel and a canvas up there, and I want you to act like you're painting when I introduce you. It will be weird. It will be funny. Watch." So for several nights, I was introduced as Dr. Fink, and I'm up there painting.

COLEMAN He's really controlling, but he was also kind of a puppy. He'd say it in a way where you couldn't say no. If you said, "I'm not going to wear that," you'd probably get fired.

MELVOIN I didn't want to wear bustiers. Wearing that stuff, I just felt like a transvestite.

Despite an R rating, Purple Rain *grossed more than $7 million in its first weekend, prompting Warner Bros. to add 1,000 more screens its second week. The movie eventually earned $68 million in the U.S., making it the ninth-highest-grossing movie of 1984. And though critics were divided—the* New York Times *praised the concert scenes but noted, "The offstage stuff* *is utter nonsense"—it made Roger Ebert's and Gene Siskel's year-end Top 10 lists. Meanwhile, the film's opening number, "Let's Go Crazy," hit No. 1 in September, helping the sound-track remain at the top of the charts for 24 weeks.* Purple Rain *and its creator were impossible to ignore, no matter how hard some parents tried.*

TIPPER GORE (founder, Parents' Music Resource Center, in an excerpt from her 1987 book, *Raising PG Kids in an X-Rated Society*) I purchased Prince's best-selling *Purple Rain* for my 11-year-old daughter. . . . When we brought the album home, put it on our stereo, and listened to it together, we heard the words to another song, "Darling Nikki": "I knew a girl named Nikki / Guess U could say she was a sex fiend / Met her in a hotel lobby / Masturbating with a magazine." The song went on and on in a similar manner. I couldn't believe my ears! The vulgar lyrics embarrassed both of us. At first, I was stunned— then I got mad! Millions of Americans were buying *Purple Rain* with no idea what to expect.

CAVALLO We just didn't pay attention. Any time Prince got bad publicity, it helped him.

BOBBY Z. I thought she was kind of late. Where was she during "Head"?

The Purple Rain *tour opened on November 4, 1984, with a seven-night stand in Detroit. Morris Day left the Time shortly after the movie wrapped. Sheila E. served as the opening act.*

COLEMAN We were a crack band. Prince would do these dances, and if he did a hand signal, we'd do this little turnaround we had discussed at soundcheck.

BOBBY Z. We'd been playing arenas, but it turned into multiple nights: seven nights at the Forum [in L.A.], 11 nights at the Summit in Houston. We put down stakes, just camped out in the city.

FINK We were in Detroit or Atlanta—I can't remember which— in this huge mall, all the members of the Revolution except

Prince, and we ran into Bruce Springsteen. He was out looking like the average street dude in a trench coat, a little bit disheveled, trying to blend in. We introduced ourselves, and we all went to eat at a restaurant in the mall. Next thing we know, everyone recognizes us, and there's a crowd gathered around us blocking the doors and we couldn't get out. We had to go through the restaurant kitchen, the secret catacombs of the mall, to get out. It was like the Beatles or something.

LEEDS In D.C., Prince needed to get his hair done, and there wasn't an adequate salon in the hotel. So our stylist made an agreement with a salon in Georgetown. With Prince, this means you close down the salon and black out the windows, and no other customers are present; even the people who work at the salon vacate the premises. The same with nightclubs: You'd have to buy out the club because he didn't want the public in. Find a local modeling agency and invite a hundred models, but not the general public. Oh God, the money wasted.

DICKERSON He invited me and my wife at the time to catch a couple shows in D.C. The first night we were there, Prince invited us to his suite, and at that point, the way they were traveling was full-blown, diamond-level status—they're hauling a grand piano from city to city for his suite. But in terms of the personal interaction, it was great. We got back to old times. As we were about to leave, I said, "Hey, we were thinking of going to Georgetown tomorrow to do some shopping," which is what we always did as a band when we were on the road. At first he got this smile on his face and was about to say something, but then he stopped—I'll never forget, the look on his face changed and his voice dropped—and he said, "You know, I really can't go anywhere anymore."

In the spring of 1985, Purple Rain *won the Academy Award for Best Original Song Score. The competition: Kris Kristofferson and the Muppets. The category was eliminated the following year.*

MELVOIN The cast of *Amadeus* was right in front of me, and I was sitting next to Jimmy Stewart. He looked over at us and was like, "Who are these weird, medieval-looking, grim reaper types?"

COLEMAN When we got the award, Prince made a joke like, "We better run, because they're going to think we stole it." We were running out the back door. He let Wendy and me keep it at our house for a long time.

LEEDS There has not been a tour bus that I've been on in 20 years where the first movie played was not *Purple Rain*. It drives me up a wall. These young artists, they know every word in the script.

Prince and the Revolution didn't wait long to record a follow-up to Purple Rain: *Less than a month after the Oscars, the kaleidoscopic* Around the World in a Day *appeared in stores. It sold far fewer copies than its predecessor but yielded a pair of Top 10 hits: "Raspberry Beret" and "Pop Life."* Parade *followed the next year, as did a European tour, but relations between Prince and his band were becoming strained.*

COLEMAN He became more of a satellite. It hurt our feelings. He used to travel with us on the same bus, but then he got his own. He would always be escorted ahead of us in his own car, and we were left behind. He had his big house, and when he got the guard at the gate, it was, "Wow, dude. It's me. I did your laundry." I lived with him for a while in his house— I'd fix him a sandwich or we'd do laundry together. It was really brother-and-sister stuff. When it changed, I'd have to go through other people to talk to him. I was not into that. I'm still not into that.

DAVID Z. I think what changed him more than anything was being on tour and staying right across the street from the Dakota when John Lennon was shot in 1980. He's diminutive, and when you walk into a place and every eye is on you, he just saw himself as a target. That got to him.

LEEDS He was very protective of his image as this weird, shy, quiet, introverted, nerdy, creative genius. He really did hide behind managers and bodyguards and so on.

COLEMAN At the end of the [1986] *Parade* tour, he brought Wendy and me to his house for dinner. We always called it the "paper-wrapped chicken dinner," because it was wrapped in pink slips. We'd be here in L.A. and he'd send us tapes with a piano and vocal, just an idea, and then we'd produce it. We would do all the instruments and background vocals. He felt like, "I need to take it back and do it all myself again. I'm losing touch with myself. So unfortunately, I'm going to let you go, because you're doing everything."

Bobby Z. and keyboardist Brown Mark left the Revolution along with Wendy and Lisa.

Dr. Fink stayed on until 1991. The full group hasn't performed together since 1986.

BOBBY Z. Would I have liked to have gone on and done more Prince and the Revolution stuff? Of course. It was a band for the ages. But Prince wanted to experiment with different musical genres, which means different musical people. I mean, it happened to Lennon and McCartney. It's just human nature.

CAVALLO Warner Bros. had no rights for a sequel. I had this idea: *Purple Rain 2: The Further Adventures of the Time.* It would start with Prince in some big arena, playing one of his incredible concerts. The Time are there, about to go to Las Vegas because they won a contest to play a lounge in a big hotel. And the basic story would be the Mob were the people who booked them, so they eventually get into trouble, and the only friends that they have are the showgirls. Well, for some reason, Morris thought that character took away his manhood.

LEEDS Prince's [subsequent] musicians were always talented. But arguably, they're not of the level he once had. If they don't bring any ideas, they don't challenge him, they don't stimulate him. The Revolution were constantly bringing songs to his attention. They would leave rehearsal and go listen to a Duke Ellington record or a country-western record. He was all ears. The more money he's had, the more he's been able to isolate himself from the real world. He handpicks his input.

?UESTLOVE *Purple Rain* really started hip-hop culture, whether the historians want to view it that way or not. You have Prince himself, a very unusual-looking figure, five feet tall—pretty much anybody considered a musical genius in hip-hop has some sort of odd physical feature, i.e., Biggie's lazy eye. And then the whole idea of beefs—Prince and Morris. Morris' whole pimp attitude, that was something you didn't hear since the blaxploitation films of the early '70s. Prince sang about sex and he worked with drum machines.

MELVOIN We did keep in touch a little. I believe it was toward the late '90s that it got very strained and we didn't speak that much until—well, we've been speaking for about seven years now.

BOBBY Z. Wendy and Lisa and Prince had talked about [a reunion] a while ago, but it doesn't seem in the stars. He just launched a whole new platform and triple album that could keep him on the road for two years. You know, it's his call.

DICKERSON I did go back to Minneapolis last spring for a thing called the Prince Family Reunion. A bunch of people—basically everyone but Prince—got together and played Prince songs.

COLEMAN He has hinted to Wendy and myself recently that he can't condone who we are or be friendly in a certain way. We both have kids now with other partners—he's been a little less than Uncle Prince. So that hurts, especially because he liked that element in his band back then. We were trying to mix it up and bust the categories: Androgyny and multiracialism were the way to go. I always feel he should open up and be honest because he's a fucking cool guy.

BRIAN RAFTERY has written for *Wired, GQ,* and *Esquire.* His first book, *Don't Stop Believin': How Karaoke Conquered the World and Changed My Life,* was published in 2008.

DJ SHADOW

Mo'wax/FFRR

JANUARY 1997

by **SIA MICHEL**

Endtroducing. . . .

Minutes into *Endtroducing. . . .*, after a chorus of fallen angels open the noirish "Building Steam With a Grain of Salt," some sampled jazzcat proclaims: "It's not really me—the music's coming through me." Such leggo-my-ego rhetoric is typical of this Bay Area DJ. Mild-mannered Josh Davis, from Davis, California, romanticizes behind-the-scenes anonymity but never fails to invest his sampladelic breakbeat collages with an instantly recognizable personality few of his clubland peers have mustered.

Paradox is Shadow's forte: Alternately a self-effacing know-your-place white kid and "your favorite DJ savior," he insists that he's making "hardcore abstract hip-hop" when he's really innovating a new genre: urban classical music. Essentially, Shadow layers slinky break-beats with sampled sounds—anything from church bells to *War of the Worlds* and, egad, Tears for Fears. (One of his favorite jokes: "Groove to this, hipster!"; U2's earnest "Sunday Bloody Sunday" anchors 1994's "Lost and Found.") The so-called Jimi Hendrix of the sampler doesn't just loop his thrift-shop snippets; he splices and resplices them into impressionistic stories complete with recurring sonic "characters." Variations on a theme scurry across the landscape like stuck-up actors impatient for their next scene, only adding to the cinematic flavor.

Part of the avant-minded SoleSides crew, Shadow became one of the most influential DJs on the international beat scene with just a handful of singles. "In/Flux" (1993) is credited with helping spawn the trip-hop movement, but the squiggles'n'blurps of a Funki Porcini are aural cotton candy compared to Shadow's epic ciphers; while Tricky specializes in nihilistic paralysis, Shadow can envision "Midnight in a Perfect World," *Endtroducing*'s ghostly first single. You can always pick a Shadow track out of mixtapes or compilations like Mo'Wax's *Headz*: It's the aural Rorschach test that manages to sound minimalist, baroque, astral, earthy, melancholy, and exuberant, all at the same time.

While post-gangstas like the Fugees are opening hip-hop's door to all the music of the black Diaspora, Shadow's approach is closer to Afrika Bambaataa: an infatuation with pure sound. Not to mention the metaphysical navel-gazing of some Ram Dass muthafucka. Or maybe Jewel: When was the last time a hip-hop artist asked you "What Does Your Soul Look Like"? While normally I'd be suspicious of a whitey stripping the words and thus the representing from hip-hop, it's hard to come down on a loop guru more obsessed with the color of your aura than your skin. (On early singles like 1992's "Entropy," sampled griots obliquely reference issues of identity and oppression.)

Anyway, what else would you expect from a California boy? Proudly multicultural in rhetoric if not in real life, the Bay Area is the kind of place where hippie notions of the transformational power of music are constantly reborn, in punk and in hip-hop as well. An MC like Spearhead's Michael Franti makes sure he gives it up to all the African-Americans, Latinos, whites, Asians, Filipinos, and Others in the house; DJs take names like Invisible Scratch Pickles; and even mobstas like E40 aren't afraid to sound hella kooky. Rapper or no rapper, Shadow would argue he's merely following in the recombinant footsteps of Grandmaster Flash, Mantronix, and the Jungle Brothers. "Don't get it twisted. *Endtroducing* is a Hip Hop album," the liner notes proclaim with a zealot's fervor. Nevertheless, on this long-awaited full-length debut, Shadow loses some of his trademark rapmosphere ("The Number Song" excepted), instead opting for a cosmic-chamber feel complete with choruses of fallen angels, plucked harps, Mellotron, and cello. Stately pipe organs moan and groan while haunted voices call out from the ether in a mutated gibberish you strain to understand. Sampling live drummers at times for a warmly organic vibe, Shadow often chops and resplices beats into jarring time signatures. Pieces like "Stem/Long Stem" change genre (Eno-ish ambient to four-to-the-floor techno to intelligent jungle) and color faster than Courtney Love's mood ring.

Shadow is orchestrally welding the music of the academy to the beat of the streets, and only rarely does that subversive linkage emit New Age fumes (see "Changeling"). The airy but intricate compositional complexity recalls modern classical works by Gavin Bryars, Scott Johnson, et al., but for its determined soulfulness. While DJ Spooky attempts a similar union of the high and yo brow, illbient is too often static and distant; *Endtroducing* practically folds you into its symphonic fantasia, the coming-of-age story of a 24-year-old bunk-bed dreamer.

Shadow cheekily proclaims "Why Hip Hop Sucks in '96" (hint: it's a G-thang), but can't stop believing in the genre's old-school transformational promise, or wanting to reinstate it as the experimental, boundless force it seemed back when visionary producers like Prince Paul knotted all the sounds of the stratosphere into manifestos of refusal *and* hope. That makes him a cynical idealist, which isn't an oxymoron but a logical response to an illogical world. Someone once said that behind every optimistic act is an intellectual failure; Shadow has the goods to prove that claim all wrong.

SIA MICHEL is the pop music editor of *The New York Times*. She joined SPIN in 1996 and was editor in chief from 2002 to 2006.

Acknowledgments

If you're the sort of person who reads this type of page, you're in for a treat. In addition to the contributors who went above and beyond, allow me to introduce some other really wonderful folks without whom this book would not exist. Or if it did, it would be a much lesser book. Trust me.

Current SPIN colleagues Dylan Boelte, Malcolm Campbell, Catherine Davis, Michelle Egiziano, Tom Fernald, Sarah Hamilton, Jack Jensen, Nion McEvoy, Alan Nichols, Devin Pedzwater, and Phoebe Reilly all either pitched in with robust physical labor or gave this project their very valuable, if somewhat less tangible, two cents. Props to distinguished alumni Bob Guccione Jr., Alan Light, Craig Marks, Sia Michel, and others who originally commissioned a number of these pieces. A fist bump with Jim Fitzgerald for sealing the deal. Whitman's Samplers are on their way to Rachel Meyers, Tom Miller, Connie Santisteban, and everyone at Wiley. And great big hugs for Rachel and Sasha, whose patience, support, and love make everything easier.

Extra special bonus thanks to Jennifer Edmondson for the photo wizardry and to Charles Aaron for the keen suggestions and additional outreach.

Credits